Transformational Reminiscence

Author Biographies

John A. Kunz, BSW, MS, has worked as a psychotherapist, author, and educator in the field of mental health since 1978. He began his practice with an emphasis on family systems and was the first practitioner to conduct family assessments within the medical community of Duluth, Minnesota, and Superior, Wisconsin, in the early 1980s. Throughout the 1980s and 1990s, Kunz worked with clients of all ages doing inpatient and outpatient individual, group, milieu, marital, and family therapy. From the mid-1980s until today he has increasingly focused in the area of gerontology and geriatrics. He has conducted hundreds of presentations, written numerous articles and book chapters, and has written and produced over a dozen educational videos. He is most known for his work in the field of reminiscence and life review. He founded the International Institute for Reminiscence and Life Review in 1995. He continues to direct this institute, its biennial conferences, and many other health and human issues programs at the Center for Continuing Education/Extension at the University of Wisconsin–Superior.

Florence Gray Soltys, MSW, LCSW, is a clinical associate professor in the School of Social Work and the School of Medicine at the University of North Carolina at Chapel Hill. She has conducted clinical work in the area of hospice and interdisciplinary assessment of frail elders since 1984. Her work in rural areas included the use of telemedicine and doing reminiscence with nursing home residents in rural North Carolina. Her work in the community has enhanced care options by planning and executing needed programs for elders. She currently serves on the North Carolina Aging Study Commission and chairs numerous committees and boards.

She has received much recognition and many awards for her work, including the Distinguished Teaching Award for Post Baccalaureate Instruction for the University of North Carolina, Trustee of the Year for the American Association of Homes and Services for the Aging of the United States, Social Worker of the Year in North Carolina, the Ned Brooks Award for Community Service, and the Hospice Service Award.

She is the current president of the International Institute for Reminiscence and Life Review.

Transformational Reminiscence

Life Story Work

John A. Kunz, MS
Florence Gray Soltys, MSW
With contributors

SPRINGER PUBLISHING COMPANY
New York

Springer Publishing Company, LLC
11 West 42nd Street
New York, NY 10036
www.springerpub.com

Acquisitions Editor: Sheri W. Sussman
Managing Editor: Mary Ann McLaughlin
Production Editor: Carol Cain
Cover design: Joanne E. Honigman
Composition: Apex Covantage, LLC

07   08   09   10/   5   4   3   2   1

Library of Congress Cataloging-in-Publication Data

Transformational reminiscence : life story work / [edited by] John A. Kunz,
Florence Gray Soltys.
    p. ; cm.
Includes bibliographical references and index.
ISBN-13: 978-0-8261-1540-9 (alk. paper)
ISBN-10: 0-8261-1540-3 (alk. paper)
    1. Reminiscing in old age. 2. Older people—Psychology. 3. Psychology—
Biographical methods. I. Kunz, John A. II. Soltys, Florence Gray.
[DNLM: 1. Aged—psychology. 2. Mental Recall. 3. Psychotherapy—methods.
    WT 150 T772 2007]
    BF724.85.R45T73 2007
    155.67—dc22   2006038957

Printed in the United States of America by Bang Printing.

Photographs with permission for use provided in part by Elders Share the Arts, Roots &
Branches, Stagebridge, Liz Lerman Dance Exchange, Memoirs, Inc., Life Story Services,
University of Wisconsin–Superior, University of North Carolina at Chapel Hill, and
University of British Columbia. Montage design by John A. Kunz and Patrick Lind.

Contents

CONTENTS

SECTION THREE: CONTENT VERSUS PROCESS

Contributors

Barbara K. Haight, DrPh, Professor Emeritus of Gerontological Nursing at the Medical University of South Carolina, is a fellow in the American Academy of Nursing, the Gerontological Society of America, and the Florence Nightingale Society and has presented and published nationally and internationally on life review and reminiscence. She was co-editor with Jeffery Webster of the *Art and Science of Reminiscing: Theory, Research, Methods, and Applications* and *Critical Advances in Reminiscence Work From Theory to Application.*

Anita Hecht, MSSW, LCSW, Director and Founder of Life History Services, LLC, has conducted over 200 life history interviews over the past 10 years. Since 1996, Life History Services, LLC, has produced video, audio, and printed archives for individuals, families, organizations, and businesses. Hecht assists laypersons and professionals in life review, reminiscence, and life history training and projects. She works nationally and internationally and is fluent in German, Spanish, and English. She served for 6 years on the board of directors of the Association of Personal Historians, Inc., and is currently its international liaison. She is a licensed psychotherapist, professional writer, lecturer, and yoga instructor.

Daniel W. L. Lai, PhD, received his doctoral degree in social work from Case Western Reserve University. He is currently professor of social work at the University of Calgary and holds the title of Alberta Heritage Health Scholar funded by the Alberta Heritage Foundation for Medical Research. For over 18 years, his teaching and research interests have been in culture and health of the aging population. As an expert in cultural diversity issues, he has been awarded grants to conduct research with special focuses on culture, ethnicity, healthy aging, and family caregiving.

Renya T. H. Larson, MA, is a training and organizational development specialist with the Paraprofessional Healthcare Institute. She provides support to nursing homes, home health agencies, and other long-term care employers that seek to improve the quality of jobs for direct care workers and the quality of care for consumers. Larson also has over 10 years of experience as a playwright and director of community-based theater, with particular interest and expertise in projects based on oral history and reminiscence. She is the former associate director of the National Center for Creative Aging.

Holly B. McLean, MA, is completing her doctorate in counseling psychology at the University of British Columbia. Her dissertation research is a narrative study of the spouses of soldiers healing from posttraumatic stress, using a life story autobiographical method.

Susan Perlstein, MSW, is the founder and executive director of the National Center for Creative Aging. She is also an educator, social worker, administrator, and artist. She has written extensively on creativity and late-life learning. Her articles appear in numerous professional journals, including *Arts in the Public Interest* and *Gerontology,* and in ASA's *Aging Today, The Older LEARNer,* and *Dimensions.* Perlstein is the author or coauthor of several books, including *Alert and Alive, Generating Community: Intergenerational Programs Through the Expressive Arts,* and *Legacy Works: Transforming Memory Into Visual Art.*

Mary O'Brien Tyrrell, MPH, BSN, president of Memoirs, Inc., has assisted hundreds of elders to write and publish their life stories in hardcover books that are distributed to family and friends at a book signing party. A nurse for more than 40 years, in addition to practicing in hospitals, clinics, and home care settings, she was employed as associate director of the Minnesota Board of Nursing, has published articles in professional journals, and has coordinated health care research. In December 2003, her article "Memoirist of Ordinary, Yet Extraordinary Elders" in *Generations: The Journal of the American Society on Aging* was the first in the professional gerontology literature to describe the burgeoning memoir industry.

Marvin J. Westwood, PhD, is a professor in the counseling psychology program at the University of British Columbia (UBC) and is an associate member of the UBC Faculty of Medicine. His teaching and research areas include group counseling and psychotherapy, trauma repair, and therapeutic applications of life review. Westwood has developed several personal development programs for professionals across a wide range of groups (counselors/psychologists, nurses, physicians, soldiers, clergy, etc.) using guided autobiography and group-based therapeutic enactment methods. He has been invited to present his research at numerous national and international conferences. He taught at St. Francis University and McGill University before coming to UBC.

Preface

As our lives and those near and far from us unfold, we further develop, and both we and they are transformed. Each time an individual tells part of his or her life story, those who listen are like a mirror. The conversation not only has an effect on the listener, but the listener's reactions, questions, and comments then have a reciprocal impact on the storyteller. Thus, the original meaning and understanding of the story evolves into something new. The telling of a humiliating experience may result in a new understanding of the situation; for example, the feelings of humiliation may turn to anger about or even pride in managing and surviving the past situation. This then propels the individual telling the story to another level.

At the same time, listeners incorporate the storyteller's experience into their own knowledge, and their thinking also evolves. This may stimulate a variety of emotions and reactions that lead them to change.

The sharing of life experiences is a universal part of human existence. This sharing of experiences happens in everyday conversations, intimate and public exchanges, and through such formal venues as writing and performance.

ABOUT THIS BOOK

This book takes a close look at these transformational processes to identify the clear benefits, as well as the risks and responsibilities, of engaging in life story work. The goal is to present clear and practical concepts and approaches that will help readers understand the issues and opportunities so they can apply this information in their own work and lives. Each chapter contains real-life examples of lessons learned from older adults. These life stories help readers gain from the experiences of older adults, and they also shape the storytellers' knowledge and wisdom.

Each chapter begins with learning points that reflect content and factual information contained in that chapter. These learning points prepare readers for the content to follow, and they are useful for discussing and teaching the content. Each chapter also contains one or more exercises that can be done individually; in study groups, classrooms, and workshops; or at conferences. The first exercise in chapter 1 is titled "Life Story Interview" and has two phases. Phase 1 walks readers through their own life review using a guided interview workbook. The second phase of the exercise is designed to be completed after reading the entire book and completing all of the other exercises. At that point, readers should be prepared to do a life story interview with an older adult. As a safety net and to further the learning process, readers are instructed on how to select and utilize an experienced mentor to complete the exercise.

After the first and last assignments are completed, readers are invited and encouraged to fill out a short, anonymous impact evaluation at www.reminiscenceandlifereview.org. This survey will assist the authors and others in the field with future endeavors and may be published or presented at appropriate venues.

THE LIFE STORY MATRIX

Chapter 1 introduces a broad framework for conceptualizing and comparing the many informal and formal ways that we reminiscence and review our lives. The *life story matrix* describes continuums from reminiscence to life review and from private to public with constant attention to the reciprocal relationship and outcomes related to content versus process. The remainder of the book is divided into three sections with particular emphasis on each of the three dimensions of the life story matrix.

REMINISCENCE TO LIFE REVIEW

The first section, Reminiscence to Life Review, starts with a look at normal human psychosocial development and the continuum from reminiscence to life review.

Chapter 2 examines a number of theories about this subject—the most famous being Maslow's Hierarchy of Needs, Erik Erikson's Stages of Psychosocial Development, and successful aging through adaptation. The concept of *elementality* is part of an appreciation of living and achieving an ultimate level of consciousness toward the end of life. Compelling new brain research is included that suggests between the ages 60 and 80 the brain begins a new stage of cognitive and psychosocial development in which reminiscence and life review play a critical role.

Chapter 3 includes a brief review of the literature followed by the Sol-Cos Reminiscence Model, which provides a structural framework for the practice of reminiscence and life review as part of this dimension of the life story matrix. This chapter includes a description and examples of the reminiscence engagement process that is essential for such work.

Chapter 4 presents a thorough and historical review of the literature by one of the pioneers in the field of life review. This includes Haight's Life Review and Experience Form, which has served as an instrument in hundreds of studies since it was first published almost 30 years ago.

PRIVATE TO PUBLIC

The second section, Private to Public, examines the continuum of the life story matrix. It emphasizes the social importance of talking about life experiences with others, sometimes in a controlled setting and sometimes in a public manner.

Chapter 5 discusses the importance and uses of a variety of reminiscence group processes for older adults. It provides guidelines and suggestions for what techniques to use and how much direction is needed for different older adult populations. These include community-dwelling older adults who want to learn and grow, have fun, or participate in a personal growth process as well as older adults who may be participating in day care or residential care and may be experiencing severe levels of sensory or cognitive impairment.

Chapter 6 focuses on the emerging industry of documenting and producing life story records through written word or other media. This trend is described with a close look at what credentials are needed to ethically carry out such work. All aspects of the production process are described in detail, beginning with negotiating the form and use of the final product and ending with the important celebration at its completion.

Chapter 7 looks beyond the written or audiovisual documentation of an older adult's life and focuses on art-based methods of reminiscence. These include the stimulation of senses combined with verbal and non-verbal processing of such stimulation, which leads to social engagement and bolsters individual identity. This type of lifelong learning can better integrate older adults into their communities.

CONTENT VERSUS PROCESS

The final section, Content Versus Process, looks at the third dimension of the life story matrix, which examines the reciprocal relationship between a focus on content as well as the experience of the process of telling one's life story.

Chapter 8 discuses how this process is impacted by the ever-present and overshadowing multicultural influences of doing life story work. This contributes significantly to how the interaction of content versus process comes into play. How culturally appropriate is it to disclose what information? What is the impact of an entire culture's experience on the telling of culturally specific life stories? How does society react to the telling of stories that challenge historical beliefs?

With culture in mind, chapter 9 discusses the intimate ways in which reminiscence and life review can be used in the psychotherapeutic setting. This is where the process is more important than the content, yet the content should guide the process. Particular focus is on ways in which reminiscence can help prevent, assess, and treat the full spectrum of mental health problems faced by older adults. These approaches may be used informally by caregivers or family members or may be integrated into psychiatric and psychological treatment plans that use cognitive behavioral therapy or other efficacious modes of individual, group, marital, family, or milieu therapy.

Many older adults have experienced trauma during their lives. Chapter 10 emphasizes competent ways to handle these memories to minimize the risk of retraumatizing the individual. The trauma recovery process is discussed with particular emphasis on prevention, management, and healing.

Finally, chapter 11 examines the uses of reminiscence and life review as part of the grief process and at end of life. Grief is described as a healing process that is individualistic, dynamic, and evolving. Reminiscing with an individual or a group is a valuable way to explore and clarify grieving. The chapter concludes with a discussion of how much or how little reminiscence life review should be facilitated at the end of life to help to sort out the ifs and whats of finishing life with peace and dignity by letting go of and passing on what has been essential in one's life.

WHO IS THIS BOOK FOR?

Health Care and Social Services

It is crucial that professionals working with elders understand the elders' values concerning health care. Learning about their lives through reminiscences helps to clarify these wishes and assists in the professional's understanding of the individual. To know the person is often more important than to know the disease. Interdisciplinary teamwork is essential when working with frail elders, and the ability to learn from each team member's perspective provides a more complete picture of the situation.

Helping the individual look at past situations in which strengths were utilized can help them recognize that they have the coping skills to face current difficulties.

Assisted Living and Long-Term Care

Being able to share one's successes and failures enables the exploration of both past and current situations. It is important that assisted living and long-term care staff understand the value of listening and affirming an individual's life. The need for reminiscence should be part of staff training, and the importance of knowing each individual should be a strong value for the institution. When people are facing the end of their lives, there needs to be an appreciation for their contribution and assistance in facing closure as they pass.

Service Learning at Secondary, Postsecondary, and Graduate Levels

There is a strong trend for high schools, colleges, and graduate schools to incorporate formal service learning in their curricula to promote better communities and provide learning experiences that are more than just volunteer work. Nursing, health, social work, psychology, counseling, sociology, anthropology, visual and communication arts, English and literature, history, first nations, music, and many other disciplines can benefit by doing some type of life story work. This book is an excellent resource for students and instructors to help them prepare for and carry out this important work. In these situations, creativity knows no bounds.

Civic Engagement

Retired individuals who volunteer in civic engagement activities involving older adults want to do more than help out at a senior center. This book can raise their awareness and inspire them and the agencies that recruit them about the many ways they can give back to the community by doing some sort of life story work. As this occurs, this book can serve as a resource and guide as the agencies develop programs and approaches.

Oral Historians and Researchers

Oral history is said to be the "history of the people." Families and communities value the sharing of stories and happenings that define their lives. These stories help us clarify who we are as a society and thus express our values. Those who ignore history tend to repeat past mistakes rather than use them as a learning tool. Reminiscence is a strong method to achieve and maintain personal histories.

Creative Arts Programs

The ability to express oneself through music, theater, dance, and painting is a joy. Reminiscence is a natural tool to enhance these expressions through the chosen work. Many older individuals begin to express their creativity after they have retired and have more time to pursue their latent talents. Some of the world's greatest music and paintings have been completed after the artist reached his or her later years. Sharing life experiences through creative arts can be both fun and educational.

Businesses That Focus on Life Story Work

This book is essential for anyone who is going to do life story work with older adults. It will help prepare individuals who want to volunteer or make a profit by interviewing older people and documenting their life stories. In fact, reading this book and doing the exercises could be considered an important ethical step before undertaking such work. Many individuals age 50 and older realize that they either will have to work for another 20 years because of financial reasons or simply want to keep working in some way. However, they want flexible hours, rewarding work experiences, and often something that helps them make use of their creative talents. Many such individuals and others have begun work documenting the life stories of others in various forms. This book will help them feel more confident that they are prepared and competent to offer such services.

We hope that you will be able to benefit from this book to continue your own transformational reminiscence processes and to assist those you know and love to further theirs.

John A. Kunz
Florence Gray Soltys

Foreword

We struggle to understand the world in which we live. Questions about the origins of the universe and the purpose of life remain beyond our grasp. But with work and over time we can achieve some understanding of the greater meaning of our individual lives.

Poet and essayist Patricia Hampl observed that "the memoir is the signature genre of our age." Yet as recently as 50 years ago people believed that reminiscing was a sign of senility—what we now call Alzheimer's disease. In that era, many geriatrics researchers confined themselves largely to the study of people who were long-term residents in chronic disease hospitals and nursing homes. The results of these studies only served to reinforce the stereotypes of old people as confused, decrepit, and leading meaningless lives. Their reminiscences confirmed that they were living in the past.

For 11 years I worked with healthy volunteers. In 1961 I postulated the existence of the life review as a normal function of the later years and not a pathological condition. Memories, reminiscence, and nostalgia all play a part in the process. Far from living in the past or wandering, as was commonly thought, older people were engaged in the important psychological task of coming to terms with the life they had lived. They sought to make amends for acts of omission and commission, resolve conflicts, and reconcile alienated relationships.

Today, along with a greater understanding of the significance of reminiscence we have seen the rising popularity of private memoirs in various forms, from oral histories by universities to audio and videotapes for family archives.

John A. Kunz and Florence Gray Soltys have made a major contribution to the field by providing a framework for individuals and groups engaged in this enriching and important work.

Robert N. Butler, MD

Acknowledgements

Fifteen years ago I nervously entered a small conference room and met for the first time my two copresenters for a session on reminiscence at the American Society on Aging Conference in New Orleans. The three of us—a nurse, a social worker, and a psychotherapist, who had never met before—were asked to do a 90-minute session. The room was soon packed and people were standing in the hall. We each took a turn presenting and were amazed at how well coordinated our session appeared. At the conclusion of the presentation, the audience commended us and said they could tell that we had presented together many times in the past!

Since that time, the social worker, Florence Gray-Soltys, and I have presented together at conferences throughout the United States and Canada over 20 times. I am always honored to be at her side and have learned a great deal from her as my mentor and friend. I greatly admire Florence's modesty, genuineness, acceptance, respect, and love for all who she encounters. I am very pleased to have the chance to coauthor this book with her. Thank you, Florence!

During these 15 years, we have both met and collaborated with so many others who practice and do research in the field of reminiscence and life review. I'm happy that we have been able to include some of these individuals as contributors to this book. Thank you, Barbara, Daniel, Mary, Anita, Susan, Renya, Marvin, and Holly for your contributions. And thank you, Dr. Butler, for your Foreword.

When I was growing up, my mother told me that when she was a young child she asked her grandparents, my great-grandparents, about their life history. My mother soaked it all in and recounted their stories to me as I was growing up, helping transmit their experience and wisdom to another generation. Both of my parents' respect and love for their parents and other community elders have taught me a great deal. Thank you, Mom and Dad, for modeling these important values and skills.

I wish to dedicate this book to my parents, Betty Lou Lillian Nichols Kunz and John (Jack) Albert Kunz. Thank you for your love and support.

I want to thank my late grandparents, Lillian Rose (as grandpa used to say, "Lillian Rose sat on a pin—Lillian Rose!") and Martin Nichols; and Helen (as she used to tell me, "You are a good kid, but who likes kids!") and Carl Frederick Kunz, for all they taught me about reminiscence and life review during my growing up and adult years.

I would also like to thank my friend and university associate, Donna Sislo; office assistants Tatiana Korsnsted, Beth Constance, Suzanne Finkler; and student intern Patrick Lind for their tremendous help in putting this book together.

John A. Kunz

It has been a joy to be associated with John Kunz over the past 15 years. He is one of the most creative people I know. He networks easily and has friends and colleagues all over the world. He founded the International Institute for Reminiscence and Life Review and remains the stabilizing force behind the organization today.

Dr. Butler, Daniel, Mary, Anita, Susan, Reyna, Marvin, and Holly are most appreciated for their consistent contributions to the field and to this book.

My personal admiration and respect go to the many elder clients with whom I have worked over the years. Their stories and their achievements, despite arduous hardships, are a part of who I am. Much of my career has been spent working with elderly African Americans in the South, who were deprived of equal rights for so many years, yet they are some of the most generous and kind people I know.

My grandmother, D. Gray, and mentor, M. Tippett, were major supporters and shared their unconditional love.

To my family—my husband, John Soltys, and two daughters and sons-in-law, Jacqueline Soltys and Stuart Henderson and Rebecca Soltys Jones and Brett Jones—I owe much.

The three special joys in my life are my granddaughters, Sophia Soltys Henderson, Grace Soltys Henderson, and Mia Wynne Jones. It is my hope that they will live in a world with peace and treasure the many memories from their youth and that the memories will enrich their lives.

Florence Gray Soltys

Transformational
Reminiscence

CHAPTER ONE

The Life Story Matrix

John A. Kunz

Robert N. Butler coined the term *life review* in 1955 (later published in 1963) when he began to scientifically identify life review as a normal aspect of older adult development. His work led the way for U.S. society to look anew at the reminiscence and life review process as a normal aspect of human aging. Many health care professionals and society in general had previously discouraged such activities, regarding them as a sign that elders were retreating into the past due to senility or other types of mental illness. In contrast, Butler suggested that life review is normal: as people approach the end of life, it is natural for them to want to put their experiences in perspective, resolve past conflicts, grieve losses and changes, forgive themselves and others, celebrate successes, and feel a sense of completion.

Every decade since then has seen increased interest in incorporating reminiscence and life review activities into the treatment of older adults. The known advantages of doing such work include improving the attitudes of younger adults toward older adults and vice versa, finding meaning in life, improving problem-solving skills, assisting with the grief process, increasing emotional support, strengthening self-esteem, decreasing depression and anxiety, and developing interventions for individuals with dementia (Kunz, 1991).

Many individuals and organizations conduct life story work in a wide range of applications, from working with fully oriented and functional older adults to working with the very frail, confused, and dying. Often the approaches are fun and are part of other education or entertainment programs. Others are designed to help older adults further process their life experiences to make sense out of their lives and gain new insights about themselves or learn new ways to express themselves. Some approaches are used to help assess and treat mental health or unresolved grief and loss. This nonexhaustive list includes a variety of life story activities that older adults may engage in:

- Recording and/or writing life stories
- Quilting
- Blogging and posting videos and other material on the Internet
- Visual art
- Scrapbooking
- Storytelling
- Writing stories or music
- Attending or leading reminiscence groups
- Volunteering to help others by leading reminiscence groups
- Establishing memorials to ensure that history is remembered
- Documenting family genealogy
- Documenting history through formal oral histories
- Participating in intergenerational programs at churches and other organizations
- Being interviewed by students

Butler (2005) and others have called this the Age of the Memoir, hinting that some memoirs are self-serving and pretentious while others are done for the common good of catharsis and the sharing of history and wisdom. The Association of Personal Historians (www.personalhistorians.org) has hosted 12 conferences and has almost 600 members. This organization promotes the telling of life stories and is a resource for individuals and businesses that help people tell their life stories through the written word and other media.

The International Institute for Reminiscence and Life Review (www.reminiscenceandlifereview.org) was founded at the University of Wisconsin–Superior following the first international conference that brought together many life review pioneers and leaders. This biennial conference continues to draw key researchers, practitioners, educators, and others in the field of reminiscence and life review to further this work throughout the world. The National Creative Aging Center (www.creativeaging.org), based in Brooklyn, New York, is a national network of theater companies, musicians, artists, and others who promote the use of life story work through the arts—including storytelling, song writing, visual art, musical productions, improvisations, and full theater productions. Performances are often held at the American Society on Aging and National Council on Aging's (www.asaging.org) annual meetings as well as at many other venues. Both the Gerontological Society of America and the American Society on Aging have special interest or peer groups that meet during the annual meetings to network and collaborate on further work in this field. More and more graduate and undergraduate programs in psychology, counseling, gerontology, and other disciplines are offering formal credit coursework on reminiscence and life review. The Birren Center for Autobiography and Life Review at the Institute of Gerontology at the California State University, Fullerton (www.guidedautobiography.com) is also an excellent resource in this field.

The Life Story Corps (www.storycorps.net) in New York is an incredible project that has soundproofed booths and trained facilitators and is set up to record individuals' life stories at Grand Central Station and other locations in New York City as well as in their mobile studio that travels around the nation. These stories are then housed at the American Folklife Center at the Library of Congress. Please see www.lifestory.net for the latest information about this significant oral history movement.

Organizations and programs in this field are emerging at what seems to be an exponential pace; refer to your favorite Internet search engine to access the most up-to-date information. You may find sites like YouTube.com (www.youtube.com), where people post hundreds of videos per day. Some are funny, some are educational, others are political and informative. Many online diaries called blogs are very personal and represent a new way for individuals to share their innermost thoughts and angst with the world in what may seem an anonymous form. Here is an example:

> OK, I'm going to be brutally honest with you guys and I know that I'm going to regret this tomorrow between the comments and messages and all that stuff but I thought I'd be completely frank with you. I feel like this isn't going anywhere not that it should be the goal of anybody when they set out but I honestly feel like there is almost no point to what I'm doing. Maybe it entertains a few people I guess. In the grand scheme of things what am I doing that matters? In this day and age I don't think I got a chance in doing anything substantial. You know it seems like as hard as I try I'm always going to be out done by someone new or someone more attractive, anything. I just feel like I'm not really worth it you know and this is not a f——— pity party—I can't wait for the Internet jackals to get a hold of this one. Have you ever got the feeling that no mater what you do it is not adding up to anything, nothing at all, I'm getting that feeling right about now and I'm wondering whether or not if in a couple of years down the line I going to look back at this and think what a dumb ass—why was I spending all this time thinking about videos, making videos, editing videos for the internet when it really didn't amount to anything that I am now or am I going to look back on it and realize that if I didn't have the balls to do that I wouldn't be where I am today. I really just don't know anymore—yeah OK f——— it you guys don't even want to hear about this—I'm posting it anyway—yeah. (*Just a Flicker of Vulnerability*, 2006)

Many of the participants in the YouTube phenomenon and related venues are of younger generations. As the aging baby boomers and older adults in their 80s and 90s further their skills with and exploration into the Internet world, we can expect increased spontaneity in sharing and experiencing life stories. In most instances, this will serve to enhance this important work. In some cases, it may not. Consider the possibility of stumbling across someone's suicide posting.

Because reminiscence and life review work is multidisciplinary and varied in application, it is difficult to formulate an overall conceptualization of the field. In a video I directed, *The Joys and Surprises of Telling Your Life Story* (2002), I propose the life story matrix as a framework for understanding the three dimensions of life story work: a continuum from reminiscence to life review, from private to public expression, and from a focus on content to an emphasis on process. This framework can help individuals interested in life story work better determine what they want to do.

The continuum from reminiscence to life review ranges from the expression of random memories (reminiscence) to a full review of one's life with the intent of evaluating it or putting it into perspective. Such attempts are not usually considered to be therapy, but their results are often viewed as therapeutic.

These approaches are experienced naturally in families and groups all the time. Think about the last time you had a really good conversation with an old or a new friend. How much of that conversation included reminiscence material? Think about your last visit with an older relative. How much of that visit consisted of that person reminiscing? Recall the common assignment when students return to school in the fall and are asked to write about what they did during their summer vacation. While the teacher gets to know the students and evaluate their writing skills, they are doing a mini life review.

Reminiscence and life review approaches also can be adapted for fun, group connection, individual growth, historical purposes, social and therapeutic goals, as well as to deal with normal human grief and loss at the end of life.

REMINISCENCE TO LIFE REVIEW

I'd like to introduce you to Gladys Roberts.

Gladys Roberts

We were born and raised on a farm back in Oklahoma I thank the Lord because we learned how to appreciate the natural things in life. I don't want to say that we are children of the soil but we worked in the ground and the fields and we raised many crops vegetables, fruit trees and all of those things and to have that some of that brought to light so that my children my grandchildren and now of course great grandchildren. I expect them to enjoy some of my background. I have a grandfather that was a boy during the slavery this country a young boy he told us of thing first hand we didn't read them in a book because they weren't recorded in the history book anywhere. He was such a wonderful man he had no bitterness in his heart no revenge or nothing like that he loved people and he got along with everybody. And he loved everybody and I liked being around him and I was proud to have him and my grandmother but I remember going to grandpa and grandma's house for Thanksgiving and my brothers John and Edward, after we had eating and eating all of the turkey grandma's could make some of the best plain cakes I tell you but anyway I'm getting ahead of myself here. After we had eaten and had a good time I remember waving goodbye to them they would come out to the wagon and they would see mom and dad and help load the kids on and all that and so we say we had a good time and I remember my brother John says "my turkey" well the turkey was already gone anyway I mean we had already devoured that sucker but anyway we had so much fun. But we didn't realize we were having fun and we didn't realize that like my brother Edward would say Oh we didn't realize we were poor it was just a way of life but we adjusted to it. And I tell you it was a time that we cared for each other. (Kunz, 2002)

This interview with Gladys represents the reminiscence end of the continuum. Although there was some structure provided by the interviewer, most of her content was free flowing and at times almost stream of consciousness. This interview conveys the emotions of love, pride, determination, and strength that were evident as she spoke. By asking broad questions and listening closely to the way Gladys answered them, we are able to learn a great deal about her.

Some things you probably learned about Gladys include

- Her strong sense of family across the generations
- Her pride in and love for her grandparents and what they taught her
- Her determination in making sure her family knew their history
- Her value of love over material items
- Her strong Christian beliefs

An artist's rendering of Gladys's life story is available for viewing in *The Joys and Surprises of Telling Your Life Story* (Kunz, 2002). It is meant to be cut out and shaped into a six-sided cube. The pictures show Gladys working in the fields as a young girl, her family visiting her grandparents, the blue Cadillac she purchased when she learned to drive, and her preaching on her radio program.

Imagine how helpful this brief glimpse of Gladys would be if you were caring for her in some way across the continuum from direct care provider, to physician or nurse, to minister or neighbor or family member. How would this help you better understand her and enable you to maintain or improve her quality of life? How would it benefit you?

It is important to note that, as Gladys chooses to share her life in a short interview that is expected to be included in a widely distributed video, she is also making choices about how public she wants to make her life; in her case, it is evident that the process is joyful and that precise details are not as important for her as that joy.

Section 1 of this book focuses more on the importance of reminiscence and life review as people age.

PRIVATE TO PUBLIC

Now I'd like to introduce you to Hy Berman. This interview especially demonstrates his desire to make his life story public by writing a book about it. He wants family members and others to understand the intricacies and intimacies of his life. To that end, he engaged in a formal life review process that reflects the reminiscence end of the life review continuum. Although he was interested in accurate content, it was his daughter who encouraged him to write this book because he had had some health problems and life changes and she thought such a project would help him. Indeed it did, and during the process he experienced the many benefits of reminiscence and, as is often the case, used the life review to further grieve the loss of his wife and other changes in his life. By the time the video that contains his interview was released, Hy attended the premiere with a new woman in his life as his guest.

Section 2 of this book focuses on the life story continuum from private to public.

Hy Berman

Five years ago I decided to write the book and we picked a good title I think it was bytes and pieces of the story of my life. One of the memories that came up was my first memory. I was able to talk about my first memory when I was four years old. I don't think people remember much before four and this was put in the book. I had been sick and this was at a time when houses were quarantined. Most people haven't heard of that. When the health department finds things like scarlet fever, diphtheria, whooping cough, the houses were quarantined and people couldn't come and go other than the doctors and so forth and I remember strangely enough is that I had pneumonia downstairs and three of my siblings had scarlet fever upstairs therefore the house was quarantined. But I remember the big crate of toys I still remember (have a clear memory) because they had to take my toys and burn them, you know, because of the danger of spreading disease.

An artist's rendering of Hy's life story is available for viewing in *The Joys and Surprises of Telling Your Life Story* (Kunz, 2002). This artist's rendering, designed to be cut out and formed into a cube, shows the horse-drawn fire truck that Hy enjoyed watching, his toys being burned because of illness, his wife, the Star of David, and the two toy companies and other businesses that he founded and named after his two daughters.

The continuum from private to public expression is the second factor to consider in using life review and reminiscence in therapy. When doing group work with clients, mental health professionals should consider whether all the members of the group will understand and respect the rules of confidentiality necessary in such work. If not, the clinician will need to protect clients from saying too much in the group setting and will be required to follow up on some issues individually.

A related question arises when the treatment approach involves clients opening up and disclosing personal material due to the communication skills of the interviewer or clinician, then expressing themselves in a story or another creative form. In such circumstances, do clients need to be provided with some level of protection from their creative work becoming too public outside the intimacy of the clinician-client relationship? Professionals who incorporate life story work in their practice must take such concerns into consideration when using creative activities in the life review framework.

It is also important for those who are helping individuals publish their life stories in some form to be sensitive to the nature of the material being disclosed and to whom it is being disclosed. Keen awareness of privacy issues is critical throughout this process. Sometimes it is better to encourage someone to discuss material on an individual basis rather than in a group or other public format or to restrict personal reflections in written or other forms for disclosure only to a preselected group.

There have been many instances in which people have disclosed material about themselves in relation to someone else's private issues and as a result "outed" the other person in a humiliating and hurtful manner. An awareness of this issue is especially important in areas of sexual relationships, pregnancies, sexual orientation, and gender issues as well as other secrets. Sometimes it is appropriate and fun to tell the stories of rogue friends and relatives, while other times is it destructive.

Geriatric 27

In August 2006, a 79-year-old widower from Great Britain known only as Peter with the screen name of Geriatric 27 posted his first video blog on YouTube.com. It appears that he initially had intended to use it for "geriatric gripes and grumbles," similar to the many young members of the site who blog about the trials and tribulations of their lives. Peter was well received by people of all ages. Early on there was a nicely done welcome and tribute to Peter that attempted to counteract some of the ageist attitudes and behaviors of some who were watching Peter's blogs. After three or four postings, the YouTube community wanted to hear about Peter's war stories and lifelong interest in motorcycles, and they loved the pictures and music he chose for his uploads. He opened all of his postings with "hello youtubers." He was soon given the title of "grandtuber" by the membership. The local and international press picked up on this unique blogger and the tremendous response he was having. In just over a month, almost 2 million people of all ages from around the world had watched his initial posting. He broke the YouTube all-time record for the number of hits and number of subscribers. This example illustrates the extreme of the private to public continuum.

By the time of his last posting, there were almost 1,000 written and hundreds of video postings saying how much they would miss him and how much he meant to the members. These included teenagers and people of all ages and backgrounds.

Peter's life stories are great but are no different than most people's. The difference is that he shares them via a technology that matches the technical skills and communication styles of younger generations. Peter reaches out to connect, and he transcends the old standards of communication by using the new standard. Few of the thousands who subscribe to Peter's blog would take the time to read his book or attend a presentation about his life story. But in a format that matches their own methods of sharing their interests and lives, they are incredibly intrigued and, in most cases, thrilled to include him. Of course, some are threatened and become angry that someone from such an old generation is infringing on their space, as evidenced by their insults. For each of those disrespectful individuals, though, there are many more YouTubers who put them in their ageist places.

This example reveals much about how many younger people feel about hearing the life stories of their elders. They value older adults' candid and honest reflections upon their lives. Viewing the video responses to Peter's postings is an excellent way to understand stages of human development, because each response reflects the developmental stage of the person who wrote it. For example, a teenager responded to Peter's au revoir posting with a tribute that included talking stuffed animals.

CONTENT VERSUS PROCESS

The final dimension of the life story matrix is the reciprocal relationship of content and process. How important is the exact detail of the material versus engaging in the process of telling one's life story? What is the emotional impact on the storyteller of disclosing traumatic experiences? What effect will sharing this information with others have on the listener or reader? Will there be consequences for the individual telling his or her story and others involved due to the nature of the experience?

Analyzing a person's social history often means obtaining critical details about his or her life as a means of exploring unresolved issues and identifying lifelong patterns of coping and problem-solving. A professional using life story approaches can gather this information in a straight-forward interview or in more creative ways; in either case, it should be remembered that the process is just as important as the content.

A trusting, emotionally supportive relationship with a professional using life story approaches, combined with creative approaches using reminiscence, will create surprises for the client. Sometimes these surprises can be strong enough to be diagnosed as posttraumatic stress disorder. Life story work is very potent, often unearthing repressed memories that may frighten clients and their families. Professionals must be able to guide people through these difficulties or refer them to others who can. Thus, if these approaches are being used clinically, they need to be framed within the context of the client's diagnosis and overall treatment plan.

In nonclinical applications, life story professionals must be prepared to screen for such issues and know how and where to make referrals for assessment and intervention, making sure that they conduct appropriate follow-up.

Elise Officer

Born in Indonesia, an orphan at age three, Elise Officer was raised in a convent. During World War II, she and her young son were taken prisoners of war by the Japanese and were forced to share a 6-by-8-foot cell with two other adults and three other children. Elise tried to shelter her son from seeing the daily torture of other prisoners. Immediately following World War II, Elise was separated from her son when she was taken hostage during the Indonesian Civil War. She eventually escaped and was reunited with her son, and they later immigrated to the United States.

> It went fast on my own because I was not born in a big family, I lost my parents when I was very young and I had to start through life by myself and finding it out so I thought on my own was kind of a nice title. Especially that it turned out fairly nice that I didn't stay on my

own. I thought they should know something. I had never known anything about my parents or mom and dad and I had so many times asked
myself I wished I had known, I had known more of my heritage I didn't
know anything about my heritage except for what people had told me
here and there a little bit and I thought they might someday ask too
what grandma's life all about because the only thing they know is that
she came from another world. I was scared to open up about so many
memories that you have tried to forget most of them that you didn't
want to think about it was not very easy to have that all down to remember and put it in the right order that the children would understand
what it is all about.

An artist's rendering (see www.yourlifestory.org), again designed to
be cut out and made into a cube, shows Elise as a child being raised by
nuns, the garden with flowers and animals where she raised her son, the
jail cell they were confined during the war, and her life in later years after
she married.

As with Hy, this interview demonstrates how Elise did a full-scale
life review, choosing to make public the many traumatic details of her
life that she might have preferred to forget and put behind her. However,
she felt it was her duty to make her children and grandchildren aware
of what her life had been like. As a result, she confronted frightening
and confusing memories from her past. In these types of situations, it is
extremely important for the interviewers to have excellent interviewing
skills, training in mental health to screen for posttraumatic stress disorder symptoms, and a willingness and knowledge of how to make appropriate referrals if necessary.

Most situations do not involve such dramatic and traumatic situations as Elise's. Much of the emotion connected with self-disclosure has
to do with the individual's:

- Self-perception of the situation at the time and in the present
- Level of cognitive and psychosocial development at the time of
  the experience
- Current level of self-esteem and physical and emotional health
- Family and cultural belief systems then and now
- Historical framework of the issues involved

For example, it should be taken into account that having a child out
of wedlock was a totally different experience during the 1930s than it
would be today. Or being openly gay or lesbian in high school today is
an entirely different experience than it would have been in the 1960s. It
is important to use great sensitivity with these issues and to always keep
in mind the subjects' perception of the experience and their physical and
emotional responses in the here and now.

Section 3 of this book focuses especially on the importance of such content versus process issues. People's life stories are with them wherever they go. The difficulties and joys they have faced are with them no matter what they do. By tapping the strengths and resources elders have developed over the course of their lives, while resolving the pain and sorrow they still face, we can help them maximize their physical and mental health and promote their further cognitive and psychosocial development.

EXERCISE

Life Story Interview

This exercise provides a guideline for someone new to doing life story work. It is designed to be completed in two phases. The first phase should be completed early on as you begin reading the book. The second phase should not be completed until you have read the entire book. In order to carry out Phase 2 in an ethical manner, it is important to recruit a mentor who has had experience in working with older adults. This may be a volunteer director, nurse, social worker, teacher, historian, or anyone who has had experience with interviewing older adults and is comfortable in this role. It is important to take this mentor relationship seriously and to complete all the suggested assignments related to that work.

Here are the instructions for each phase:

Phase 1: Your Life Story

1. Use the *Recapturing Past Resources in Times of Change* workbook to review your own life experiences. Write down your answers. Write a brief essay about and/or discuss what this experience was like for you.
2. Ask someone you know who is experienced in working with older adults to be an informal mentor as you proceed with this exercise. Ask them if they would be willing to read and discuss your essay about your life story. Tell the mentor about this book and Phase 2 of this exercise and ask him or her to be available to help you troubleshoot any issues that may develop during the life story interview that you will conduct in Phase 2.

Phase 2: Life Story Interview

1. **Do not** complete Phase 2 without first reading this book and completing the other exercises.
2. Once you have completed Step 1, find an older adult to interview, keeping the following points in mind:

- Make sure that the interview is within the bounds of your role with the older adult.
- Make sure that your client understands and agrees to the limits of the interview in terms of all three aspects of the life story matrix.
- Agree on the form of the final product of the interview. It can simply be an oral interview that is not represented in writing or any other way; however, if it will take some public form, this should be discussed before the process begins.
- Discuss any issues that develop with your mentor.

3. Take some time to discuss what this process was like for your client, and make sure that you make appropriate referrals or follow up on any unfinished business that arises.
4. Discuss with your mentor the outcome of this process for both you and your client. Pay particular attention to any surprises that my have arisen and what you did about them.
5. To contribute to the growth of this field, please consider taking a voluntary, anonymous, and quick survey about this exercise and book at www.reminiscenceandlifereview.org. Click on the survey button. The survey can be completed in 3 minutes or less.

RECAPTURING PAST RESOURCES IN TIMES OF CHANGE WORKSHEET

The *Recapturing Past Resources in Times of Change* worksheet (see Table 1.1) is designed to help individuals review their life experiences in a chronological manner so they can identify markers during their lifetime when they developed new problem-solving or coping mechanisms that led to higher levels of maturity and more advanced perspectives on their life history. It also provides an opportunity to explore and identify intergenerational life experiences, family legends, family wisdom, and family values that have become part of each individual's sense of being.

The worksheet is a guide for recording and discussing the content related to the steps described below. It is designed for use in a flexible and fluid manner. Some examples are included. The worksheet can be used as a simple tool for personal reflection, or one can take notes, write down experiences, or audio- or videotape the responses. The worksheet may be helpful for preparing and later conducting an in-person interview that is recorded or transcribed. It may be helpful to record the information on separate pages using the categories contained in the worksheet.

Step 1: Recalled Events

Relax and think back to experiences—including images, sounds, physical sensations, tastes, smells, and emotions—that you recall in relation to each stage of life listed in the guide. Try to get in touch with all five senses as your memories resurface.

Step 2: Resources Used or Developed

After you have completed Step 1, reflect on your level of cognitive and psychosocial development at that time in your life. Try to identify particular problem-solving, intellectual, and/or coping skills and values you developed as a result of these experiences at that time in your development.

Step 3: Retrospective Wisdom

As you look back at that time from your current level of development, what do you think you learned at that time?

Step 4: Intergenerational Resources and Wisdom

Think about your parents, grandparents, and other family members or close family friends. What stories, myths, or legends do you remember? How have the experiences of others shaped and influenced your experiences? Try to identify particular problem-solving, intellectual, and/or coping skills and values that you adapted for yourself as a result of their experiences.

Step 5: Application of Your Individual and Intergenerational Resources and Wisdom

Identify current or anticipated challenges or transitions. Think about ways that you can apply your individual and intergenerational resources and wisdom in these situations.

TABLE 1.1 *Recapturing Past Resources in Times of Change* Worksheet

Transitions, Changes, and Trauma

From Birth to Age 2

Events	Resources	Retrospective Wisdom
Example: Fell off the bed and head caved in.	Mother prayed.	Spirituality is very helpful.

Ages 3 to 7

Events	Resources	Retrospective Wisdom
Example: Took three years to learn how to ride a bicycle.	Mastery, independence.	Perseverance pays off. You need to laugh at yourself.

Ages 8 to 12

Events	Resources	Retrospective Wisdom
Example: Had own boat and motor.	Learned how to drive boats, independence, pride.	You can learn a lot from your father.

Ages 13 to 18

Events	Resources	Retrospective Wisdom
Example: Almost ran over Mom when she tried to get out of the car when the brakes failed.	Calm response during crisis.	Panic can cause accidents. "Someone" is looking out for you.

Ages 19 to 25

Events	Resources	Retrospective Wisdom

Ages 26 to 35

Events	Resources	Retrospective Wisdom

TABLE 1.1   *(Continued)*

Ages 36 to 45

Events	Resources	Retrospective Wisdom

Ages 56 to 65

Events	Resources	Retrospective Wisdom

Ages 66 to 75

Events	Resources	Retrospective Wisdom

Ages 76 and beyond

Events	Resources	Retrospective Wisdom

Intergenerational Resources and Wisdom

Great-grandparents and beyond

Person	Legends, Myths, Metaphors, and Wisdom About Change and Transition
Example: Great-grandparents	Great-grandmother emigrated from Norway through Canada to Wisconsin. Great-grandfather emigrated from Norway through Ellis Island to Wisconsin. They met, married, and had children. They later discovered they had been on the same boat and that she played the accordion and sang religious songs to help seasick passengers, and he rescued a baby from falling off the boat. These stories represent the family values of leadership, compassion, and heroism.

Grandparents, great-aunts, great-uncles, old-time family, friends

Person	Legends, Myths, Metaphors, and Wisdom About Change and Transition

Parents, aunts, uncles, parents' friends

Person	Legends, Myths, Metaphors, and Wisdom About Change and Transition

TABLE 1.1 *(Continued)*

Siblings, cousins, peers

Person	Legends, Myths, Metaphors, and Wisdom About Change and Transition

Approaches to facing anticipated changes and transitions

Anticipated Future Changes and Transitions	Individual and Intergenerational Resources to Apply	Wisdom to Apply	Your Future Legend
Example: Retirement.	Both grandfathers and father never stopped doing things after formal retirement.	Work can be fun. Activity keeps you young-minded and healthy.	He continued to contribute to the field after his retirement.

REFERENCES

American Society on Aging. (2006). Retrieved September 12, 2006, from www.asaging.com.

Association of Personal Historians. (2006). Retrieved September 20, 2006, from www.aph.org.

Birren Center for Autobiography and Life Review at the Institute of Gerontology at California State University, Fullerton. Retrieved September 20, 2006, from www.guidedautobiography.com.

Butler, R. N. (1963). The life review: An interpretation of reminiscence in old age. *Psychiatry Journal for the Study of Interpersonal Processes, 26,* 65–76.

Butler, R. N. (2005). The nature of memory, life review and elementality. *International Reminiscence and Life Review Conference 2005, Selected Conference Papers and Proceedings.* Superior: University of Wisconsin–Superior, 9–18.

Gerontological Society on Aging. (2006). Retrieved September 18, 2006, from www.geron.org.

International Institute for Reminiscence and Life Review. (2006). Retrieved September 14, 2006, from www.reminiscenceandlifereview.org.

Just a flicker of vulnerability. Retrieved September 9, 2006, from www.youtube.com.

Kunz, J. (1991). Case reports: Counseling approaches for disoriented older adults. *Illness Crisis and Loss, 1*(2), 91–96.

Kunz, J. (2002). *The joys and surprises of telling your life story.* Superior: Center for Continuing Education/Extension, University of Wisconsin–Superior.

Life Story Corps. (2006). Retrieved September 16, 2006, from www.storycorps.net.

National Creative Aging Center. (2006). Retrieved September 20, 2006, from www.creativeaging.org.

SECTION ONE

Reminiscence to Life Review

CHAPTER TWO

Older Adult Development

John A. Kunz

- Life, from birth to old age, can be divided into stages or cycles:
  - Dependent infants must learn to trust.
  - Very young children learn autonomy.
  - Play-age children learn to take initiative.
  - School-age children become industrious.
  - Adolescents develop their own identity.
  - Young adults develop mature, intimate relationships and bring new generations into the life cycle.
  - Middle-aged adults launch their own children, care for their parents, and look toward future generations and the community to maintain active involvement in the life cycle.
  - Older adults watch their children and grandchildren grow through the same stages of life they have gone through. Realizing they are growing through the final stage of life, older adults integrate their lifetime experiences and tie up loose ends to feel content and fulfilled.
- The strengths, knowledge, and understanding learned only by living through the earlier stages of life result in the wisdom of old age so highly respected in many cultures for centuries.
- Older adults strive to view their lives realistically, to accept past failures and future limitations, and to feel a sense of satisfaction with their lives.
- The unfinished life tasks from early stages remain in older adulthood until they are resolved as the growth cycle continues.

- Grieving the many changes and losses of a lifetime is an important task of older adulthood. Loss of physical or intellectual functioning, deaths of significant people or pets, loss of possessions, and changes in living arrangements are issues older adults must face.
- Some older adults become disoriented or confused, but this altered reality enables them to continue the tasks of old age and also serves as a poetic, expressive reflection of their inner conflicts, issues, and needs.
- Many older adults are masters at adapting to the changes in their life-style as they age.
- Successful aging is maintaining a balance of physical function and health, a high level of cognitive function, and active involvement in society.
- New brain research shows that from age 60 to 80 is a time of cognitive and psychosocial development whereby both sides of the brain are used equally, leading to a different and higher level of functioning in later adult years than was previously believed.
- *Elementality* in old age and at the end of life is the time when older adults live in the here and now, experiencing and appreciating life through their senses, while remembering the past and enjoying each moment.

EVELYN BEDORE

Born in September 1900, Evelyn Bedore still lives in her own home in Ironwood, Michigan, where I first interviewed her in 2003. She was still living at home in 2005, when the DVD *We'll Have These Moments To Remember: The Life and Spirit of Evelyn Bedore* (Kunz, 2005) premiered at the Ironwood Memorial Building. She gave a 20-minute impromptu speech at the event after everyone sang "Happy Birthday" because she had recently turned 105. Evelyn represents a living history of the entire twentieth century. Legally blind due to macular degeneration and plagued with brittle bones, her mind is as alert and sharp as ever. Her attitude is bright and cheery. She reads a book each month with her reading machine; helps with fund-raising for her church and other causes; and has a very positive outlook, enjoying each day of life while also looking forward to her death.

Evelyn worked full time at a catering business that she began in the 1940s. At age 87, she cut back and only catered part time. She now makes pastries for the annual family reunion of one long-time customer.

She makes a few at a time and freezes them. She also continues to make her Linzer torte for the church bake sale each Christmas. She measures out all the ingredients and gets the pans ready one day. The next day, she assembles the ingredients and makes the torte. She no longer makes a dozen at a time, but she has adapted to her age limitations while still continuing her lifelong passion of cooking and contributing to society.

Here is an excerpt from the video:

INTERVIEWER: How old are you?

EVELYN: I am 103. I will be 104 on the 29th of September. If I make it, and I really don't care if I do or not. Priscilla [Evelyn's daughter] will be disappointed; she said "I want you to go to 110," but I don't want to.

INTERVIEWER: Why don't you want to live to be 110?

EVELYN: Well, there are many things I can't do. I do what I can. I can talk on the telephone and I do. Last year I still did the organizing for the In Gathering, where handicapped kids receive two and a half months of rehabilitative care. . . . I get too tired of it, and more and more I need more help than I used to. You see, after I had that second fall, my right side was trashed and it never has really come back. My right side, I can't reach as far with my right arm. The shoulder was badly broken as well as the cuff. The arm has three compound fractures . . . that's when I had a stay at the rehab center. . . . I had a hard time convincing the rehab staff at Ashland that what I needed was to lay perfectly still so the bones could rebuild and fill in the cracks because he [the doctor] said, "We can't open that up, there are too many little pieces that would have to be put together and we can't do that." His nurse said "you'll eat lots of Jell-O and it'll help to form new bones." . . . I hadn't been in the hospital since 1914 except for overnight stays. As was the custom, my three children were born at home with no special excitement. Once or twice I had stayed overnight for tests and that's all. Here was all this good care and I was practically carried on a golden plate.

ADAPTIVE AND SUCCESSFUL AGING

Evelyn is an example of both successful aging (Rowe & Kahn, 1987) and adaptive aging. Through the use of adaptation and increased ways of coping with her physical changes associated with aging and health problems, Evelyn is able to maintain each of the three components of successful aging:

- Physical and functional health
- High cognitive functioning
- Active involvement in society

There is no doubt that, by maintaining her life in each of these three domains, she is better adapting to the continual physical changes associated with her age. Evelyn has always maintained a healthy diet; had plenty of exercise and hard work; didn't smoke or drink; and actively engaged in problem solving, volunteer work, and other social and productive activities. This reflects the activity theory of aging that hypothesizes that active older people are more satisfied with their lives, and their self-concept is validated through their participation in roles played in earlier life and/or through substituting such roles in a way that enables them to continue to be a vital part of society. By maintaining her interactions with the environment and a diverse variety of individuals and groups, Evelyn has been able to maintain her lifelong beliefs and identity during her aging process, as suggested in the theory of symbolic interactionism.

MASLOW'S HIERARCHY OF NEEDS

As Evelyn tells her story, it is interesting to consider how she is reflecting the aspects of Maslow's (1968) Hierarchy of Needs (see Figure 2.1). All of her physical needs are met, and, although she has a number of health complaints, she receives excellent care. Although she needs to use a walker, she rejects the idea of building a ramp because she considers ascending and descending the stairs to be a form of exercise. She is comfortable in her home and life. She is a member of the women's club and continues to socialize, especially via telephone. The community adores her. When she was in her mid-90s, the mayor wanted to tear down the Memorial Building that she had watched being built during the early 1920s. She announced publicly that he would tear that building down "over her dead body!" She then led an effort that raised $50,000 to restore the building's stained-glass windows. More recently, she and her daughter led a fund-raising campaign to re-roof her church and the attached community hall. Up until recently, she cooked and delivered a full Thanksgiving dinner to the local women's shelter each year. Evelyn represents the epitome of self-actualization. Part of this level of satisfaction with her life is, no doubt, the result of facing the many challenges throughout her life to provide for her and her family's basic needs. For example, she once fashioned a snare out of a broken fence to catch rabbits that she then butchered and cooked for supper. One week, all she had was rice, jam, and salt pork to feed her family, so she was creative and made rice cakes and rice pudding. One time a doctor told her to give her son one orange each day to

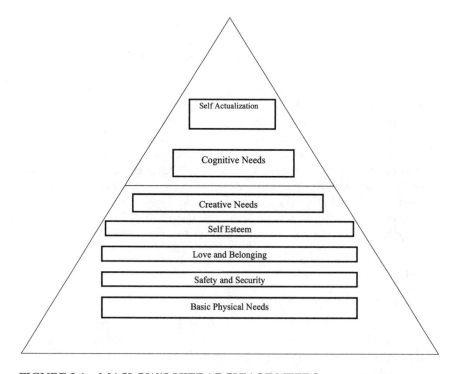

FIGURE 2.1   MASLOW'S HIERARCHY OF NEEDS.
1. Physiological Needs
     Water, food, shelter
2. Safety and Security Needs
     Freedom from fear and threat of injury, need to depend on someone, to orient oneself for order, for security for an ordered world
3. Love and Belonging Needs
     Affiliation, affection, companionship, relationship, comfort, communication, giving and receiving love
4. Self-Esteem Needs
     Dignity, respect, deserved praise, self-esteem, individuality, sexual personal identity recognition
5. Creative Needs
     Self-expression, usefulness, creativity production
6. Cognitive Needs
     Knowledge, understanding, comprehension, stimulation, personal mastery
7. Self-Actualization Needs
     Realization of potential, personal autonomy, beauty, truth, privacy, spiritual goals

help him recover from an illness. She told the doctor she couldn't afford to even give her son a slice of bread each day, let alone an orange. The doctor laughed in disbelief.

Having survived, and even thrived, in response to her life's challenges contributes to Evelyn's level of satisfaction and contentment at her current age.

ERIKSON'S STAGES OF PSYCHOSOCIAL DEVELOPMENT

The explanation of why reminiscing is so effective and validating for older adults lies in part in the principles of human psychosocial development as described by Erikson (1980). Life from birth to old age takes the form of cycles within the overall life cycle. With each stage of development lies the challenge of mastering important psychological developmental tasks in order to develop the wisdom needed to effectively carry out the tasks of the next stage. At each stage, we develop an increased knowledge base about the world around us, the roles we and others play, the values we base our decisions and actions upon, and the meaning life has for us. Each stage has its own biological and cognitive tasks and challenges as well.

Infancy

Trust Versus Mistrust (Up to Age 2)

Imagine what life is like for newborn babies. Because they are so dependent, their mother or other primary caretaker is the most important person in their world. They need to be fed, bathed, and diapered quickly and gently. If their needs are met and they are not abused or neglected, they learn to trust and feel hope. If their needs are not met, they became overly accustomed to frustration, fear, and despair. People who do not learn to trust and have hope may continue to struggle with this developmental task their entire lives. They may have great difficulty anticipating and facing changes and losses that are inevitable as they age. Their fear of abandonment and death may be quite strong. They may need an unusual amount of attention if being cared for by caregivers. They may continually test those who are most important to them as they attempt to resolve their trust issues, many times paradoxically developing abandonment situations by pushing others away.

Early Childhood

Autonomy Versus Self-Doubt and Shame (Ages 2 to 6)

Search back to your earliest memories of your childhood, piecing together the bits of memories with knowledge your parents and others have given you about yourself. Think about when you learned to walk, eat, toilet properly, and do things on your own. Imagine the willpower these tasks entail. Young children assert or often demand their ability to make decisions and become autonomous. If parental figures are supportive, accept the child's need for autonomy, and provide the balance of permissiveness versus direction needed, then young children develop a sense of pride, confidence, and independence. If young children are not able to successfully accomplish this developmental task, they may feel shame, have low self-esteem, or be reckless and uncaring toward others. These unresolved issues may plague their relationships throughout their lives. Related personality problems may become obstacles to receiving care from others. This type of older adult may become the victim of resident dumping, whereby long-term care facility staff become burned-out on providing care.

Play Age

Initiative Versus Guilt (Ages 6 to 10)

Remember the childhood games you played? Children's play activities may include birthday parties, playing outdoors, or building a fort in the living room. During the play age, from ages 3 to 6, children are still very self-centered, but they also become aware of the consequences of actions and thus develop a conscience. At this stage, along with parents, playmates also become significant. It is a time for showing off, looking for approval, and having a sense of purpose. This drive of doing things may result in decisions based on sound or poor judgment.

If the resources of playmates are supportive, yet directive parenting is not available, children at this age may feel further shame or morally bad and may utilize poor decision making their entire lives. It may be very difficult for an older adult who never successfully completed this stage of development to make appropriate or realistic choices regarding his or her own health care. The personality problems associated with unresolved developmental issues at this stage may result in these individuals being social isolates, poor roommates, and difficult for caregivers to deal with.

School Age

Industry Versus Inferiority (Ages 10 to 14)

"School days, school days, good old golden rule days." This whimsical song represents the fond memories many older adults have regarding their childhood. This era of psychosocial development is a time for achievement, positive social interaction, and competition. Children at this age find their peers as well as other adults helpful as role models and mentors as they learn about many of life's fascinating activities. When the developmental needs of family security and support as well as ample opportunity for challenge and knowledge at the child's level of cognitive ability are present, children develop a sense of intellectual and social competence. Great life satisfaction is derived from initiating, participating in, and completing intellectual and social activities.

When children are not challenged at an appropriate level or are preoccupied with family, health, or related stressors, they may withdraw at this stage, feel left out, have low self-esteem, and may engage in antisocial acts. Individuals who did well at this stage of development generally remain involved in prosocial activities throughout their lives. As older adults, they are usually seen as model participants in community or long-term care settings. Individuals who are unable to accomplish these developmental tasks may continually perceive themselves and act as though they are social outcasts in any setting. They also may have difficulties with roommates and have personality conflicts with staff, instigate problem situations, dislike group activities, and generally be antisocial.

Adolescence

Identity Versus Role Confusion (Ages 14 to 20)

Recall what life was like during your adolescence, when you developed secondary sexual characteristics and experienced hormonal changes, crushes, confusion, and erratic, intense mood swings. Children this age are withdrawn and exhausted one moment, pulsing with energy and drive the next. This is a time when children begin to question or perhaps totally disagree with their parents' beliefs and join with the values of peers and other adult mentors instead. What was your hairstyle when you were 16? What music did you listen to, what clothes did you wear, and what activities did you pursue?

Adolescence is an incredible stage of development in terms of physical and emotional changes, all yielding a further developed individual identity. The questions "Who am I and what is my purpose in life?" are prominent in thought and behavior. The heightened sense of social awareness and self-consciousness is a result of having a broader sense of the world. Individuals who do well at this stage of development have a strong sense of their personal values and direction they want their life to take. Decisions about career and future plans come relatively easy. Social relationships become increasingly important, and, although social skills are improving, many of these relationships are the educational resources

needed to move adolescents toward the interdependent relationship competence they need as adults. Lack of opportunity, inadequate resolution
of earlier developmental tasks, preoccupation with family, emotional or
physical illness, chemical abuse, dysfunctional peer pressure (i.e., gangs),
or other stressors may result in significant problems for adolescents.
Interpersonal relationship problems, social or sexual confusion, social
withdrawal, delinquent behavior, depression, and thoughts of suicide
may all become evident. Without timely and appropriate assessment and
intervention, these issues may result in lifelong personality patterns that
may negatively affect their relationships throughout their lives. As older
adults, these patterns remain and may contribute to continual refusal of
care; dishonesty; substance abuse; and aggressive, problematic behavior
toward others, including verbal, physical, and sexual abuse. Having driv-
en family and friends away, these older adults are commonly alone and
lonely. Their personality problems continue to drive those trying to help
them further away. Older adults who have not successfully completed the
tasks of adolescence make frequent, unjust complaints and sometimes
threaten lawsuits.

Young Adulthood

Intimacy Versus Isolation (Ages 20 to 30)

"First comes love, then comes marriage, then comes [insert name] pushing the baby carriage." Another whimsical view of this stage of life
as portrayed by children at play. By young adulthood, individuals are
most likely able to develop and participate in independent, intimate
personal relationships with friends and potential life partners. Careers
are crucial as individuals at this stage become independent and self-
supporting. Social patterns become more set. Frequently, this is a time
when young adults consider love, commitment, and children. As a
result, partners, children, close friends, and work relationships become
most significant.

Earlier developmental task failure, poor relationship and societal
options, emotional or physical health problems, abuse by others, or ad-
diction problems can all hinder the accomplishments during the early
adulthood stage of life. This may result in a string of relationship failures, employment problems, poor relationships with children, disability,
isolation, and other ongoing difficulties. Older adults who encountered
difficulties at the early adulthood stage of development will likely continue to have difficulty being direct in their communication style and
may have stormy relationship issues with family members, roommates,
and staff members. They may appear as emotionally needy, but efforts

to meet their needs frequently may be unsuccessful. The emotional maturity of caregivers to this population needs to be high because it is tested regularly.

Adulthood

Generativity Versus Stagnation (Ages 30 to 60)

Given the demands placed on adults, it is difficult to imagine the opportunity for middle-aged adults to become stagnant. However, when the resolution of earlier developmental tasks has been unsuccessful or emotional, physical, or other types of abuse have taken their toll, middle-aged adults may be old before their time. They may become self-absorbed with their personal issues, give up on a purpose in life beyond their own existence, and exploit others. These individuals frequently become involved with caregivers at a younger age and may be demanding of time and draining of staff energy.

Usually people at this stage of life are filled with creative energies, are strongly involved with families or community, and are at the epitome of their careers. They've launched their children and have discovered the joys of grandparenthood. They feel fulfilled with their existence, have a sense of satisfaction with their lives so far, and set goals for future plans and adventures, perhaps including retirement. Similar to each stage of development, but often with more awareness, middle-aged adults reexamine their beliefs and values to further adjust their life course before old age. They often report having a broader, more flexible outlook on life and the choices people make.

Old Age

Integrity Versus Despair (Age 60 and Over)

The wisdom acquired as a result of living long enough to reach the highest level of psychosocial development is what Erikson (1980) sees as available to older adults. Older adults in this stage strive to integrate past psychological themes into a new level of psychosocial meaning. Just as adolescents see the world differently than young adults, older adults have a unique and wiser perspective about the world and their lives. Looking at one's overall lifetime and achieving a sense of integrity about one's life is what Erikson sees as the final stage of life.

Older adults strive to put their lives in perspective. They look at life more realistically than ever. They attempt to resolve their feelings about past failures and guilt about mistakes they've made. They continue to grieve the changes and losses they've encountered throughout their lives.

They remember and celebrate their successes and the many good things that have happened during their years.

This life review process is what Butler (1963) described as a normative process engaged in by anyone, regardless of age, when aware that they are approaching death. As part of the life review process, individuals look back at their entire lifetime, try to resolve past conflicts, accept negative experiences, celebrate or relish accomplishments and experiences, and, overall, feel a sense of accomplishment and closure. Memories from the distant past become more vivid as one goes into the 80s and beyond.

Older adults are more aware than any other age group that death is inevitable. Reading the obituary column usually is a standard practice for people in this age group. The task of resolving feelings about the meaning of death and facing death with dignity is primary for older adults throughout this stage of development.

Watching younger generations mature through the same life cycle as they did helps older adults better appreciate the lives they've led. Older adults have a realistic and wise perspective to offer to younger people, which, unfortunately, is often overlooked. Frequently characterized as rigid and unchanging, older adults have actually had their limits of flexibility expanded more than any other age group.

It is interesting to think about Erikson's Stages of Psychosocial Development as Evelyn talks about her life story. The following quote reflects her resolution of ego integrity versus despair:

> We were planning my funeral about ten years ago. I had a couple of pretty shocking incidences of stomach trouble and I thought, you know, this could kill me. I'll get my funeral taken care of, so we had my funeral planned in a week. . . . We haven't had a chance to use any of them [the plans] yet. But we will. We will celebrate the life that I had—the good parts. The bad parts are pretty much forgotten or appear as blemishes on the sky. You can't dwell on the bad parts, but if you do you're done for. . . . If you want it [life] bad enough go for it!

ELEMENTALITY

Building upon his work with his collaborator and wife, Myrna Lewis, and the work of Erikson, Robert Butler (2005) has begun to rework earlier discussions of elementality. He states that elementality is

> the capacity to enjoy the fullness of the moment . . . , a return to the spontaneity of childhood and its pleasures, memories and emotions. . . . When we recover such memories of a distant childhood, we gain

strength and a sense of peace. Elementality, pensive and evocative, is a way to freedom from anxiety. . . . One of the tasks of late life is learning not to think as much in terms of the future but to confront and deal with the past, and to live to the fullest in the moment, emphasizing the quality of the time remaining rather than the quantity. (Butler, 2005, pp. 9–18)

The question of how much these ideas relate to normal aging and human development versus death and dying is like looking at two sides of a coin. The more we age, the more we realize the inevitability of death. When we face death at any age, the more we realize how precious life is.

NEW BRAIN DEVELOPMENT IN OLD AGE

Is Evelyn an exception to the rules of old age or is it possible for many people to age as she has? Until recently, there were few role models like her, and the medical community—including psychologists—gave little credence to any psychosocial development beyond the age of 65 or so, let alone thought that cognitive development may continue into very old age.

Things have changed, and now Gene Cohen (2005) and others are saying that there is brain and psychosocial development past the age of 65. Cohen posits that:

- The brain has the capacity to "remodel" itself—that is, certain genes are activated by experience as we age, allowing our personalities to grow and change in surprising ways.
- The brain can "recruit" areas of itself that were underused in earlier years. These reserves of strength and agility can compensate for the effects of aging in other parts of the brain.
- It is in the latter stages of life, ages 60 to 80, that the brain's "information processing center" achieves its greatest density and reach.

COHEN'S FOUR PHASES OF THE
SECOND HALF OF LIFE

Most of the theory discussed earlier in this book defines old age and retirement at age 65 and above. In his book *The Mature Mind,* Cohen (2005) points out how little attention has been paid to this period of later life that can span over 50 years if someone lives that long. Everyone ages differently, and those differences between older adults continue to expand as their unique paths further unfold. Cohen offers a valuable framework for studying and discussing older adults' cognitive and psychosocial development.

Cohen postulates four phases during the latter part of life. The first phase—mid-life reevaluation—is characterized by reevaluation, exploration, and transition. "The brain changes during this phase spur developmental intelligence, which is the basis for wisdom" (Cohen, 2005, p. 52).

The second phase—liberation—occurs in what many call the "third age" and includes liberation, experimentation, and innovation. The plans of older adults in this phase are the result of the realization that if they are going to do something different, now is the time. Cohen says "new neuron formation in the information processing part of the brain is associated with a desire for novelty at this time of life" (Cohen, 2005, p. 52).

Cohen's third phase—summing up—is a time when people engage in much more of what Erikson described as old age. This is a time when unresolved issues are dealt with, and people engage in the life review described by Butler. At this point, "bilateral involvement of the hippocampi contribute to our capacity for autobiographical expression" (Cohen, 2005, p. 53).

Most previous theories leave older adults at this summing up phase, assuming the completion of this phase will eventually lead to a good death. This is the stage that Evelyn, who was featured earlier in this chapter, was in when she planned her funeral in her 90s.

However, many people now move past the summing up phase to what Cohen describes as the encore phase. Older adults in this fourth phase continue their lifelong interests and themes but also explore what Cohen (2005) says are "novel variations on those themes" (p. 53). Their desire to live well to the very end of life fits well with the concept of elementalism discussed earlier in this chapter.

Evelyn's life story includes many such encores: saving the memorial building from being destroyed, fund-raising for a new church roof, and continuing to bake her Linzer torte each Christmas. How do people like Evelyn maintain such a positive outlook? Cohen (2005) says that "further changes in the amygdalae promote positive emotions and morale" (p. 53).

As with any stage or phase theory, these phases are not set in stone, and older adults may revisit these stages as the health and psychosocial issues in their lives evolve. For example, a woman caring for a disabled husband for a decade or two may find herself at phase one (reevaluation) or phase two (liberation) following his death and the successful completion of her grief process. These phases may end up being incorporated into her grief process. Someone who survives a serious cancer treatment and hadn't expected to live may then experience the encore phase or even the earlier reevaluation and liberation phases.

We are at a new crossroad in understanding the aging brain and human development past age 65. For years, gerontologists have cited lists of older people—such as artist Grandma Moses—who accomplished great feats when over age 65, but these people typically have been viewed as the exception rather than the rule. However, with the latest research and understanding of human development combined with new medical treatments, we have the potential to appreciate and cheer on the creativity and productivity of the aging baby boom generation. This group has always brought change with it, and now again the world will benefit from a more conscious aging process.

These new concepts about development help me better understand two observations that I've made about the newly retired and people in their 80s. There are changes in behaviors and thought patterns of newly retired individuals and increased reminiscing in people around the age of 80.

Many people that I used to work with who have since retired have a new energy and freedom about them. Their personalities flow more easily, they are brutally honest about themselves and sometimes other people, and they seem to converse and problem solve in a much more circular manner. I've particularly noticed this when they are in their 60s. Cohen (2005) writes that people who have aged successfully in the absence (or good management) of physical and mental health problems think more with both sides of their brain rather than the previously dominant side. Younger adults tend to think more with only the dominant side of their brain. This may help explain what I've seen in my former colleagues who have retired.

Furthermore, Cohen (2005) writes that autobiographical memory is essential in old age, because the aging brain creates a kind of backup copy of the lifelong memories of an individual on the less-dominant side of the brain, thus protecting memories for further use since there are now two identical copies of a lifetime of memories, one on each side of the brain.

Fifty years after Robert Butler (1963) coined the term *life review* and suggested that the process of reviewing one's life was a universal part of the aging process, Cohen (2005) presents scientific evidence that life review is part of successful and normal aging. This explains my second observation that, around the age of 80, reminiscence and life review activities seem to become much more significant in people's lives.

These developments bring up many questions to consider when doing life story work with older adults:

1. What are the best ways to facilitate specialized adult development in old age?
2. Should we rethink and rework our life story approaches to reflect both the summing up of life and the further development of life?

3. Is it possible that, even with cases of dementia, there may be a way to facilitate continued development?
4. What will be the impact of this paradigm shift?

I had the honor of speaking with a prominent gerontological nurse at a conference. She had just fully retired at the age of 75. She talked about how much she enjoyed spending a full day simply watching DVDs of a television series she had always wanted to watch but had never had time for. She chose to attend her granddaughter's high school musical concert the night before instead of attending a book signing for what she believed was her last book about the history of gerontological nursing. Vibrant, alive, and brimming with life satisfaction balanced with sincere modesty, she talked about human development and aging. Her priorities had become realigned. As we talked about conscious aging and the fate of the baby boomers, she was frank in raising the question of how much was really new material about aging and how much was simply coming to light because of the denial of the forces of aging by the latest members of U.S. society to go there.

We are at a pivotal point in the understanding of the cognitive and psychosocial functions of old age and human development. More than ever, it appears that life story work is crucial in facilitating such development in old age. The future of this field is filled with opportunities to demonstrate such impact and evaluate the results.

The Rocking Chair

A woman in her 80s once told me that she would have brought the rocking chair that had belonged to her grandfather to her reminiscence group's "show-and-tell," but when she'd sold her home and moved into an apartment, she'd given the chair to her granddaughter and never saw or heard about the chair again.

This unfortunate situation and lost opportunity demonstrates how the woman's material loss was compounded by the lack of response from her granddaughter. In such a situation, the loss could have been supplanted and the grandmother's memories and life role expanded if her granddaughter had taken further action. The granddaughter could have taken a photograph of her own daughter sitting in the chair and had it enlarged for her grandmother. The grandmother would then have an intergenerational photograph of her great-granddaughter sitting in her grandfather's chair that she'd given to her granddaughter. The loss would have been transformed into an asset that represented several aspects significant to the grandmother's identity. The grandmother could be reminded of this by the photograph, and caregivers could utilize it as a reminiscence or life review cue.

Communication is a key to understanding and responding to older adults:

- First, establish attention using a combination of touch, voice, and eye contact.
- Maintain appropriate physical closeness or distance where you sense the older adult is best able to feel comfortable.
- Adjust the volume and tone of your voice so you can best be understood.
- Remember that 90 percent of communication is nonverbal. Mirror the older adult's posture. Stand or sit at the same level.
- You are the one with the greatest flexibility. Adjust your physical placement, closeness, voice, etc. to best communicate with them.
- Go at their pace. Don't talk too fast or change topics too quickly.
- Look and listen for feedback from them to know whether you're being understood.
- Start at their level and, if necessary and possible, try to lead the conversation to a more functional level.
- Utilize information about reminiscence and life review.
- Make sure you have their attention when making shifts in conversation or when introducing new topics.
- Plan what you have to say beforehand so you can present yourself in the most easily understood manner and minimize misunderstandings.
- Consider breaking information into small segments to be introduced one at a time.
- Keep your expectation of the older adult to the here and now.
- The more disoriented or confused the older adults may be, the less important it is for them to recognize you or understand your role with them. You should use fewer words to make greater use of their shorter attention span.
- Respect their role in the relationship with you. Be gracious in accepting their best wishes, expression of interest, and care for you.
- Remind yourself of their perspective, issues, and feelings when they are critical, blaming, or attacking you. Protect yourself, show your feelings, but remember why they're acting the way they are.
- Get support for yourself. Caring for older adults can be very demanding and stressful.

EXERCISE

Greta Spindler was 98 years old at the time of this interview by John A. Kunz (Kunz, 1997). As you read the interview, keep this chapter in mind, and then answer and/or discuss the questions that follow.

JOHN: You've said that it's different being 98 years old. What do you mean by that?

GRETA: Because you think differently when you are old, differently and when you are visiting with younger people they don't see the things you see and that you enjoy. They enjoy other things. I enjoyed those things when I was young but now when I'm old I have my special things that I enjoy. I sit out here and look at the beautiful hillside and thank God for giving us such a beautiful world to live in and to try to make the most of it every minute. I meditate, I don't dwell on myself and my problems, I try to think of better things. I try to make the day a good day. Sometimes I wish I was younger and I wish I had done a lot of things I didn't do. You know, you think about the past and then you have the future to think about. I wish I had been a great musician, I love music and I appreciate music.

JOHN: So you love music and appreciate listening to it.

GRETA: I love good music, I especially like going to opera.

JOHN: You love opera?

GRETA: And I have attended opera and it is wonderful the singing and the acting and the story, I just love grand opera.

JOHN: Now what about your long-time friends and family?

GRETA: Well, you see they are all gone. I have no real close friends left, and my family is mostly my brother's children. He has two nice daughters and they come to see me and we have a nice visit.

JOHN: Do they live near here?

GRETA: Yes they live in Duluth.

JOHN: So they see you often?

GRETA: Quite often, then they're real busy girls.

JOHN: And then you have your daughter?

GRETA: And of course she is away, thousands of miles away.

JOHN: Your daughter is?

GRETA: In Florida, Orlando. We talk on Sunday ever since she left Duluth. We have set aside an hour on Sunday to visit.

JOHN: Do you miss your parents?

GRETA: Well, you know, that happened so many years ago that, well, you miss them at first but you gradually get accustomed to not having them. You can get used to anything if it lasts long enough, I think.

JOHN: I see.

GRETA: They were old and frail, you know, now with my mother, she just went to bed and went to sleep, that was it. Wasn't that beautiful?

JOHN: It was.

GRETA: She lived with one of my nieces and they went up to see her and she just wouldn't wake up, we were grateful.

JOHN: I imagine so, I would be too.

GRETA: Yes, she was old and frail and didn't have much to live for; you know, that's the way you live when you get old. Look at me, I'm old, I don't have a great deal to live for, but make the most of what you got is my philosophy.

JOHN: That's a great philosophy. Do you think about your family and parents when you were young?

GRETA: Oh yes. I think the older you get the more you think about when you were young and your parents.

JOHN: That's what I've been told by many older people. What do you remember best about your days when you were young?

GRETA: I think that I remember when we were all at home and lived in a big house and we had four bedrooms, every bedroom occupied with two or three people. My sister and I had a beautiful big room and the two boys the two rooms together and two boys in each room and my mother and father were down on the ... there was a bedroom on the main floor so they were away from all this restlessness.

JOHN: Sounds like it was just perfect.

GRETA: We had lots of fun. My mother was a good cook and the kids would be hanging around the kitchen while she was cooking a meal and she would say, "Now leave me alone and I'll get it done quicker."

JOHN: Do you remember some of your favorite things that she made?

GRETA: I remember pancakes. Isn't that funny? We had a stove with two lids that you could take off and then she had a pan that fitted into that. It filled in that area and she could make about six pancakes at a time and they would be gobbled up as fast as she could make them.

JOHN: Now I remember you telling me that when you were, I don't know, 18 or so that when World War I was going on and that you ended up taking a man's job.

GRETA: For the express company, the railway express company. At first, I did some work in the office and then I went out and collected, if you know what that is. People would send express prepaid and I would go to the offices and collect the prepaid, the money. I'd get the bills. I was called the collector.

JOHN: So you were the collector?

GRETA: I liked it. I met so many nice people.

JOHN: I bet you were good at that.

GRETA: Oh, I don't know but I was happy with it. I know when we were married that people—Bridget and Russell—sent ice cream, individual molds of ice cream, for my wedding as a present, and the Duluth Oil Company made my wedding bouquet and my bridesmaid bouquet. These were gifts from the people I collected from. We went down to Lake Nebagamon one weekend with some neighbors that took me along with them and we went several times and then this lady, this Misses Spindler, a neighbor lady, said there's the nicest young man that I'm going to invite to go, and that was my husband and we met that day and then we saw each other. I wasn't too crazy about him at first, you know, I wasn't, I wasn't interested in getting married, but he was a wonderful husband, he was so, he was wonderful. And, you know, I think his happy life helped him in his work because, you know, he got one promotion after another; he ended up in the top of the department. It was an office in a loading building and I like to think that it was our happy life that made him a likeable man.

JOHN: I bet it was. I bet your life with him helped him tremendously.

GRETA: I didn't let anything interfere with his work, I thought that was very important. If he was tired, we didn't do anything. If he had something to do important, then I said, well, we could make other plans, but his work came first and he went to the very top in his work. I was proud of him. I was live in Saint Ann's, we were living in Saint Ann's and something happened. I fell, I might have had a heart attack or stroke or something, that's why I'm here and he died. I can't get that all straightened out in my mind.

JOHN:　That's all a little confusing?

GRETA:　It's all mixed up.

JOHN:　That was awhile ago?

GRETA:　Oh yeah.

JOHN:　Now what's happened to all your friends?

GRETA:　They have died, they're not living and I've lost contact. You know what? You don't want to think about that. I don't want to think about that. Who died, who didn't and I didn't and I'm not in contact with any that are living so I just don't think about it. That's why I listen to a lot of music, it takes my mind off myself. Or in the morning when I got to wake up early I shed a few tears nearly everyday but maybe that's good. I'm lonesome, but it's not that I feel sorry for myself, that's the worst thing that people can do is to feel sorry for themselves. Maybe I'm lucky that I didn't commit any crimes. I have earphones and I can tune in, I put on the phones in the afternoon and they pick up news around the city. I know what is going on, and then in the evening there is music and you know me and music more important than lobster. So I know how to manage.

Study Questions

1. How do you see Greta adapting and adjusting to the changes in her life?
2. How has Greta adapted to the changes in her life-style over time?
3. Would you consider Greta to have been successful at aging?
4. Discuss Greta's life in terms of Maslow's Hierarchy of Needs.
5. How does the interview with Greta reflect Erikson's Stages of Psychosocial Development?
6. Does Greta reflect any type of new brain development in this interview?
7. Has Greta reached the stage of elementalism?
8. What role does reminiscence and life review play in Greta's life satisfaction at this point in time?
9. Where do you see Greta in terms of Cohen's Four Phases of the Second Half of Life?

REFERENCES

Butler, R. N. (1963). The life review: An interpretation of reminiscence in old age. *Psychiatry Journal for the Study of Interpersonal Processes, 26,* 65–76.
Butler, R. N. (2005). The nature of memory, life review and elementality. *International Reminiscence and Life Review Conference 2005, Selected Conference Papers and Proceedings.* Superior: University of Wisconsin–Superior, 9–18.
Cohen, G. (2005). *The mature mind.* New York: Basic Books.
Erikson, E. (1980). *Identity and the life cycle.* New York: Norton.
Kunz, J. (1997). *Older adult development, mental health and aging video training series* [Video]. Chicago, IL: Terra Nova Films.
Kunz, J. (2005). *We'll have these moments to remember: The life and spirit of Evelyn Bedore* [Video]. Superior: Center for Continuing Education/Extension University of Wisconsin–Superior.
Maslow, A. H. (1968). *Toward a psychology of being.* New York: Van Nostrand.
Rowe, J. W., & Kahn, R. L. (1987). Human aging: Usual and successful. *Science, 237,* 143–149.

CHAPTER THREE

Reminiscence and Older Adults

Florence Gray Soltys and John A. Kunz

- Remembering past events and reviewing certain aspects of life is healthy and common to do at any age.
- As part of the human life cycle, older adults especially need to integrate their lifetime experience and tie up loose ends.
- The heartwarming, joyous memories from the past contribute to daily contentment.
- Remembering and sharing painful life experiences promotes greater emotional healing and acceptance of life's unfortunate circumstances.
- Remembering the way difficult times were faced in the past helps people better face difficult times today.
- Reminiscing helps people grieve the loss of people, pets, and material items no longer in their lives.
- Reminiscing helps people maintain an awareness of who they are, where they have been, and what roles they have played in their lifetime.
- Reminiscing helps bridge the gap between generations and passes on important life events, values, and beliefs.
- Reminiscence is often seen as more random and spontaneous, while life review is seen as more evaluative and contemplative.
- Normal reminiscence has been identified as serving distinct functions.
- Specific applications of reminiscence and the life review process guided by the Reminiscence Engagement Process and the SolCos

Reminiscence Model can be helpful in a full spectrum of approaches.

- Reminiscing may serve the purpose of copying memories from the dominant side of the brain to the less dominant side of the brain to help preserve brain function and facilitate cognitive development in later life.

One of Florence Gray Soltys's most precious possessions is the written memories of her 95-year-old mentor and friend. She lived to be 97.

It was a December Sunday in 1892 that I came to my mother. Though I was too young to remember any of the details, I had a perfect mental picture of my arrival that has persisted through the years.

"Where did I come from?" I asked Letty, our maid. "I found you in a rosebush," was her reply. If she ever pointed out the particular bush to me, I do not know, but I have always pictured it as the first in a row of three bushes on the north side of the house.

"Was I crying?" I asked Letty. "No, you were just laying there smiling," she answered.

"A rather intriguing picture of myself I always found it; a wee, naked baby, oblivious to the chill of December's wind or the briers or thorns that made up my bed—just lying there smiling."

Then the best question of all, "and what did you do then?" I asked. "I picked you up and carried you into the house [to Miss Mattie], and she didn't have no clothes for you so I wrapped you up in an old flannel petticoat." It was a lovely story that was repeated again and again during the early years of my life.

The term *life review* was coined by Butler (1963) when he began to scientifically identify life review as a normal aspect of older adult development. This research led the way for society to look at reminiscence and the life review process as a part of normal human aging. He also asserted that life review was normal for anyone approaching death. It is natural for people at the end of their lives to want to put their lives in perspective, resolve past conflicts, grieve losses and changes, forgive themselves and others for wrongdoings, celebrate their successes, and feel a sense of completion. Erikson (1980) also discusses older adults' reconciliation with the inevitability of death. The wisdom acquired as a result of living long enough to reach the highest level of psychosocial development is what he called "ego integrity versus despair." Looking at one's lifetime and achieving a sense of integrity about one's life is what Erikson believed to be the final stage of life.

Since Butler first introduced the term life review, there has been a great amount of discussion and investigation regarding the definition and usefulness of reminiscence and life review (see Haight & Webster, 1995, for an overview). Parker (1995) cited a number of both positive and negative outcomes of studies of the effectiveness of reminiscence and found that there were clearly two camps with regard to the utility of reminiscence; she concluded that reminiscence has no influence on well-being. She hypothesized that continuity therapy may best explain the adaptive process of reminiscence.

In defining reminiscence and life review, Haight and Webster (1995) synthesized the existing literature into four areas with five dimensions in each area. The four categories of recall were reminiscence, life review, autobiography, and narrative. They defined the five dimensions of reminiscence as highly spontaneous, frequent in practice, requiring little structure, noncomprehensive, and only moderately evaluative. Life review, on the other hand, was seen as highly structured and evaluative, very comprehensive, only moderately spontaneous, and lower in frequency. Autobiography was seen as the least spontaneous, low in frequency, moderately comprehensive and evaluative, and highly structured. Narrative was seen as relatively low in evaluation and comprehensiveness, low to medium in structure and frequency, and medium to high in spontaneity.

WEBSTER'S REMINISCENCE FUNCTION SCALE

Webster (1993, 1997) and Webster and McCall (1999) identified eight separate reminiscence functions by administering questionnaires to males and females of various ages and of diverse educational, cultural, and ethnic backgrounds. From a factor analysis of these results, Webster produced a robust 43-item Reminiscence Functions Scale (Gibson, 2004, pp. 25–26, summarizes the scale well) organized according to eight functions described below that apply across all age groups, from young adulthood to late life (Webster, 1997, p. 140):

1. Boredom reduction: having something to do.
   "Our propensity to reminisce when our environment is understimulating and we lack engagement in goal-directed activities."
2. Death preparation: valuing the life lived and becoming less fearful of death.
   "The way we use our past when thoughts of our own mortality are salient and may contribute to a sense of closure and calmness."

3. Identity: discovering and better understanding a sense of who we are.
   "How we use our past in an existential manner to discover, clarify, and crystallize important dimensions of our sense of who we are."
4. Problem solving: drawing on strengths and experience from the past for coping in the present.
   "How we employ reminiscence as a constructive coping mechanism whereby the remembrance of past problem-solving strategies may be used again in the present."
5. Conversation: rediscovering common bonds among old and new friends.
   "Our natural inclination to invoke the past as a means of connecting or reconnecting with others in an informal way."
6. Intimacy maintenance: remembering personally significant people.
   "Cognitive and emotional representations of important persons in our lives are resurrected in lieu of the remembered person's physical presence."
7. Bitterness revival: sustaining memories of old hurts and justifying negative thoughts and emotions.
   "The extent to which memories are used to effectively charge recalled episodes in which the reminiscer perceives themselves as having been unjustly treated."
8. Teach/inform: teaching younger people, including family members about values and history.
   "The ways in which we use reminiscence to relay to others important information about life (e.g., a moral lesson). It is an instructional type of narrative."

This taxonomy also fits well within the framework of this book as we look at the three dimensions of the life story matrix and the role of these functions on each of the three dimensions. The SolCos Model and Reminiscence Engagement Process provide methods to facilitate these eight functions of reminiscence.

Subsequent chapters demonstrate the application of often-overlapping functions of reminiscence in more specialized areas or fields. For example, the chapters on mental health, posttraumatic stress, and end of life focus heavily on Webster's reminiscence functions of death preparation, problem solving, and bitterness revival. Section 2 of this book, which examines the continuum from private to public, especially involves the functions of boredom reduction, identity, conversation, and transfer of knowledge.

Only recently has scientific evidence suggested that autobiographical work in the later years is a function of cognitive development. In his groundbreaking book, *The Mature Mind,* Cohen (2005) asserts that high-level-functioning individuals begin to copy memory from the dominant side of the brain to the less dominant side of the brain at age 60 and beyond. This leads to their ability to eventually protect brain function by using both sides of their brain on an equal basis rather than relying only on the dominant side of the brain. This discovery shows great promise for future uses of reminiscence and life review approaches that may better facilitate this recently identified phenomena.

Precise definitions are most helpful in conducting research, but the processes become blurred when they are used in a clinical setting or as part of normal day-to-day life. Some older adults naturally engage in activities that enable them to accomplish the developmental tasks of life described by Erikson and accomplish what Butler referred to as life review. Family or class reunions, annual events, and even funerals are examples of events when natural reminiscing occurs (Kunz, 1991).

As individuals age, more and more significant people in their lives may die, become disabled, move, or for some other reason become unavailable. Thus, there are fewer contacts available to promote natural reminiscence, and more structured approaches may be needed to promote quality of life through the facilitation of normal developmental processes. Such techniques may be particularly useful in enabling older adults to apply the wisdom of providers and other multidisciplinary professionals, particularly if the client has some level of cognitive impairment (Kunz, 1997). Grief therapy can result in desired changes in a single session.

As one ages, the need to put one's life experiences into an understandable perspective becomes an important life task. This may not be true for some whose lives have been especially painful with experiences such as sexual abuse or crime victimization. The inability to resolve these painful experiences may result in late-life depression.

Conflict for some can bring strength and growth. As John Dewey (1922) stated: "Conflict is the gadfly of thought. It stirs us to observation and memory. It instigates to invention. It shocks us out of sleep-like passivity, and sets us at mating and contriving—conflict is a 'sine qua non' of reflection and ingenuity."

Depression can occur as a result of illness or life events, such as the loss of a loved one. But even with loss and difficulties, life offers pleasure and happiness. It is not normal for older people to be "down in the dumps" for a long time. Older persons without depression are able to bounce back from hard times and find joy in life.

It is important to recognize that anyone can get depressed for a while, but when someone gets stuck in a depression, they should be evaluated for a depression illness. When depression lasts for two weeks or more, it requires attention and probably treatment.

Individuals with painful memories may resist reminiscing about their lives. It becomes too painful, and they are uncertain of a resolution. But sometimes our thinking, if left to itself, may become biased, distorted, partially uninformed, or downright prejudiced. Yet the quality of our life and what we produce, make, or build depends precisely on the quality of our thoughts. Shoddy thinking is costly, in terms of both money and quality of life. Excellence in thought, however, must be systematically cultivated (Paol & Elder, 2002).

Providing the opportunity for individuals to share their joys, experiences, and sadness can bring an inner peace to their lives. Reminiscence can create thinking that is self-directed, self-disciplined, self-motivated, and self-corrective. For clinicians who work to help clients embrace their quality of life, the use of reminiscence can be a gift to bring together the wholeness of clients' lives.

Whether one is facing a critical time such as the loss of a loved one, terminal illness, retirement, or another life-changing event or seeking enjoyment and growth related to the exploration and passing of his or her life history on to the next generation, the use of reminiscence allows one to put life into perspective and define one's hopes for the future. It can help one see the circumstances in which a decision was made and appreciate the road taken versus the road not taken. It further allows one to forgive and to express one's love for family and friends. Indeed, forgiveness is essential for healing and reaching peace with one's life.

SOLCOS REMINISCENCE MODEL

Soltys and Coats (1994) developed the SolCos Reminiscence Model (see Figure 3.1) to enhance the art of reminiscence. Not only does the model provide a framework to help with reminiscence work, but it expresses the enrichment that clinicians gain from the interaction. The model is flexible rather than linear in its approach. The model was conceptualized and articulated visually based on the Soltys's experience in using reminiscence with various individuals and in various situations. The model outlines strategies and suggests outcomes for both the facilitator and the client.

The model was generated based on experience and logic. Conversations between the authors (Coats and Soltys) about reminiscence activities yielded a process pattern. Subsequently, the pattern components were sequenced and verified through repeated appreciation. Finally, the components were analyzed to elucidate subcomponents, and all elements were put together in a visual design. The basic components were then further defined. The model consists of three major components: processes, items, and outcomes.

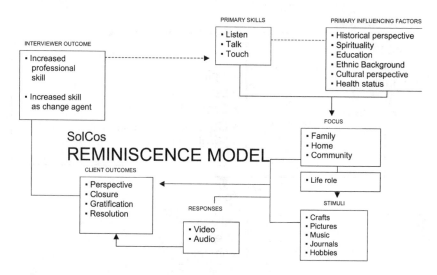

FIGURE 3.1   Facilitator and client outcomes. © Soltys and Coats (1994).

Within the processes component, three subcomponents exist: primary skills, primary influencing factors, and focus (see Figure 3.2). The items component has two subcomponents: stimuli and responses (see Figure 3.3). The outcome category has two subcomponents: client outcomes and interviewer outcomes (see Figure 3.4). Client outcomes are defined as benefits to the interviewee as a result of the reminiscence process.

A client, Mrs. T, recalled entering first grade when she was 6 years old. She recalled a verse that her teacher, Miss Lottie, taught the class:

School is begun
So come everyone
And come with smiling faces
The older you grow
The more you will know
And soon you will learn your places

Mrs. T and the other students used slates as well as pencil tablets. Each slate had a small sponge attached to use as an eraser. That first year set the tone for her love of reading, and the challenge of and quest for learning continued throughout her 97 years.

She continued her education with a master's degree from Columbia University. She later served as a supervisor of the Raleigh Elementary Schools, then taught at the prestigious Lincoln School in New York City. She taught children who later became college presidents, governors, and

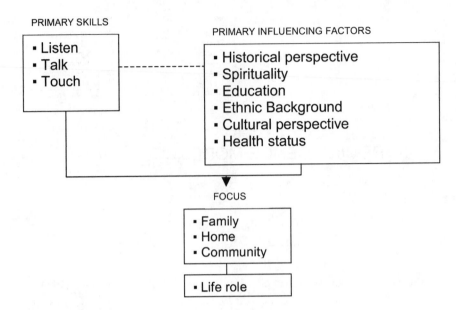

FIGURE 3.2   Processes components.

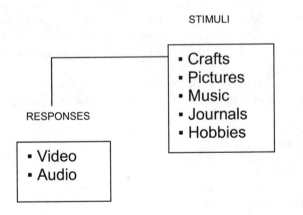

FIGURE 3.3   Items components.

a vice president of the United States. Many of her students kept in contact with her over the years, which demonstrates the value and appreciation placed on an excellent teacher. She wrote:

> In the summer vacation following my first year in school, my brother, McClure, took Emily, Mother, and me on a trip to a lake in Wisconsin.

INTERVIEWER OUTCOMES

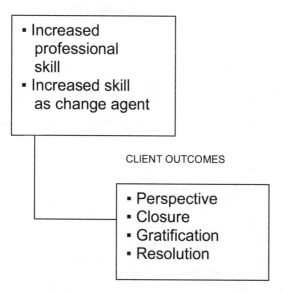

FIGURE 3.4   Outcome categories.

We left Hopkinsville by train and spent two days in Chicago. (It was her first trip to a city). We stayed at the Lexington Hotel, where I soon made friends with Walter, who ran the elevator. I was so fascinated with the ride that my brother tipped him to let me ride up and down with him as often as I wished.

I do not know how many floors above the room was but I remember the fascination of looking down on the traffic of trucks, horsedrawn cabs, and an occasional horseless carriage.

I also remember the powdered sugar that was served on my oatmeal and going to a High Episcopal Church and hearing my first boys choir. When we left for Wisconsin after our weekend in Chicago, McClure ordered a "horseless carriage" and I had my first ride in an automobile.

Although her family had adequate middle-class resources, many did not, and she recalled that,

from time to time there would be a knock at the back door, and a ragged unshaven "tramp" would ask for food. My mother could not bear the thought of someone being hungry while she had food aplenty, so she got together a plate of cold food and he sat on the back step and ate it. On one occasion my brother, Fairleigh, watched with interest as the tramp had his meal and mother asked Fairleigh to see if he would like a piece of cake. When he said he would be obliged, Fairleigh asked, "Do you want a piece of cake with white icing or caramel?" The man broke into a laugh and replied, "My little man, I don't often have a choice, but since you asked me, I'll have the caramel."

One summer while visiting a cousin, I was exploring her garden. There were many flowering shrubs with which I was familiar—snowball bush, bridal wreath, Rose of Sharon, Althea, burning bush. Most were past the blooming season but I wandered along the paths alone and there I had an experience that mystified me for nearly eighty years. Only a year or two ago did I find the answer. I never spoke of it to anyone, for it seemed too preposterous to mention, but I *knew* I had not imagined it.

As I stopped in front of one of the shrubs, my eyes caught sight of one of the tiniest of little creatures peering out from a sort of nest of leaves hung in the bushes. To me, it looked like a *very* tiny fox, its head about the size of my thumbnail, the body hidden in the tiny nest it had made. I watched in amazement as it looked at me with bright eyes, and its coat, what I could see of it, was a golden brown. We stood staring at each other for a long moment and suddenly I was struck with fear—perhaps it was a witch in disguise and if I stayed longer it might cast a spell on me. In real panic I turned and ran from the garden and the gaze of the bright-eyed creature, whatever it was. I did not mention it to anyone for fear of being laughed at but all through the years, especially after I was grown past a belief in elves and fairies and animals that could take strange forms, the memory stayed with me and I wondered what I had seen.

In the winter of 1980 I came across a book by the naturalist, John Terres. He described many of the animals and birds who preferred night life to daytime and gave several interesting descriptions of such creatures he had observed. He had seen the rare, tiny golden mice, rodents rarely seen by man. He described the beautiful golden tan coat, its bright eyes and sharp nose, and its habit of sleeping in the daytime in a small nest in a low bush. At last, I knew that was what I saw and feared and ran away from, was a rare encounter that many a naturalist would have welcomed—a face-to-face meeting with a golden mouse.

In 1929, at the age of 36, she married Mr. T, who was 42. It was the first marriage for both, occurring much later than was the norm among their peers. She joyfully described the next 29 years as the happiest of her life. She felt that her marriage (despite meaning the end of a career she loved) provided for her the greatest period of satisfaction in her life. The respect, admiration, and love she shared with her husband were a strong memory and source of great joy to her.

Mr. T headed a private boarding school in New England and wrote children's books. In 1939, the couple decided to move to Chapel Hill, a small academic community, so he could devote his time to writing.

In the late 1930s, Mr. T attempted to publish a textbook specifically for the "colored students." Even though he had many successful publications, none of the major publishing houses would accept the manuscript, indicating they would become known as the "colored publisher." Mrs. T recalled her husband's great distress at this inequity.

Mrs. T shared that her greatest fear was dependence—the loss of control over her life. "I could adjust to an institution, if necessary, but as Scarlett O'Hara said, 'I'll worry about that tomorrow.'" (It is a joy to report that she died in her own home on an early summer evening surrounded by author Soltys and some family saying goodbye as she crossed over to be with her dear husband, parents, siblings, and friends.)

When asked what advice she would give to others, she offered the following:

1. Establish a firm spiritual faith. The attributes derived are optimism, confidence, patience, strength, charity, and love.
2. Have younger friends as well as contemporaries. They can be a great source of joy and happiness.
3. Recognize and tolerate differences. Always remain open-minded to issues and individuals.
4. Be involved in community affairs. Contribute your skills and be willing to take a stand even when unpopular.
5. Take advantage of the availability of openness of careers for women, such as medicine, law, aeronautics, and politics.
6. Remember the value and joy of nurturing young children. This is more important than any career, because the future of the world is involved.

Mrs. T was like a grandmother to my daughters. She spent most holidays and special times with us. Once at dinner, she asked my daughter, who was a high school freshman at the time, what she was studying in history. My daughter responded that she was studying President McKinley. Mrs. T immediately began a very detailed description of McKinley's assassination, the country's mourning, and the aftermath. No history book could have given more vivid details. Much to the delight of her teacher, my daughter shared the information with her classmates.

Mrs. T also marched with the women's suffrage movement. She often spoke of the need for more involvement of women in all areas. When the Women's Rights National Park Museum opened in Seneca Falls, New

York, I made the trip to honor my friend (she was deceased) and to "close the gap" for her and myself.

Mrs. T

Born: December 11, 1892

Died: June 9, 1989

Education: BS, Peabody College, 1912; MA, Teacher's College of Columbia University, 1926

Career: Peabody Demonstration Faculty, 1916–1922; Raleigh Supervisor of Primary Grades, 1922–1924; Lincoln School Faculty (Columbia University), 1924–1927; Louisville Supervisor of Primary Grades, 1927–1929

Marriage: 1929

Major losses: older sister, age 32, 1924; father, 1929; mother, 1930; three brothers lived to their late 60s; husband, 1958; younger sister lived to age 103.

Historical events remembered: turn of the century ceremony; women's suffrage movement; the Great Depression; 15 presidential administrations; five wars (Spanish-American, World War I, World War II, Korean, and Vietnam)

Greatest impacts during her lifetime: civil rights—great strides toward equality; women's rights; free education for the masses; advances in health sciences and availability to the masses; technological advances (now considered essential but not available during her youth), including central heat; bathrooms and indoor plumbing; washing machines and dryers; television and radio; cars; convenience and variety of food available.

Her life spanned the period of the horse and buggy to man's walk on the moon.

> Man is like breath: His days are as a fleeting shadow.
> In the morning, he flourishes and grows up like grass.
> In the evening, he is cut down and withers.
> So teach us to remember our days that we may get a heart of wisdom.
>
> B. Myerhoff, 1995

Regardless of the specific definition or designation, reminiscence can be used for a variety of reasons. It may inform, help evaluate life, or even be a symptom of guilt (LoGerfo, 1980). It may be designated as storytelling, providing material of life review, or being defensive (Molinari & Rechlin, 1984–1985). Reminiscence may be used to learn about and appreciate an individual's life and to gather valuable information concerning psychological factors, underlying health beliefs, coping skills, and cultural perspectives. It can assist in the establishment of rapport between the speaker and the listener and help the client share sensitive information. This sharing can be particularly valuable in adjustments related to declining health, loss of a spouse or loved one, institutionalization, or approaching death. Because long-term memory remains intact longer, the ability to share recollections also may help energize and increase self-esteem in individuals diagnosed with dementia.

Recalling past successes provides strength and stability to face crises. If the facilitator can help the individual recognize and appreciate his or her coping skills during previous hardships, the individual can gain strength from understanding previous methods of problem resolution.

For the older individual who has experienced discrimination or lacks a formal education, the sharing of stories in an oral format can facilitate the release of anger related to injustices and the sharing of cultural norms of his or her time. It also allows for expression and sharing of memories not available in written form. In many cultures, the art of storytelling is the method used to carry on the values and traditions of the culture.

Reminiscence may provide linkages for family history and strengthen family connections. Such sharing can create a sense of belonging, thus enhancing self-esteem and appreciation for the uniqueness of each individual within the context of his or her time. These exchanges also can provide younger relatives or listeners with insight into the past and a greater sense of security and legacy. Landmarks such as weddings, graduations, births, funerals, and holidays provide opportunities for building memories and sharing through reminiscing; for families, the events may become the tie that binds.

Helping an individual see how his or her life has made a difference can improve both professional rapport and the coping skills that relate to the stressors of aging. Intergenerational reminiscing can help health care providers better understand the individual's health care beliefs and values, which in turn can improve compliance and the ability to cope.

Reminiscence is a normal activity that may assist the older person to successfully accomplish the development tasks of older adulthood. One of these tasks is to achieve a sense of integrity in one's life by finding meaning and purpose.

As our society changes and the values reflect our thinking, the need to recognize and appreciate our heritage becomes paramount. The need to respect individuals and families and their contributions becomes more important than money and physical things. The test of an advanced society is not in how many millionaires it can produce, but in how many law-abiding, hard-working, highly respected, and self-respecting citizens it can produce. The success of such a venture is a measure of our national enterprise (Franklin, 2005).

REMINISCENCE ENGAGEMENT PROCESS

The Reminiscence Engagement Process can serve as an entry point to the SolCos Model and other reminiscence and life review approaches. Many people engage in this naturalistic process without thinking about it. They may think of it as simply making conversation or visiting. However, upon further analysis, it becomes evident how rapport and trust can be established by initially modeling reminiscence behavior, then facilitating reminiscence through genuine care and interest, and then moving it into the business at hand. That business may include engaging older adults in community activities; business and marketing interests; and health care, mental health, and chaplaincy applications.

This process can, unfortunately, be used in a contrived, artificial, and condescending manner in an effort to patronize or exploit older adults. Fortunately in many situations, the experience and superior wisdom that older adults have acquired over their years of development help them see right through such attempts. This process is not intended as a 20-minute formula to help someone sell the latest youth-producing tonic or become the sole beneficiary of a rich uncle's will. It requires sincere and ethical motivations in order to be truly effective.

Step 1 (1 Minute): Introductions

Greet the client with respect and culturally and socially appropriate levels of formality.

Step 2 (1 to 2 Minutes): Model Reminiscence

Based on prior knowledge or observations about the client's surroundings, clothing, or interests, initiate brief, self-disclosed memories of your own in order to model reminiscence behavior and stimulate this type of response from your client.

Step 3 (5 to 15 Minutes): Listen and Empathize

As soon as appropriate, facilitate the client's response to the topic. Listen and empathize as you find and show genuine interest through nonverbal and verbal responses. Keep the focus on the client's memories, but balance this with appropriate short disclosures of your own memories that reflect the topic at hand. Make good use of the communication skills outlined at the beginning of chapter 2 of this book.

Step 4 (Length Varies): Business at Hand

Letting instinct and tact be your guide, segue into the main purpose of your visit. As you introduce the topic, take more control of the communication process.

Step 5 (2 Minutes): Conclude Visit

Again with respect and utilizing a socially and culturally appropriate level of formality, say thank you and good-bye. This is a good time to end with a brief reflection of what you learned about your client during Step 3.

Examples of the Reminiscence Engagement Process

The following two interviews are real-life examples of how the reminiscence engagement process can be utilized by investment advisors to build trusting and meaningful relationships with their clients.

LAVERNE JIRAL, INTERVIEWED BY JOHN A. KUNZ

JOHN: Hello, Mrs. Jiral.

LAVERNE: Hello, Mr. Kunz, nice to meet you.

JOHN: Good to see you. I see that you are going to be canning some tomatoes today?

LAVERNE: Yes—tomorrow.

JOHN: Oh, tomorrow.

LAVERNE: Yes—I'm just getting them ready today.

JOHN: My mother says that my grandmother used to can chicken, venison, and beef and that it was so delicious, that the texture was so good and the flavor was so good.

LAVERNE: It was—my mother-in-law used to can chickens, but, of course, that was many years ago and people don't do that anymore.

JOHN: How did she do that?

LAVERNE: Well, you kind of cold-pack into a jar as I recall, and then you have to water-boil them for, I don't know, quite a long time, and I think sometimes you pressure cook them but she never pressure cooked them—she water-packed them.

JOHN: And you used to eat those too?

LAVERNE: Sure, they were good.

JOHN: Do you do other cooking yourself?

LAVERNE: Oh, yes, sure.

JOHN: Do you enjoy that?

LAVERNE: Well, not as much as I used to because it is no fun cooking for yourself, but I do cook.

JOHN: I see. What were some of the things that you used to cook that you really enjoyed?

LAVERNE: Well, my husband used to like gravies. Like a Bohemian extraction so we cook like a lot of tomato gravy and dill gravy and pork and dumplings and sauerkraut and spareribs for the sauerkraut.

JOHN: Delicious, I'm a quarter Bohemian.

LAVERNE: Are you?

JOHN: I enjoyed kolache.

LAVERNE: Oh yes.

JOHN: Kolaches, have you ever made kolaches?

LAVERNE: Many times.

JOHN: My favorite were poppyseed kolache; they were so delicious.

LAVERNE: I liked the apricot.

JOHN: Apricot—how do you make those exactly?

LAVERNE: Well, there a lots of different recipes that I have calls for, sour cream, butter, flour, and you mix it together and then you chill it for overnight and the next day you roll it out to whatever thinness you want and you can make them as big or small as you want, just put your fillings on. Now my grandmother used to make them and they called them *hopaches* and they were little squares and they use to fold the dough over like in four strips so they were like a little pillow and I think that is what *hoopdy* means.

JOHN: Interesting. So, your grandmother made them while you were a little girl?

LAVERNE: Yes, they were made out of yeast and my mother-in-law was an excellent baker and made all these different coffee cakes, yeast coffee cakes. Never had a recipe, just throw in a little of this and that but one thing she used to use a lot was chicken fat; she thought that made the dough very short. I don't know, I never used it.

JOHN: Jewish people use a lot of chicken fat.

LAVERNE: Yes they do; in fact, I used to work with Jewish people and they would pay me in chicken fat.

JOHN: Oh, so you did cook with the chicken fat then too.

LAVERNE: No, my mother-in-law did; I never did. They would bring me the chicken fat so she would make coffee cakes and I would bring it to the office and then we would all eat it.

JOHN: That was during your working years.

LAVERNE: Yes.

JOHN: How long did you work, it was at a credit union, right?

LAVERNE: Yes, but before that I worked at a food wholesale place that is where all the Jewish people worked. It was very nice but then they moved it and it was so far I would have to take like two or three buses to get to it and it just took too long so I left there and went to this other job at the credit union where I worked for 25 years.

JOHN: That's a long period of time.

LAVERNE: Yes, but it was a nice place to work though.

JOHN: What did you enjoy about working there?

LAVERNE: The people and the atmosphere. There was a wonderful atmosphere there and I don't think anybody ever got fired there and if you did get fired you were the worst person in the world. We used to manufacturer automobile parts and we had big presses that would punch out the side of the car. Huge presses, maybe three or four stories tall. It was interesting.

JOHN: That is, and what was your role there?

LAVERNE: I was the assistant treasurer in the credit union. Making loans to people who joined. We used to have payroll deductions so it was a matter of posting it to each account.

JOHN: So you probably got to know everybody in that place.

LAVERNE: Anybody who belonged to the credit union I did.

JOHN: So you have a lot of experience with finances?

LAVERNE: Yes.

JOHN: What was your best experience that you have ever had in terms of investing?

LAVERNE: Well, actually some government grants in which I goofed up on because I didn't take it for a long enough period of time and all the interest rates dropped in the meantime. That was my best and worst.

JOHN: Your best and your worst at the same time. What is your biggest worry concerning making investments?

LAVERNE: The interest rates are dropping so much and if you live on a fixed income and have investments, well, each month your checks keep getting smaller and smaller so then you have to try and make it stretch and then with taxes and all the house things that is not easy so I wish that would go up little.

JOHN: So your biggest concerns right now are the interest rates being so low.

LAVERNE: Yes. I need the money, which is almost anybody in my situation. I'm sure your parents are feeling the same way.

JOHN: Certainly. Well, it has been really nice talking to you.

LAVERNE: Nice talking to you too, John.

ARNOLD AND VIVIAN HOVEY, INTERVIEWED BY JOHN A. KUNZ

JOHN: Good morning, Mr. and Mrs. Hovey, good to see you.

VIVIAN AND ARNOLD: We're glad you could come this morning.

JOHN: Yes, I'm very happy to be here. Thank you for the coffee and date bread.

VIVIAN: Yes, it is a pleasure.

JOHN: Boy, you have a lot of antiques here!

VIVIAN: Yes, we do, and many of them have a little history and most of them have been in the family.

JOHN: When I was about 6 years old, there was a gas station next to my parent's house and I went over there and they were cleaning it out and I saw this clock, an axonal schoolhouse clock and I said, "Oh, I sure like that clock, gee that is sure a neat clock, I sure like that clock." Finally, the fellow that was cleaning that stuff up said, "Johnny, would you like that clock?" So I said, "Oh, I sure would," so I carried it home and it filled up my whole arms and that was my first antique.

VIVIAN: Well good for you. Then you have an eye for things like that. Our eyes have developed over the years because for years that desk was on the porch all dirty and then one day we looked at it and that was my grandmother's.

ARNOLD: You learn not to miss anything.

VIVIAN: Yes—if you watch the *Antiques Roadshow,* then you understand.

JOHN: That is a beautiful piece; whose was that again?

VIVIAN: My grandmother's, my grandparents'.

JOHN: It is so nice when it is things from the family.

VIVIAN: Yes it is. And this was Arnold's parents', the table and the chairs were Arnold's Aunt Lena's and my dad bought those when she was selling.

ARNOLD: Do you remember Lena?

JOHN: Lena Larson.

VIVIAN AND ARNOLD: Yes.

JOHN: So that was your aunt?

ARNOLD: Great aunt.

JOHN: Your great aunt?

VIVIAN: Yes.

JOHN: Okay, I didn't know there was a Larson-Hovey connection like that.

VIVIAN: Yes, there is and Arnie has a lot to thank Aunt Lena for because she helped him get though the last years of high school.

ARNOLD: When I was finishing high school the Depression was in full swing and my folks were thinking of taking me out and she said, "no way, you can't do that," so she helped me through.

JOHN: Isn't that something?

VIVIAN: She was the most interesting character in this neighborhood really at the time.

ARNOLD: She used to teach school down here.

JOHN: At the school that you have here, Nobelton School?

ARNOLD: Yes, she taught my dad; it is a weird set up.

JOHN: So that was your dad's sister?

ARNOLD: No, my aunt.

VIVIAN: No, now wait a minute; that would have been your dad's mother's sister. Okay, yes, that is right, that would be your aunt.

JOHN: She must have thought a lot of you?

VIVIAN AND ARNOLD: She did.

ARNOLD: I don't know why but she was a rather eccentric person. That's my interpretation.

JOHN: What was that house like? I never saw that house.

VIVIAN: Oh, Aunt Lena's house, it was just lovely—beautiful curved porch.

ARNOLD: It flowed all the way around.

VIVIAN: Yes, and she was an immaculate housekeeper and she loved books. She had some wonderful books and I still treasure one of the books she gave me.

JOHN: Really?

VIVIAN: Yes. Oh, I can't remember the name right now, but it is a classic, however.

JOHN: She must have valued education a lot. A teacher and making sure you [Arnold] got a high school education, which in that day and age not everybody had. It is not like today.

VIVIAN: That's right, and of course they didn't have TV so she always did creative things and she made the most beautiful quilt. I don't know what happened to her quilts. She gave one to my grandmother and my sister has that. Quilts are really works of art.

JOHN: That's neat.

VIVIAN: Yes, and you are really finding out a lot about this.

JOHN: Yes, well I never knew. Where was the house on that property?

ARNOLD: Right where, I think Peter and LaVerne's.

JOHN: Oh it was right near the water then?

ARNOLD: Not too far and it used to have a boat house. You probably remember the boat house.

VIVIAN: I was going to guess the house was situated further this way but I could be wrong. I could show you a picture after this if you're interested.

JOHN: That would be great. I would like to see what it looked like then. They had to tear that old house down?

VIVIAN: Well, I guess nobody wanted it. My mother wanted it and she wanted to move it because it was moveable, a little farm if you will, and it was a big project. And so at the time we didn't encourage her and then the house was falling down, which was too bad.

ARNOLD: There were other buildings along with it like the barn, usually farm buildings.

JOHN: So that was a real working farm?

ARNOLD: Oh yes.

JOHN: So how did the two of you meet?

VIVIAN: Well, he was up here visiting his parents because he had gone to Chicago to seek his fortune and I was up here visiting my grandparents who had purchased that farm from Aunt Lena; matter of fact, this farm, the farm Mary Ellen has, she purchased from Aunt Lena.

JOHN: Oh, she had all of these.

ARNOLD: She had all of these around.

VIVIAN: She was a shrewd businesswoman; she really was, although I think she had lots of expense in taxes and things. So, somehow we met on the lake. I think I was fishing and my fishing line was caught in a tree—

ARNOLD: The usual tree story.

VIVIAN: And I need to untangle it. And then I had also met Arnold's brother and he also introduced us and then when I went back to Chicago and Arnold was there he called me and I was thrilled, you know, and then we I think we were engaged before he went into the service, the Air Corp.

JOHN: I see. So you were engaged then but not married until afterwards?

VIVIAN: It was just as well; we were too young, not just young—like I was 20 or something, which is young in every way. So when Arnold came home ... we got married.

JOHN: Were you writing then the whole time while he was in the service? Did you keep in touch with each other?

VIVIAN: Yes, Arnold did. He wrote me letters and I wrote him letters.

ARNOLD: Sandra Dee called them not e-mail but V mail for victory.

VIVIAN: And, unfortunately, I don't think we kept any of those letters.

JOHN: Oh, what a shame.

VIVIAN: Well, every now and then we get overzealous about tossing stuff out.

ARNOLD: And, of course, being in a POW camp, the mail was all censored.

JOHN: You were actually able to write right from the POW camp?

ARNOLD: Oh, yes, but we could write just general things.

VIVIAN: Like "the weather's nice."

ARNOLD: Or like "I'm feeling fine" and things like that.

JOHN: Which would have been important for you to hear that he was alive and doing okay?

VIVIAN: Yes, and then the Red Cross gave us advice as to what to send the men and we sent them the wrong things. They were only interested in food. We would send things like handkerchiefs and underwear and ice skates—they were so disappointed.

ARNOLD: It didn't cost them to send anything regardless of what was sent, but most of what was sent ended up being firewood.

JOHN: What did they think you were going to do with those things?

VIVIAN: As though they would have the energy to even make a skating rink or go skating.

ARNOLD: They didn't realize what it was like, they thought we had a country club.

VIVIAN: I guess they meant well.

JOHN: That's interesting. So you have actually written down your life story. Your POW experience?

ARNOLD AND VIVIAN: Yes—I think there is a copy somewhere if you want a copy.

VIVIAN: For awhile it was in one of the chronotype sections. I don't remember what section.

ARNOLD: Senior section.

VIVIAN: Yes, senior section. I don't even know if they have that any-
            more.

JOHN: And your father wrote his life story. I have that—I have a
            copy of that somewhere. I got it a long time ago.

ARNOLD: It was very factual from a date sense.

VIVIAN: It could be edited now, though, because he speaks of farms
            where people don't live there any more so the names don't
            mean that much anymore, and if I ever had the inclination I
            should go through that.

JOHN: That would be a fun project.

VIVIAN: My niece had them printed into about 12 books and each of
            our kids has a book.

ARNOLD: Most people around the lake have read it.

JOHN: I read it when I was about 14 I think.

VIVIAN: Oh good for you. It is kind of fun if you have forgotten some-
            thing you can rescan.

JOHN: I want to ask you a couple of questions about investments.
            What was your best experience with investing, your most
            exciting and positive experience that you have ever had with
            investing.

ARNOLD: Well, I'll tell you one thing: my brother-in-law was a broker
            and he clued me in on Chicken Unlimited and I invested in
            that and it doubled in a week but then we sold it.

VIVIAN: We aren't as savvy about or I'm not as savvy as I should be
            because we have been accustomed to buying high and selling
            low it seems to me. But we have some Wrigley stock that we
            just love because there is a reinvestment plan and Wrigley
            stays pretty much the same about $50 a share but there were
            a couple of years that it zoomed up to over a $100 a share.
            Vern sold some of his and Beck sold all of hers when it was
            high—

ARNOLD: Had kids through school.

VIVIAN: And I kept mine. But reinvestment plans are just one of the
            nicest investments and we bought our kids Disney because
            we though that was a fun investment for them to have and
            to get started on having a little portfolio, but then Disney
            discontinued it, the reinvestment plan, and maybe they have
            reinstated it, I don't know, but then I sold my Disney be-

cause I didn't care. So that is the kind of investment that I liked; even though the dividends are low, it's just automatically done, which is kind of nice when you get to just stay at home and then, oh, you have another share of stock.

JOHN: What about your worst experience?

VIVIAN: Well, just now with Van Camp because the principal has gone way down and down so far that we don't even like to sell because it would go badly but—

ARNOLD: It is starting to inch up. Last month was a gain of about $1,000, so it is coming back.

VIVIAN: We hope it comes back. The principal has gone down and it is about $12,000, which is a lot of money for us as we're not rich and our income has gone down because the interest rates are so low. The checking account is about one and a half percent and a few other things. CDs are low, you know, and then our broker, Edward Jones, said why don't you get a bond? Well, a bond the interest rate is good but it is long term.

ARNOLD: 15 years.

VIVIAN: 15 years at our age, that doesn't seem to make sense so we are kind of debating.

ARNOLD: It's a lifetime.

JOHN: It seems like you are going through some rough times right now with the economy?

VIVIAN: Yes, yes we are and I am perturbed.

ARNOLD: But we are not hungry, we're not going hungry.

VIVIAN: No, we are very grateful for a lot of things but I am perturbed at the democrats that they don't speak out about all these issues. The economy, women's rights, and the environment. I think they're uneasy about doing that because it won't seem patriotic now days. I think everyone is just waving the flag and the president is anxious for us to get into war and I don't understand, so I'm a little disappointed in some of the democrats that seem to lack the courage to speak out about this situation, about all the domestic issues that are so important, prescription drugs.

JOHN: Well, I really enjoyed our visit today and thank you very much for taking the time to meet with me.

VIVIAN AND ARNOLD: Oh, you're welcome, John. This was short and sweet.

The Year Moves On

The snow has melted;
The ice has gone
Spring rain is falling
The year moves on
Spring rain is washing
Everything clean
And bringing fresh clothes
Of new soft green
Birds are peeping
With heads half out
From holler and places
Round about
Across the fields
The Sun shines through
And it's come-come-coming
To shine on you.

James S. Tippett, 1998

EXERCISE

Using the Reminiscence Engagement Process as your guide, select an older adult family member, friend or acquaintance and ask if they would like to have a short visit with you. Make sure that you plan enough time to complete this process. [Arrange a time and plan for encounter visit use the process as your guide.] As you the complete this exercise do the following:

1. Note the emotional and physical responses to this process by both you and the older adults.
2. Ask what this conversation was like for the older adult you were visiting with.
3. Share your reactions to the visit.
4. Thank them.

REFERENCES

Butler, R. N. (1963). The life review: An interpretation of reminiscence in the aged. *Psychiatry, 256*, 65–76.
Cohen, G. D. (2005). *The mature mind.* New York: Basic Books.
Dewey, J. (1922). Morals are human. In *Human nature and conduct: An introduction to social psychology* (pp. 295–302). New York. Modern Library.

Erikson, E. (1980). *Identity and the life cycle.* New York: Norton.

Franklin, J. H. (2005). *Mirror to America.* New York: Farrar, Straus & Giroux.

Gibson, F. (2004). *The past in the present.* Baltimore, MD: Health Professions Press.

Haight, B. K., & Webster, J. D. (Eds.). (1995). *The art and science of reminiscing: Theory, research, methods, and applications.* Washington, DC: Taylor and Francis.

Kunz, J. (1991). Reminiscence approaches utilized in counseling older adults. *Illness Crisis and Loss, 1*(4), 48–54.

Kunz, J. (1997). Enhancing quality of life for older adults. *Ed-Cetera, 2*(2), 6–7.

LoGerfo, M. (1980). Three ways to reminiscence in theory and practice. *International Journal of Human Development, 12*(1), 63–65.

Molinari, V., & Rechlin, R. E. (1984–1985). Life review and reminiscence in the elderly. A review of the literature. *International Journal of Aging and Human Development, 202*(2), 81–92.

Myerhoff, B. [1995] 1980c. *Number our days.* New York: Simon and Schuster.

Parker, R. G. (1995). Reminiscence: A continuity theory framework. *The Gerontologist, 35,* 515–525.

Paul, R. and Elder, E. (2002). *Critical thinking: Tools for taking charge of your professional and personal life.* Upper Saddle River: Financial Times Prentice Hall.

Soltys, F. G., & Coats, L. (1994). The SolCos Model: Facilitating reminiscence therapy. *Journal of Gerontological Nursing, 20*(11), 11–16.

Tippett, M. K. (1988). *Kentucky babe.* Unpublished gift to Florence Gray Soltys of early childhood recollections.

Webster, J. D. (1993). Construction and validation of the reminiscence functions scale. *Journal of Gerontology: Psychological Sciences, 48*(5), 256–262.

Webster, J. D. (1997). The Reminiscence Functions Scale: A replication. *International Journal of Aging and Human Development, 44*(2), 137–148.

Webster, J. D., & McCall, M. E. (1999). Reminiscence functions across adulthood: A replication and extension. *Journal of Adult Development, 6,* 73–85.

CHAPTER FOUR

The Life Review: Historical Approach

Barbara K. Haight

- The life review has been mentioned in the literature since the times of Socrates.
- Academic interest in the life review was created by Butler's seminal article in 1963, noting the presence of reminiscing and life review in older people.
- Erikson's Eight Ages of Man is the theoretical model most commonly used by scholars doing life review research.
- There were only a few publications on life review and reminiscence in the 1960s.
- By the next decade (1970s) there were at least 20 new manuscripts.
- The 1980s saw confusion and mixed methodologies among scholars trying to examine both reminiscence and life review.
- By the 1990s the work in reminiscence expanded to recognize other reminiscence modalities such as oral history, narrative therapy, and autobiography.
- Charges made to researchers ask them to differentiate methods, use similar labels, describe methodologies, and create a universal understanding.
- Practitioners are called upon to identify the purpose of their interventions and then to tailor their interventions to meet the identified purpose.
- Many people benefit from life review, especially those with dementia, AIDS, and minor depression.
- By the year 2000, practitioners were being reimbursed for life review as short-term therapy.

- Marjorie's story exemplifies the beneficial effects of a life review.
- A group of nurse aides learns how to do a life review with their homebound patients.
- The Life Review Form helps beginners to conduct a life review.

HISTORICAL APPROACH

The life review has a long and illustrious history going back at least to Socrates, who said, "the unexamined life is not worth living." The exact beginning of the process is unknown, but we do know that the phenomenon of scanning one's past has served innumerable individuals over time. For example, religious orders use a life review of sorts when they go on retreat, as they review their lives and activities during the past year to ascertain whether they have been following a righteous path. Hence, the life review has been used for many reasons in many ways and has been noted in literature over the centuries.

In *The Death of Ivan Illych*, Tolstoy used the life review as a tool for his protagonist's death preparation. Tolstoy described Ivan as a simple bureaucrat whose life was ordinary. Ivan is a man attracted by the outer trappings of success such as wealth and power who married a woman suitable to his station and position. They raised a family, but the marriage was not a happy one, so Ivan devoted much of his energy to his work. One day Ivan felt ill and visited his physician, who diagnosed cancer. The following is a description of Ivan at the end of life.

> Ivan saw that he was dying and he was in continual despair. He took morphine for the pain and to entertain himself thought of the pleasant days of childhood. He experienced great loneliness in his dying and lived only in the memories of his past. He kept thinking, what if my whole life has really been wrong? He lay on his back and began to pass his life in review in quite a new way. He screamed to his family, go away and let me die in peace and for three days his family heard moaning and groaning coming from his room. Then there was quiet. Ivan called his family and said, "Though my life has not been perfect, it can be rectified." He no longer feared death. He drew in a breath, stopped to sigh, and died. (Tolstoy, 1960, p.150)

THEORY AND RESEARCH

Each of us has found reference to the life review in its many forms even before the aforementioned times. Those who have a scholarly interest in reminiscence and life review were made acutely aware of the phenomena in the 1960s, when an astute psychiatrist recorded his observations of older people's reminiscences in a seminal article. "The Life Review: An Interpretation of Reminiscence in the Aged" (Butler, 1963) has served as the basis for numerous discussions since it was published, and, although some of its assertions have been challenged and others have been misinterpreted, it still stands as a treatise on life review. Butler described the two-pronged effect of life review when people conduct the process by themselves, often internally. He described the life review as a naturally occurring universal mental process characterized by the progressive return to consciousness of past experiences, and particularly the resurgence of unresolved conflicts. Simultaneously and normally, these revived experiences can be surveyed and reintegrated. Butler's conception is used repeatedly today as an introduction to many life review articles.

Along with Butler's description, most modern authors use the Eriksonian developmental framework as a theoretical base on which to build their research. Erikson (1950) described the Eight Ages of Man and posited that one must complete the first age successfully to be able to move on to the second age. Life review researchers have historically worked with older people and are interested in the last developmental task put forth by Erikson, which is integrity versus despair. Erikson characterized integrity as accepting one's life as it was lived. If an individual could accept the way he or she lived life, then the individual would also achieve wisdom and be happy and content in old age. Conversely, Erikson described despair as a combination of depression and hopelessness. Thus, for those testing the efficacy of the life review, it is seen as a tool to help older persons accept their lives and reach integrity.

RESEARCH BY DECADE

Few other publications and a scant amount of research on the topic of reminiscence and life review appeared in the professional literature in the 1960s. McMahon and Rhudick (1964) conducted a research study with veterans and concluded that reminiscing is an important means of successful adaptation to old age. Two social workers, Liton and Olstein (1969) presented four case studies in which they found reminiscence helpful to elderly patients as a way for them to gain a sense of relief from their troubles.

Interestingly, in the 1960s, the autobiographical literature was also looking at the therapy provided by autobiography. Annis (1967) discussed the use of autobiographies as a source to help therapists understand their clients' psychobiological processes. He described autobiography as an individual's own written introspective report of life, and he described several psychological uses of the tool starting in 1904. Annis concluded that the autobiography allows people to gain sufficient perspective on their problems and thought it was unfortunate that scientific psychology had not studied a communication instrument with the potential of the autobiography more extensively.

The 1970s saw increased interest in reminiscing and life review, producing 20 new manuscripts of various sorts: clinical observations, research, and theoretical discourse. Havighurst and Glasser (1972) interviewed older people to see how often they reminisced and reported that reminiscence was therapeutic and common. In addition to the excited clinicians and researchers, there were naysayers. Lieberman and Falk (1971) failed to find empirical support for the adaptive value of reminiscence. Boylin, Gordon, and Nehrke (1976) conducted a project and reported that increased ego integrity was not correlated with a favorable attitude about the past. During the 1970s, methods and techniques were seldom described, and there was little differentiation among studies; thus, the controversy began as to whether doing a life review was a good thing.

The controversy may have piqued a surge of interest in the 1980s, as this decade saw the publication of 71 new studies about life review and reminiscence. In the 1980s, the research was mixed and needed to be examined closely to determine methodology and the adaptive function. Coleman's (1986) research from Great Britain stating that there were two types of reminiscing—one more adaptive than the other—was groundbreaking and could have served as a guide for all future research. However, many of the publications during this decade took a different scholarly approach than Coleman's and instead described the author's experience with the concept (Babb de Ramon, 1983; Chubon, 1980). Participating in a life review is a great experience, and reading the published research, one can detect an "ah hah" experience in each author's work as they discovered the life review for themselves. We who have worked with these modalities, whether by chance or design, think we have discovered a unique and useful way of communicating and want to share it with others. There was an excitement in much of the research of this era, as people shared their thoughts and wanted others to know about the life review.

In the 1980s, the interventions ranged from 8 hours to 1 hour, to just asking people if they reminisced; thus, the work was difficult to compare. The group work using reminiscence often had more positive outcomes than individual reminiscence, but it was not known whether this was due to the group effect or to the longer intervention, usually 6 to 8 hours. In the 1980s, there were seven reviews of the literature, each offering sage advice. Molinari and Ruchelin (1984–1985) stated that we needed to separate life review from reminiscence and examine the differences in similar samples. Following Molinari and Ruchelin, Haight and Bahr (1984) structured the life review as an intervention and created a form for individuals to follow that they tested in research. Their findings and future findings found the life review to be therapeutic for varied populations in diverse situations. Canadians joined the fray in the late 1980s to examine the process variables in the life review (Webster & Young, 1988). They echoed the findings of Coleman, although labels had not yet been put on the variety of reminiscence modalities used at that time. Very little theory was used to guide the research, but lip service was given to both Butler and Erikson as models to guide the work.

During this time, many books were also published on the topic. Most were how-to books written by therapists to share their way of conducting life reviews and suggest that others use their techniques. Magee (1988) produced a professional's guide, and Lehman (1989) published a guide for writing the life story. Kaminsky (1984) edited a book about the different ways to reminisce, and this volume described the use of theater, poetry, etc. as tools for looking at the past. No historical view is complete without mentioning the use of autobiographical writing groups fostered by James Birren (1987). Many researchers studied with Birren at the UCLA Center for Aging and worked on the topic of autobiography (Birren, Kenyon, Ruth, Schroots, & Svensson, 1996).

Many were unaware of parallel but related work going on in other countries. Oral histories were being collected and qualitative work was being done on the content of the life story (Bornat, 1994). Narrative therapy was coming into its own (Kenyon, Clark, & deVries, 2001), as was a movement toward the use of the autobiography (deVries, Birren, & Deutchman, 1995). Along with the growth in the modality and with the giving of labels, many more countries were becoming involved. In Great Britain, an organization called Age Concern sponsored Age Exchange to open a reminiscence center near London and produced a journal entitled *Reminiscence* (Schwietzer, 1998). In Northern Ireland, Faith Gibson (1998) shared her expertise on using reminiscence with those who have dementia. Japanese researchers were studying group reminiscing and created a reminiscing network across the country (Nomura, 1998). Presently, students in Africa, China, Australia, and France are working on projects that will make the life review a truly international topic and a modality for all nations.

As a result of the work conducted prior to the 1990s, several charges were made to researchers, many from reviews of the extant literature. Researchers were charged with differentiating their methods, using the same labels across studies, describing their methodologies, and creating a universal understanding across disciplines and across countries (Haight,

1999). Charges were made to practitioners as well, especially those who publish research (Haight, 1999). Practitioners were asked to determine the purpose of their intervention and tailor the intervention to the purpose. For example, in a study looking at 10 ways to reminisce, Haight and Dias (1992) found that random reminiscing in groups was the most effective way to conduct reminiscence for newcomers in a congregate living setting. Through a group modality, newcomers become acquainted with one another and with older residents. Two newcomers discovered that they were friends and classmates in the first grade. In this same study, the individual evaluative structured life review process was the most effective way to improve mood and decrease depression. Practitioners should also state their desired outcomes and then report their actual outcomes. If they did not reach their goals, they should determine why. They must also describe their methods and interventions fully so others can learn what is effective and what is ineffective.

The 1990s ushered in 115 new manuscripts and much new thought. Several provocative books were published (Freeman, 1993; Schafer, 1992). Authors were discussing the need for theory; and, using theory, labels became more similar or at least they were compared to one another (Haight & Webster, 1995). Researchers were discussing the use of reminiscence and life review with children and diverse populations, not just elderly people (Fivush, Haden, & Adam, 1995). Researchers were beginning to look at the content of the intervention and to examine the story qualitatively. The story was every bit as important as the process. Some researchers looked at the therapeutic effects of the life review across time (Haight, Michel, & Hendrix, 1998, 2000), while others looked at the functions of life review (Watt & Wong, 1991). There were many more experts to consult, and applications differed among groups. The life review/reminiscence tool was tested across different populations for different reasons (Webster, 1993).

Autobiography was used in psychoanalysis, as Annis suggested in the 1970s (deVries et al., 1995). Life review was used to create life storybooks for people who have dementia (Haight, Bachman, Hendrix, Wagner, & Meeks, 1998). The storybooks offered entertainment and provided caregivers with a tool for communication. A variety of studies reported life review/reminiscence as an aid to dying, helpful with AIDS patients, and a preventive measure for suicide. According to the literature, groups that have received benefits from life review include nuns, drug addicts, nursing home residents, other seniors, survivors of sexual abuse, surgical patients preoperatively, those with a psychiatric diagnosis, those with depression, and a variety of ethnic groups. In some states, the life review is seen as a short-term therapy, and its use is reimbursable by Medicaid (McDougal Blixen, et. al, 1997).

MARJORIE

Marjorie was a patient who had shared her life with a nurse and who had made great psychological strides with the help of this modality. When the nurse met Marjorie, she was a confused client who, for many years, had been homebound in a high-rise apartment building for the elderly. Her husband had been her caretaker, and he had recently died. Marjorie had not left her apartment for several days, and the nurse visiting the building was asked to look in on her.

When the nurse knocked on the door, Marjorie answered in a state of disarray. She was in her nightclothes, and her hair had not been combed or washed in weeks. She was chain-smoking and pacing the floor in agitation. She began searching for something to drink, and the only visible items in her kitchen were cigarettes and cola. This had been her diet for the last few weeks because it was all she could remember to order from the grocery store.

As the nurse questioned Marjorie to thoroughly assess her functional status, Marjorie digressed and spoke of inconsequential events in her past. She spoke of her life as a child, her two marriages, physical abuse by her first husband, the great love she shared with her second husband, her incapacitating illness, and her isolation. The stories continued for several visits while the nurse struggled to acquire assessment information and to devise a care plan. One day Marjorie cried and shared that the act of caring hurt.

Each week, Marjorie repeated this emotional breakdown, worked through her sorrow, and eventually went on to ask questions about the grocery store, the hairdresser, and the outside world. One day, a taxi ride to the grocery store was arranged. It was Marjorie's first trip out of the high-rise in 7 years. The miracle continued as Marjorie pulled her life together and became an independent woman for the first time in her life at the age of 55. Marjorie's nurse-teacher was a firsthand witness to the power of the life review.

EXERCISES

Teaching the Life Review

Class Members

The class members were all women over the age of 55 and of a low-income group. Most were African American. They were all state-certified nurses aides but otherwise had little formal education except for grade school, which was often interrupted by the need to work in the fields. As a group, the aides seemed content with their current life status. They had survived many hardships and were doing meaningful work. A sense of camaraderie was present among the group as they gathered for their monthly in-service and shared anecdotes about patients. They were dressed in their uniforms and were tired from working all morning; yet there was a sense of anticipation concerning the afternoon meeting. After a hard morning of work, they met to socialize and to be entertained as well as educated. They possessed the wisdom of experience, as was apparent in the views they shared. It also appeared that they were open to new information. In summary, the group may be characterized as eager to learn, with little formal education but wise from life experiences.

Practicing the Life Review

Marjorie's story was shared often, and it was well received. As the story of Marjorie unfolded, the group began to relate to Marjorie's hardships: her divorce experience, her illness and marital problems, and finally the loss of her husband and the inevitable grieving. The aides empathized with Marjorie's hardships and cheered as Marjorie pulled herself out of her difficult circumstances and began to take charge of her life for the first time at the age of 55. They were inspired by what life review had done for Marjorie and ready to learn about it for themselves and their clients.

Background on life review was presented along with examples and success stories such as Marjorie's. The group enjoyed this approach to the content. It was essential that the group be involved and that class time be a rewarding experience. The poem, *The Crabbit Old Woman* was read, and copies of the poem were distributed. Copies of the life review and experiencing form (LREF) (Haight and Bahr) were also handed out. The group was given instructions for the use of the LREF, and three simple questions were chosen from the form so that the group could break into pairs and practice with one another. Typically, some group members got into reminiscing right away and others were slow starters. The experience of viewing varied styles of reminiscing prepared them for differences among their clients when they began to use life review. The following is an example of one of the three questions—about a first memory.

One of the aide participants reported her first memory as helping her father pick cotton in the fields. She said she looked forward to helping because, after weighing in a certain amount each day, she could keep the excess and use the proceeds from the excess for her own wants. Then she talked about going into town on Saturday and looking for material for dresses. As she related this vignette, she realized that this experience taught her to budget her money. As is typical of people recalling an enjoyable event, she was laughing and bright-eyed and feeling good about herself. When the pairs of aides returned together as a group, I asked her to share this early memory with the other group members. As a result of her sharing this experience, the other women in the group shared her delight and contributed similar experiences of their own.

To continue this feeling of enjoyment and worth and to allow the aides to experience more life events, it was necessary to think of an event that was a common and meaningful experience for the entire group. Since they were all women, the event that marked the physiologic passage from girlhood to womanhood, the first menstrual period, was a universal choice. A former client had shared some of the trauma associated with her first menstrual period, and parts of her story were shared with the aides.

The story began during this client's early teenage years, a time when sanitary napkins and tampons as we know them today were nonexistent. Consequently, girls of her low economic status had to use rags in place of sanitary pads. The rags were washed out each day and reused. This elderly lady grew up with six sisters, so this ritual of washing the rags was a time-consuming event in her house, but one associated with memories of her sisters and happy times they had shared together. As this memory was related, the others in the room started to buzz and hands went up as each member of the group recalled a similar event. As the aides talked among themselves, they carried the memory further, telling how they kept a bucket under the porch to soak the rags, and how they had to hide it when their brothers brought their friends home. They recalled their embarrassment around their brothers' friends. Others told how their parents kept track of the bucket to determine their daughters' innocence. For these women, this was a common and significant event and one they all enjoyed sharing, thereby giving them all the pleasure of reminiscing.

Implementing Life Review

The class had become a meaningful experience for the women, and now it was time for the more difficult task of teaching the aides to implement the life review using the life review and experiencing form. The main intention in life review is to recall the entire life span, from the earliest memory to the present time. The LREF is intended only as a guideline to accomplish the review, and the questions in the LREF are used only as probes. In discussing the use of the LREF, it became apparent that this group of nursing aides interpreted the procedure literally. They wanted to read the life review questions from the form and have every question answered sequentially. It was necessary to convince the aides to use the questions only as probes for a more flexible interview. Although it was important for clients to review the whole life span, it was not important for them to answer every question in order, from every stage of life. The aides who could not resist reading each question were instructed to put the form aside and to use it only as a guide. Life review should be spontaneous and conversational and not a question-and-answer period. The only necessity is that the life review be a structured method of recalling the entire life span.

Each aide left the meeting with two LREFs, one for the client and one for her own reference. The aides were instructed to select one of their clients and conduct a life review with that person. The aides were directed to conduct the review at any time: during a bath, while folding laundry, or while sharing a cup of coffee. Before the aides left the classroom, a meeting was planned for 8 weeks hence for the purpose of hearing the group's life review experiences and for taking an attitude posttest.

The group departed the class on a very high note. Not only had they enjoyed the session, but they were eager to begin life reviews with their clients. In the experiencing of their own past, they were able to feel the positive changes caused by life review. Consequently, they were anxious to practice life review and create the same positive change in their clients. In 8 weeks, we would learn whether the nurse aides conducted the life reviews properly, if at all, and we would see whether participating in the life review changed the nurse aides' attitudes toward their clients, as the teachers believed it would.

Epilogue

At the end of the 8 weeks, teachers and students returned to the classroom at the senior citizens' center. There was an atmosphere of anticipation, and the class convened with the posttest on attitudes. This time, taking the test seemed to be a much less threatening experience, probably because the testing was no longer a new experience and because the students trusted the teachers. When the test was completed, the topic of life review was introduced, and class members were asked whether any of them had conducted a life review with their clients.

The response was overwhelming, as the hands went up and each of the aides vied to discuss her experience. The teachers had not expected such an enthusiastic response and, in fact, had prepared additional material in the event that no one had conducted a life review. Each aide spoke in turn, with great pride, describing her experience. Each life review had been conducted differently, but all seemed successful. One aide had notes on every one of her patients; another had the rewarding experience of sharing a confidence for the first time and seeing drastic improvement in her client. All students agreed that they saw their clients in different perspectives after completing the life review, and, as a result, they could understand their clients better.

LIFE REVIEW AND EXPERIENCING FORM

Following is a protocol for conducting a life review with an older person. The questions are to be seen as probes only; the important point is to cover each developmental stage.

Haight's Life Review and Experiencing Form

Childhood

1. What is the very first thing you can remember in your life? Go as far back as you can.
2. What other things can you remember about when you were very young?
3. What was life like for you as a child?
4. What were your parents like? What were their weaknesses, strengths?
5. Did you have any brothers or sisters? Tell me what each was like.
6. Did someone close to you die when you were growing up?
7. Did someone important to you go away?
8. Do you ever remember being very sick?
9. Do you remember having an accident?
10. Do you remember being in a very dangerous situation?
11. Was there anything that was important to you that was lost or destroyed?
12. Was church a large part of your life?
13. Did you enjoy being a boy/girl?

Adolescence

1. When you think about yourself and your life as a teenager, what is the first thing you can remember about that time?
2. What other things stand out in your memory about being a teenager?
3. Who were the important people for you? Tell me about them. Parents, brothers, sisters, friends, teachers, those you were

especially close to, those you admired, and those you wanted to be like.

4. Did you attend church and youth groups?
5. Did you go to school? What was the meaning for you?
6. Did you work during these years?
7. Tell me of any hardships you experienced at this time.
8. Do you remember feeling that there wasn't enough food or necessities of life as a child or adolescent?
9. Do you remember feeling left alone, abandoned, not having enough love or care as a child or adolescent?
10. What were the pleasant things about your adolescence?
11. What was the most unpleasant thing about your adolescence?
12. All things considered, would you say you were happy or unhappy as a teenager?
13. Do you remember your first attraction to another person?
14. How did you feel about sexual activities and your own sexual identity?

Family and Home

1. How did your parents get along?
2. How did other people in your home get along?
3. What was the atmosphere in your home?
4. Were you punished as a child? For what? Who did the punishing? Who was the "boss"?
5. When you wanted something from your parents, how did you go about getting it?
6. What kind of person did your parents like the most? The least?
7. Who were you closest to in your family?
8. Who in your family were you most like? In what way?

Adulthood

1. What role did religion play in your life?
2. Now I'd like to talk to you about your life as an adult, starting when you were in your 20s up to today. Tell me of the most important events that happened in your adulthood.
3. What was life like for you in your 20s and 30s?
4. What kind of person were you? What did you enjoy?
5. Tell me about your work. Did you enjoy your work? Did you earn an adequate living? Did you work hard during those years? Were you appreciated?
6. Did you form significant relationships with other people?
7. Did you marry?

(Yes) What kind of person was your spouse?

(No) Why not?

8. Do you think marriages get better or worse over time? Were you married more than once?
9. On the whole, would you say you had a happy or unhappy marriage?
10. Was sexual intimacy important to you?
11. What were some of the main difficulties you encountered during your adult years?
    a. Did someone close to you die? Go away?
    b. Were you ever sick? Have an accident?
    c. Did you move often? Change jobs?
    d. Did you ever feel alone? Abandoned?
    e. Did you ever feel need?

Summary

1. On the whole, what kind of life do you think you've had?
2. If everything were to be the same, would you like to live your life over again?
3. If you were going to live your life over again, what would you change? Leave unchanged?
4. We've been talking about your life for quite some time now. Let's discuss your overall feelings and ideas about your life. What would you say the main satisfactions in your life have been? Try for three. Why were they satisfying?
5. Everyone has had disappointments. What have been the main disappointments in your life?
6. What was the hardest thing you had to face in your life? Please describe it.
7. What was the happiest period of your life? What about it made it the happiest period? Why is your life less happy now?
8. What was the unhappiest period of your life? Why is your life more happy now?
9. What was the proudest moment in your life?
10. If you could stay the same age all your life, what age would you choose? Why?
11. How do you think you've made out in life? Better or worse than what you hoped for?
12. Let's talk a little about you as you are now. What are the best things about the age you are now?
13. What are the worst things about being the age you are now?
14. What are the most important things to you in your life today?

15. What do you hope will happen to you as you grow older?
16. What do you fear will happen to you as you grow older?
17. Have you enjoyed participating in this review of your life?

REFERENCES

Annis, A. P. (1967). The autobiography: Its uses and value in professional psychology. *Journal of Counseling Psychology, 14*(1), 9–14.

Babb de Ramon, P. (1983). The final task: Life review for the dying patient. *American Journal of Nursing, 13*(2), 44, 46–49.

Birren, J. E. (1987). The best of all stories. *Psychology Today,* 91–92.

Birren, J. E., Kenyon, G. M., Ruth, J. E., Schroots, J. J. F., & Svensson, T. (1996). *Aging and biography: Explorations in adult development, 20.* New York: Springer.

Bornat, J. (1994). *Rethinking ageing: Reminiscence reviewed perspectives, evaluations, achievements.* Bristol, Pennsylvania: Open University Press.

Boylin, W., Gordon, S. K., & Nehrke, M. F. (1976). Reminiscing and ego integrity in institutionalized elderly males. *The Gerontologist, 16*(2), 118–124.

Butler, R. N. (1963). The life review: An interpretation of reminiscence in old age. *Psychiatry Journal for the Study of Interpersonal Processes, 26,* 65–76.

Chubon, S. (1980). A novel approach to the process of life review. *Journal of Gerontological Nursing, 6*(9), 543–546.

Coleman, P. G. (1986). *Ageing and reminiscence process: Social and clinical implications.* Chichester, England: Wiley.

deVries, B., Birren, J. E., & Deutchman, D. E. (1995). Method and use of the guided autobiography. In B. K. Haight & J. D. Webster (Eds.), *The art and science of reminiscing* (pp. 165–177). Washington, DC: Taylor & Francis.

Erikson, E. (1950). *Childhood and society.* New York: Norton.

Fivush, R., Haden, C., & Adam, S. (1995). Structure and coherence of preschoolers personal narratives overtime. *Journal of Experimental Child Psychology, 60,* 32–56.

Freeman, M. (1993). *Rewriting the self: History, memory, narrative.* London: Routledge.

Gibson, F. (1998). *Reminiscence and recall: A guide to good practice.* London: Age Concern.

Haight, B. K. (1999). Using reminiscence in research proceedings: International Conference. Institute of Reminiscing and Life Review.

Haight, B. K., Bachman, D., Hendrix, S., Wagner, M., & Meeks, A. (1998). Life review: Treating the dyadic family unit in families with Alzheimer's disease. *The Gerontologist, 38*(Special Issue I).

Haight, B. K., & Bahr, R. T. (1984). The therapeutic role of the life review in the elderly. *Academic Psychology Bulletin* (Michigan Psychological Association), *6*(3), 289–299.

Haight, B. K., & Dias, J. (1992). Examining key variables in selected reminiscing modalities. *International Journal of Psychogeriatrics, 4*(Suppl. 2), 279–290.

Haight, B. K., Michel, Y., & Hendrix, S. (1998). Life review: Preventing despair in nursing home residents: Short and long-term effects. *International Journal of Aging and Human Development, 47*(2), 119–143.

Haight, B. K., Michel, Y., & Hendrix, S. (2000). The extended effects of the life review in nursing home residents. *International Journal of Aging and Human Development, 18,* 12–13.

Haight, B. K., & Webster, J. D. (Eds.). (1995). *The art and science of reminiscing: Theory, research, methods and applications.* Washington, DC: Taylor & Francis.

Havighurst, R., & Glasser, R. (1972). An exploratory study of reminiscence. *Journal of Gerontology, 27*(2), 245–253.

Kaminsky, M. (1984). *The uses of reminiscence: New ways of working with older adults.* New York: Haworth Press.

Kenyon, G., Clark, P., & deVries, B. (2001). *Narrative gerontology: Theory, research and practice.* New York: Springer.

Lehman, J. D. (1989). *Tracing life's footprints: A guide to writing your life story.* San Diego, CA: Libra.

Lieberman, M. A., & Falk, J. (1971). The remembered past as a source of data for research on the life cycle. *Journal of Aging and Human Development, 14*, 132–141.

Liton, J., & Olstein, S. C. (1969). Therapeutic aspects of reminiscence. *Social Casework, 5*(50), 263–268.

Magee, J. J. (1988). *A professional's guide to older adults' life review: Releasing the peace within.* Lexington, MA: Lexington Books.

McDougal, G. J., Blixen, C. E., & Suen, L. J. (1997). The process and outcome of life review psychotherapy with depressed homebound older adults. *Nursing Research, 46*(5), 277–283.

McMahon, A. W., & Rhudick, P. J. (1964). Reminiscing: Adaptational significance in the aged. *Archives of General Psychiatry,*10, 292–298.

Molinari, V., & Ruchelin, R. E. (1984–1985). Life review reminiscence in the elderly: A review of the literature. *International Journal of Aging and Human Development, 20*(2), 81–92.

Nomura, T. (1998). *Reminiscence and life review: Therapy and skill.* Tokyo, Japan: Chuohoki.

Schafer, R. (1992). *Retelling a life: Narration and dialogue in psychoanalysis.* New York: Basic Books.

Schweitzer, P. (Ed.). (1998). *Reminiscence in dementia care.* London: Age Exchange Theatre Trust, The Reminiscence Center.

Tolstoy, L. (1960). *The death of Ivan Illych and other stories.* New York: New American Library.

Watt, L. M., & Wong, P. (1991). A taxonomy of reminiscence and therapeutic implications. *Journal of Gerontological Social Work, 16*, 37–57.

Webster, J. D. (1993). Construction and validation of the Reminiscence Functions Scale. *Journal of Gerontology, 48*, 256–262.

SECTION TWO

Private to Public

CHAPTER FIVE

Reminiscence Group Work

Florence Gray Soltys and John A. Kunz

- We gain our identity by interacting with others.
- Our earliest life experiences prepare us for later relationships with others.
- Knowing that we can fail and return to an atmosphere of support is essential for building self-esteem and self-image.
- Each day we experience group involvement with family, community, work, and so on.
- Rituals become strong markers for us throughout life. Our group participation provides strength to face both joys and sadness.
- Group interaction can enhance individuality by encouraging participants to share their moments of pleasure, accomplishment, loss, and sadness.
- Sharing can create a sense of belonging, thus enhancing self-esteem and appreciation for the uniqueness of each individual within the context of his or her time.
- Reminiscing can assist health care professionals to better understand the health care beliefs and values of their clients, which in turn improves the patients' compliance and ability to cope.
- The group process can look at the strengths and weaknesses of the individuals and the reciprocal impact they have on the group and thus move to the individual's life resolution with the most beneficial outcome.
- With specialized approaches, group processes can also help confused older adults who have dementia.

- Telemedicine can be an effective and economic method for working with institutionalized and isolated elders.
- Telemedicine can fill a defined need, especially with outreach services to underserved rural areas.
- Privacy can be a concern with telemedicine. Every effort is made to provide a secure connection between the sites.
- Life story circles can be utilized to propel culture change in long-term care settings.

NATURAL GROUP PROCESSES

We all participate in groups frequently: as a member of a family unit, through clubs and social occasions, in classroom settings, and with colleagues. From our earliest life, we experience being part of a family unit, school, and community and later expand into many group settings. It is from these experiences that we begin the processes of education and clarifying our roles within society. These experiences teach us to erase and retrace; to give and reciprocate; to share similar pleasures; and to support, reassure, and gain insight (Yalmon, 1995).

Moments of full recall are often triggered by sensory events such as taste, touch, and smell; physical movements and actions such as singing and dancing; and participation in rituals, prayers, and ceremonies. A lullaby sung to a young child by a parent, the smell and taste of bread baked by a grandmother, a wedding, the first day of school, meeting one's spouse, and other markers bring memories at times pleasant and at times filled with sorrow and regrets. Reminiscence can reconstitute those memories and provide an opportunity to ask for forgiveness; to reassure one's commitment and love; or to recognize that, given the situation and times, there was little option for other choices. Reminiscence can allow the individual the opportunity to become visible and to enhance the reflection consciousness. For the old, it can be work that is essential to the last stages of life.

Rituals such as holidays, funerals, births, graduations, and other times of joy and loss provide an opportunity to review one's life and place memories into perspective. One woman recalled her family's Christmas celebrations.

On Christmas Eve, we hung our stockings from either side of the fireplace mantel. We just got a clean black ribbed stocking and hung it from one of the supports of the tall mirrored cabinet mantels of the period—very lumpy they were, and from the top protruded three or four Roman candles for fireworks Christmas night. Inside would be mostly eatables—an apple, an orange (we rarely had an orange except at Christmas), some chocolate drops, some nuts and sometimes a large stick of peppermint candy.

On birthdays we usually received a nickel which we saved for Christmas shopping. A nickel would buy a very pretty piece of pressed glass at the "Rachet" store now worth many times its original price. Some grown ups showed us how to make "shaving balls" of tissue paper, on which father and Wallace could wipe the whiskered lather from their razor blades. How well they served their purpose, I cannot say. (Tippett, 1991)

Memory is a continuum ranging from vague, dim shadows to the brightest vivid totality. Memory may offer the opportunity to not only recall the past but also relive it in all of its original freshness, unaltered by change and reflection. The ability to reflect and put experiences into a more current perspective can be very helpful. The accompanying sensations, emotions, and associations of the first occurrence are recovered, and the past is recaptured. These memories often may involve childhood and young adult experiences, which provide the sense of continuity and completeness that may be an essential developmental task in old age, leading to the achievement of a balance of Erikson's (1980) ego integrity versus despair.

People know better where they are going if they know where they have been. We live our lives forward, but we understand them from a past perspective and build on past experiences to develop friendships, participate as family members, and define who we are within our lives. Value structures and community norms reflect these past experiences. Rituals such as holidays, funerals, graduations, and weddings provide opportunities to express love, sadness, and joys in life.

Funerals and memorial services serve a valuable group function, allowing the deceased individual to be remembered. The relationships to each of the participants can be shared with each other and family members. These rituals often celebrate and acknowledge the deceased individual in the areas of his or her family, community, and work. These types of rituals help to establish how one's value structure fits into the lives of others.

STRUCTURED REMINISCENCE GROUP PROCESSES

Use of reminiscence in groups is an excellent way to become familiar with group work skills. Group work within a community or institutional setting can be rewarding and bring joy to the participants. It is an economical way to provide assistance, share common interests, and problem solve. McMahon and Rhudick (1964, p. 298) were the first to pose a link between self-esteem and reminiscence: "The older person's knowledge of a bygone era provides him an opportunity to enhance his self-esteem by contributing in a meaningful way to society." Later researchers expanded:

> Human beings are not meant to live solitary lives. Talking, touching, and relating to others is essential to our well being. These facts are not unique to children or to elders but apply to all of us from birth to death. Isolation can bring depression, unusual thought processes, hallucinations, and a diminished sense of self and reality. (Rowe & Kahn, 1998, p. 39)

Often practitioners are younger than their older adult clients and have not yet faced the developmental stage the elder is experiencing; however, they may have experienced the event through older relatives or friends. Consequently, it is imperative that the group leaders have a historical perspective about the events faced by the older adult (Toseland, 1955). Typically, individuals entering the field of gerontology have a strong interest in history.

Working with a group of elders in their 90s, I (Soltys) heard about a client's personal experiences such as marching with the suffragettes, owning her first car, having electricity, riding in an elevator, and tasting powdered sugar. Especially exciting was hearing about her experience of the turn of the last century:

> I was four at the time and remember little of the ceremony [for the turn of the century] itself—I had never been up that late before, but I do remember we sang "Blow Ye, the Trumpet Blow"—the gladly solemn sound from the *Loudes Domini* hymn book. And I remember stumbling sleepily on the walk home holding to Sister's hand. I had seen the twentieth century in! (Tippett, 1991)

The best kind of therapy occurs with the deep respectful listening that happens when people listen to honor each other's lives.

Romanick and Romanick (1981)—although they did not study groups—describe four uses of reminiscence that are relevant for reminiscence group leaders: self-regard, image enhancement, problem solving, and existential self-understanding. The Romanick and Romanick (1981) study can be extrapolated and used as a guideline for goal development in reminiscence groups. As the group moves toward goal development, these following positive outcomes can be the result of the above uses of reminiscence:

1. Remembering pleasant events is enjoyable.
2. Remembering can lift spirits.
3. Remembering can entertain.

4. Remembering can further a description of self to others.
5. Remembering can identify what was best in the past.

Rowe and Kahn (1998, p. 126) define social support as "information leading one to believe that he or she is cared for, loved, esteemed, and has a network of mutual obligations." The impact of unconditional emotional support cannot be overestimated. The frequency of emotional support is a strong indicator of the likelihood of enhanced physical functioning over time. The effectiveness of supportive action, however, depends on the situation, person, and perceived needs.

According to Galinsky and Schopler (1989), when one enters a group, four stages are experienced:

1. Forming (becoming a part)
2. Storming (defining one's place)
3. Norming (clarifying role and goals)
4. Performing (meeting these goals)

Reminiscence enables the listener to understand a part of the teller's mind. It enables the teller to retrieve and rethink aspects of the past, putting memories into perspective and tempering them with other experience. Reminiscence is an effective strategy for processing information, feelings, and thoughts and for putting experiences into perspective over time. It can be used in a variety of areas to achieve various psychological, physiological, and educational outcomes (Soltys & Coats, 1994).

Reminiscence, therefore, is a strategy by which the individual or group may both affirm and discover life. It provides the opportunity for integration by offering people a chance to be recorded as existing, and to integrate and reconstruct historical experiences, thereby manifesting a valuable identity (Soltys, Reda, & Letson, 2002).

Rowe and Kahn (1998) report that elders thrive as a result of important social bonds with both family and friends. Many elders cite friendship as the key factor in keeping them active and emotionally secure in advanced age. They protect each other, share joys and concerns, and keep each other company. Research has long shown that perceived social support impacts on health issues. As a rule, people whose connections with others are relatively strong—through family, friendship, and organizational membership—live longer. For individuals whose relationships to others are fewer and weaker, the risk of death is two to four times as great, irrespective of age and other factors such as race, socioeconomic status, physical health, smoking, use of alcohol, physical activity, obesity, and use of health services. The bottom line is, we do not outgrow our need for others. The life-giving effect of close social relations holds throughout the life course (Rowe & Kahn, 1999, p. 156).

SPECIFIC REMINISCENCE GROUP APPROACHES

In an interdisciplinary clinical assessment clinic for frail elders, the author (Soltys) often uses the technique of reminiscence with the patient and family to gain information about the patient, why they sought the clinic, how they define the problem (often varies within the family), major life events, and quality of life as seen by the family. We identify and explore the five areas in the patient's life deemed to be the most important. We discuss what would they change about their life if this were possible, the availability of support systems, and their end-of-life choices. This session is free flowing and nonstructured and is more productive than a formal structured questionnaire. Interdisciplinary assessment is reserved for patient and caregiver problems that are perceived to be beyond their capacity to manage effectively (Coppola et al., 2002).

With individuals who suffer from depression, a more structured group interview may be needed. Depression is one of the most common psychiatric disorders among the elderly. The presence of clinically significant depressive symptoms range from 8 percent to 15 percent among community-dwelling elders and is about 50 percent among institutionalized elders.

Soltys and Coats (1994, p. 14) suggest the following factors to be considered when forming a reminiscence group:

a. Historical perspective
b. Spirituality
c. Individual autonomy
d. Education level
e. Ethnic background
f. Cultural perspective
g. Health status

Groups have many purposes and may be used to solve problems, express the joys in life, relate to specific disease processes, or foster cognitive growth. Toseland (1995) found that forming homogeneous groups may bring cohesion and intimacy more rapidly to the group process. For example, a group that relates to a specific disease process such as Parkinson's disease might include caregivers as well as patients. Various stages of the disease may be represented, which gives the participants an opportunity to witness the changes while realizing that each individual and his or her response(s) may be different. An educational and resource component would be a valuable addition to such a group.

In setting goals for a group, several factors are important for the facilitator: beginning where the members are; respecting differences in values, knowledge, and problem-solving styles; having a willingness to share one's knowledge, values, and skills even when they may conflict with those held by others; having the capacity to work through rather than avoid conflict; and maintaining an openness to the ideas and insights of others (Schopler & Galinsky, 1990).

Groups may be time limited or open-ended. An open-ended group allows the members to enter in various stages (for example, people may enter a bereavement group at various stages of grief). Such groups take a more skilled facilitator. No single type of support is uniformly effective for all people or situations (Barrett & Soltys, 2002).

Themes from specific decades may be used (for example, cars in the 1930s, the Great Depression, World War II, college years, jobs). For example, a nursing facility might set aside a room that houses old furniture, books, kitchen gadgets, fabrics, and pictures that individuals may visit when upset. Group activities should happen there, where members may be surrounded by the familiar objects.

The decade theme can make it easier for the practitioner to control patients who reminiscence in a compulsive and obsessive manner (Kunz, 1991). By redirecting a participant to the timeline at hand, the individual can be redirected to events of that period. Similarly, the same strategy can help keep the group on task. If a topic is brought up that will be covered in the near future, the participant can be redirected to reintroduce the subject in the appropriate session. The timeline will not always be followed, because reminiscing is not always an orderly and accurate process.

The decade format provides a sense of order and purpose to the group—qualities sometimes emphasized in the literature as characteristics of a successful group. Themes should be easily understood, precise, flexible, and organized (Burnside, 1993). If a certain topic or decade elicits stress and unpleasant memories, there are always other topics and decades that the practitioner can switch to.

The use of themes may be selected by using a life span approach—a list of events in one's life, losses in one's life, or major achievements. Birren & Deutchman (1991) suggests using the major turning points in ones' life as themes for reminiscence. He suggests thinking of life as a river winding its way to the ocean. If one chooses to use props they should be (1) culturally appropriate, (2) gender appropriate, (3) geographically appropriate, and (4) age appropriate. The authors mentioned props earlier and wanted to now provide specific examples. Props may be more effective with cognitively impaired individuals, especially if they appeal to the senses of sight, touch, smell, and taste. Such props can renew long-term memories. Old photographs may be very strong in prompting recurring memories.

For the sensory impaired, other props may be more effective. For example, in the southern United States, gospel music may be a strong trigger.

Reminiscence values have explicitly espoused or advocated respect for others, listening, and sharing. It follows that spirituality informs or is integral to reminiscence—a familiarity with and competence in spirituality work is crucial.

Humor in a variety of forms may be a positive outcome of sharing one's memories. Four southern women with some cognitive loss were discussing a recent episode of the *Oprah* television show that had been about lesbians. One woman turned to another and asked, "Are you lesbian?" She responded, "No, I'm Methodist." The first woman posed the same question to another woman, and the response was, "No, I'm Pentecostal." The third woman, upon hearing the other two answers, refused to answer, and the first woman said, "You must be a Catholic, because you have talked about coming out of the closet."

Some of the positive results of life review can be a righting of old wrongs, making up with enemies, coming to an acceptance of one's mortality, gaining a sense of serenity, having pride in accomplishment, and feeling that one has done one's best. It gives people an opportunity to decide what to do with the time left to them and work out emotional and material legacies. People become ready, but are not in a hurry, to die. The qualities of serenity, philosophical development, and wisdom in some elders reflect a state of resolution of their life's conflicts. A capacity to live in the present is usually experienced, including the direct enjoyment of elemental pleasures such as mature children, forms, colors, warmth, love, and humor. One may experience a comfortable acceptance of the life cycle, the universe, and the generations (Butler, Lewis, & Sunderland, 1998).

Reminiscence in a group setting can be very effective with the physically frail. Being physically ill is lonely and isolating. Attending a group can help bring ill or frail people into a participatory role where they can share more of themselves. The setting must be inviting and comfortable for them. The participants should identify the theme for each session. It is important to decide whether the group is open or closed. A closed group allows the opportunity to experience the personalities and get to know the individuals better; however, closed groups can be difficult if tensions develop and are not resolved between group members. An open group allows for newness, but tension may arise as members adapt to newcomers. An open group requires a more skilled facilitator.

Individuals with cognitive failing can especially enjoy group reminiscing. Long-term memory remains for a longer period, and it allows recall of energy and happier times in their lives. One may need to use props—items, music, or photographs—to enable the memories. Often individuals with dementia may mistake a group member or facilitator for a parent or other relative. To extract recall by asking about that person, what they remember, and how they felt with that person can be enlightening for the clinician and the family. Some support groups for caregivers of individuals with dementia also may have a separate group for the patients, which gives them an opportunity to have respite in a comfortable surrounding.

There are many ways in which caregiver support groups can prevent and alleviate the stress resulting from such demanding work. Toseland (1995, p. 228) suggests that the benefits include:

> (1) providing caregivers with respect; (2) reducing isolation and loneliness; (3) encouraging ventilation of pent-up emotions and sharing the feelings and experiences in a supportive atmosphere; (4) validating and normalizing thoughts, feelings, and experiences; (5) installing hope and affirming; (6) educating about the caregiver role and the aging process, the effects of chronic disabilities, and community resources; (7) teaching coping strategies and effective problem solving and (8) helping caregivers to identify, develop, and implement effective actions to resolve pressing problems.

This process of group reminiscence also assists in the resolution of grief associated with loss and the adaptation to physical changes. Knowledge gained through the group process is powerful in helping to resolve problems. We all grow the most when challenged in an arduous situation and receiving support needed to master the situation. Having this knowledge can bring about change and also offer the opportunity for growth that is positive in our lives.

The local media may also assist with valuable information, resources, and education. A weekly television show in North Carolina, *In Praise of Age*, features individuals and resources that relate to the community. Additionally, a weekly newspaper column entitled *A Touch of Gray*, started in 1994, gives detailed information about programs such as groups and respites that impact on elders and their caregivers (Orange County Department on Aging, 2005).

GROUPS FOR CONFUSED OLDER ADULTS

The group setting can be structured in a way that is therapeutic for older adults with dementia who may be moderately to extremely confused. Facilitating such groups requires balancing the various reality orientations of group members.

Naomi Feil (1992) is a pioneer in using what she calls validation therapy groups. She has spent the past 40 years traveling the world to help care providers of older adults understand when to stop pushing reality on an older adult and go with them in their creative thought process. Validation allows the confused older adult to lead the listener to where he or she needs to be. If a confused older adult is looking for a dog from when he or she was a child, the listener should understand that the older adult may have any of the following needs:

- Wants to be needed like any pet owner
- Is frightened and vaguely aware that something is wrong, and this cues a memory about a time his or her dog was missing
- Is bored and wants to play like when she or he had the dog
- Never had a dog but would like one now.

By asking some questions and entering the confused person's world, the listener can usually figure out the older person's needs and then adjust the environment, care plan, etc. In the example, a motion-activated mechanical dog might amuse the person as well as reduce that chances that he or she may wander off to look for the dog.

Feil identified a group process that unites confused older adults in order to explore unmet human needs and to use the group process to help resolve these issues. Over the years, a number of group facilitators have tailored the groups process. Mary Lucero (2001) adapted the process into a grief group, and Kunz (2005) has incorporated reminiscence approaches in such groups. Using Reisburg's theory of retrogenesis and the stages of cognitive decline outlined in Reisburg's Global Deterioration Scale, Kunz tailors the group activities and expectations and roles for each member to their level of declining cognitive development. When the activities, questions, and other approaches are at the correct cognitive level, the group participants are better able to make use of residual memories and skills.

These groups are often conducted in long-term care facilities. Before beginning such groups, it is best to do facility-wide training to empower the facilitators, who are often activity staff. It is important to sensitize staff at all levels that, in order for the group to be effective, they cannot bring residents in and out of the group for hair appointments or pass off a resident who is having behavior problems. It is also helpful to emphasize the huge amount of energy that is needed to make these groups successful. It is very important to keep the number of group participants small and to have adequate staff and volunteers to help the participants stay focused.

These highly structured groups follow the same social ritual each time. These rituals are similar to those used by the Lion's Club, Rotary

Club, and many other social organizations. This social process feels familiar to the participants and cues them into appropriate behaviors. It is not
uncommon to hear profound statements from an individual who is very
demented. When family members observe the groups or watch video foot-
age of the group, they are often amazed at how their loved one interacts.

Dementia Group Format

1. Set up physical space.
2. Announce group and suggest that there be no interruptions.
3. Place "do not disturb" sign on door.
4. Escort members and place in a circle.
5. Greet each participant individually with a handshake, touch,
   and welcome.
6. Resident greetings are encouraged.
7. Participant leader greets group.
8. Pledge of allegiance led by participant while another participant
   holds a flag.
9. Sing a long-time familiar song led by one or more participants.
10. Announce theme for the group and demonstrate through appro-
    priate props.
11. Randomly discuss theme
12. Show and tell related to the theme, giving each participant the
    opportunity to have the group's full attention.
13. Facilitator connects individuals with similar interests, experi-
    ences, and behaviors.
14. Facilitator "translates" between group members.
15. Facilitator checks in with group and individual members to
    see how they are doing, directing the discussion toward shared
    human values, emotions, and basic human needs.
16. Facilitator summarizes group discussion.
17. Serve refreshments with the help of participants, as appropriate.
18. Participant leader concludes group.
19. Sing closing song led by one or more participants.
20. Facilitator individually thanks and says good-bye to each resident.

LEVEL OF DIRECTIVITY IN GROUPS
FOR OLDER ADULTS

Groups with older adults should be framed within the context of older
adult developmental issues and make use of lifelong wisdom of the group
to solve problems, support each other, and promote well-being. To accom-

plish this, social workers need to feel comfortable altering their style, voice level, and physical presence when working with older adults. This is often challenging for students or inexperienced, self-conscious workers.

Certainly not all, but many older adults, particularly in residential settings, have mild to severe sensory and/or cognitive impairment. Thus, group workers must adjust both their expectations of the client and group outcome as well as the way they structure and facilitate the group to the abilities of the clients. Figure 5.1 provides a visual representation to help select different approaches to group leadership according to the needs of the participants.

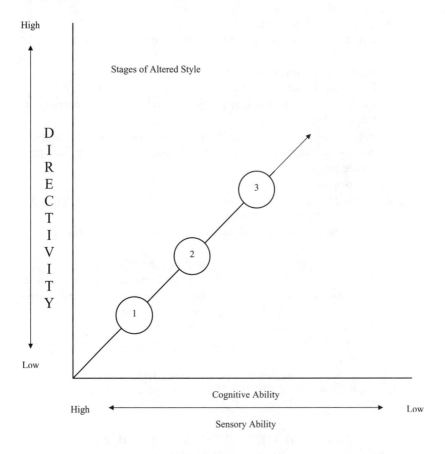

1. Standard group techniques.
2. Concrete and moderately directive group techniques.
3. Fully directive group techniques

FIGURE 5.1   Levels of Directivity in Groups for Confused Older Adults

The horizontal axis of the diagram shows the levels or cognitive and/or sensory abilities of group members, ranging from excellent to poor. The vertical axis of the diagram shows the level of directivity, from low to high, needed to lead the group effectively. This directivity needs to be fluid and may vary from person to person and change over time. Stages 1, 2, and 3 represent a continuum along which the leader may need to alter his or her communication and facilitation style.

At Stage 1, the facilitator uses standard group techniques ranging from open discussion to formal therapy with explicit rules of confidentiality. Reminiscence and life review techniques as well as other approaches are easily understood and applied by the participants. If the group worker is seeking third-party reimbursement for such work, it is important to frame these approaches within established treatment modalities and the treatment plan. Reminiscence and life review approaches can be easily integrated within brief and cognitive behavioral models of therapy. At Stage 2, the worker should become more concrete and use more directive group techniques. Confidentiality may not be guaranteed on the part of the clients, and the worker may need to respectfully redirect or otherwise shut down a participant in order to keep him or her from sharing what might be inappropriate in a group context. The worker must later follow-up on the issues raised by the client with an individual approach or via referral to other qualified personnel. The facilitator will need to be more forceful in keeping the group on task and may need to be repetitive in communicating the purpose of the group and more frequently summarize the group progress. At this stage, the worker must often "translate" between group members due to their sensory and/or cognitive impairment. It is helpful to include direct care staff to help some of the members communicate and focus on the group process. The facilitator must slow down yet maintain group momentum. Props are often needed to maintain group attention and appeal to members' more concrete level of cognitive development.

This facilitation style likely conflicts with styles of group leadership found in many group work textbooks. The leader's success in resolving conflict and facing the challenge of altering his or her physical and emotional presence will either make or break a group at this stage.

At Stage 3, the facilitator must use fully directive group techniques. The level of translation between members now becomes even more repetitive. The facilitator may need to move around the room physically to maintain group attention and connection between members—perhaps to the point of connecting with participants who may not see, hear, or realize that someone else is there. Even more props are needed at this stage. The worker must connect the reactions and discussion that results in feelings and issues related to any of the stages of adult development.

This is done for the group to better meet the emotional needs of each group member while at the same time tying these feelings and needs to the group as a whole.

By structuring the group at the correct cognitive level, the participants can make use of residual memories and skills, resulting in rich and often surprising discussion and insight. Given the proper structure, the group process promotes a sense of well-being (and more confident positive behavior) that often continues long past the period of time the participant can remember what happened in the group (Kunz, 2005).

TELEMEDICINE

Telemedicine, which has been defined as "the use of telecommunications technologies to provide medical information and services" (Perednia & Allen, 1995), is being used increasingly with older clients (Williams et al., 1995). The growth of telemedicine in recent years has been impressive, both in terms of the number of programs and new applications that are being developed rapidly. Generally, telemedicine involves two or more people at a distance too great for traditional face-to-face conversation conferring over two-way audio and video. However, it is misleading to think that telemedicine is only about cables and television capabilities (Soltys, 1999). Telemedicine is a viable therapeutic strategy for groups and frail older adults.

Telemedicine should first fill a defined need. One area that has been identified as appropriate for telemedicine is rural healthcare. Problems of the rural community include poorer overall health status, lower income for elders, difficulty attracting practitioners, and transportation (Parker et al., 1992).

The University of North Carolina School of Medicine (Program on Aging) has telecommunication hookups in two remote facilities: a nursing home facility and a rural clinic. The interdisciplinary team from the university visits the facilities monthly.

Working with groups utilizing telemedicine allows practitioners to supplement scarce resources in underserved areas and may include work with individuals, families, and various groups. For example, these sessions may include education to certified nursing assistants, explanations of disease processes to older adults and their families, exploration of feelings that need to be recognized among family members, completion of unfinished business, or social enhancement.

It is important to have a person at the remote site to support the client-patients if they become upset. Graduate students are invited to participate and not only learn the methodology but also become familiar and comfortable with the technology. Graduate students completing their field practicum in the distant areas are supervised weekly through the telemedicine network. If the instructor wishes to observe the student interviewing a patient, telemedicine offers a unique way to achieve this.

An interdisciplinary team may use telemedicine to work with a patient and his or her family to identify problems and work toward resolution, respecting their values and utilizing available resources. Among the innovation services are the reminiscence sessions with both individuals and groups via telemedicine by the author. The benefits of reminiscence therapy have been generally recognized as improved mood, elevated self-esteem, expression of life satisfaction, and maintenance of cognitive functioning. Some residents, who have mild to moderate dementia, enjoy sharing their earlier life and often connecting to their present being. They often respond to music with hymns being a strong preference. As individuals face major crisis, such as health decline, institutionalization, spousal death, or terminal illness, the need to review achievements and put relationships in order becomes increasingly important (Soltys and Coats, 1994).

Group members seem to have no more difficulty with reminiscence telemedicine than in traditional face-to-face reminiscence. The sessions can be videotaped (with the participant's permission) and may become a keepsake for individuals and their families. After the participant's death, family members often express appreciation for and joy about having the tape and the stories. The telecommunication lines are secure and therefore confidentiality is ensured.

Groups have used telemedicine in a variety of ways:

1. Telemedicine was used to videotape nursing home elders in small-group (seven to nine participants) discussions about the end-of-life treatment that they would like. Reminiscence was used to explore the participants' value structures and experiences related to end-of-life issues. The tapes were then given to the facility and/or to the participant to help them in their decision-making. It has been noted that African American nursing home residents are less likely to have advance directives than other elders. This is generally believed to be the result of problems with illiteracy and fear that medical treatment will be withheld because of discrimination. This is especially true of older African Americans in the South, who suffered from segregation. Many, in fact, will say they want family members to make decisions for them. When questioned specifically, however, the situation is more complicated. Many fear ending up attached to complicated machinery with no expectation for quality of life to return.

2. Groups from two nursing facilities about 20 miles apart partici-
    pated in video sessions to discuss what their lives were like and
    explore some common issues regarding institutional placement.
    This led quickly to reminiscing about earlier lives. Many par-
    ticipants had known each other when they were younger, and
    the sessions renewed earlier times when they were healthy and
    productive. The interaction between the groups brought energy
    to the group members, and they were able to glean strength to
    face their current situations.
3. The technology has been used with groups of individuals with
    fairly advanced dementia. Hymns were used to engage them.
    Participants sang all the verses of "Amazing Grace," even though
    many had low verbal skills. They were a group from a day health
    center, and the caregiver was on-site to support them.
4. Telemedicine works well for families who are facing difficulty,
    especially families who are facing an uncertain future. Through
    the use of reminiscence—exploring relationships, defining issues,
    and looking to the future—many are able to begin to plan for
    the future and say "I'm sorry, I love you, and it is the best I could
    do under the circumstances."

Telemedicine has the disadvantage of the facilitator not being immediately present with a participant who may become upset and need to be
comforted. Having a staff member on-site to serve in that role is crucial.
Telemedicine is a technology that can work with older frail individuals
and bring the outside world to isolated institutionalized elders. It is an
effective method to expand clinical services into underserved areas, both
rural and urban.

Additional Groups

1. Eight women ranging in age from 70 to 89, all widows living
    alone and not previously known to each other, began an 8-week
    closed reminiscence experience at their local senior center. The
    first week was devoted to developing the topics for the group.
    Topics chosen were: their earliest childhood recollection, first day
    of school, parents, how they met their husbands, World War II
    and its impact, their first child and other children, and how they
    want to be remembered. Many women brought photographs,
    early readers, wedding dresses, and other memorabilia. Pretest-
    ing was done with standardized tests for depression and life
    satisfaction. All eight women had mild to moderate depression.

Posttesting was done 5 weeks after the group ended, and improvement was shown in all areas—in some areas the improvement was dramatic. Many had established friendships and were attending social events, having dinner together, and sharing common interests. The members were more interactive within the group and in other settings. The members reported being happier with their lives, and the posttest showed less depression. The group participation enhanced their quality of life (Soltys, Reda, & Letson, 2002).

2. In the early 1980s, before the cause and effect of AIDS were widely known, a local hospice developed an open-ended bereavement support group. The group consisted of 10 55- to 75-year-old women. At the time, the hospice experienced its first death from AIDS, and the partner of the deceased called and asked to join the group. He joined the group, and the other group members—not knowing he was gay—presumed that his wife had died.

   He was handsome, articulate, and gentle. As weeks passed, he became friends with the other participants—teaching one to drive, teaching another to balance her checkbook, taking another to lunch, etc. One could see the reaction—the women were getting dressed daily and feeling more confident about themselves.

   He and the facilitator eventually explained to the rest of the group that he was gay and what AIDS was. They were very accepting and supportive of him. It was a learning experience and a growth time for all. Group experiences can expand members' attitudes about formerly close-minded topics. Group work creates an atmosphere where participants are able to see themselves and others in a different light.

3. Reda (Soltys, Reda, & Letson, 2002) conducted group work with six men ages 82 to 87. The 10 decades of the twentieth century provided the structure for 10 weekly sessions and elicited the men's recollections of wartime interests, major sporting figures, presidents' legislation and achievements, World War II, and favorite automobiles. Reda reported that the group was fun, provided social stimulation, and achieved intergenerational communication. Reda developed a close bond with the men and developed a greater appreciation for their contributions to society.

Everyone has a story to tell—if only someone would listen ... if only someone would ask.

Reminiscence allows individuals the opportunity to express their belief systems and value structures with health care providers, family members, and others involved in their lives. The group structure provides a method for the members to put into perspective important events in their lives, to bring closure to many issues, and often brings gratification and resolution to concerning events. With current economic concerns about health care, the use of groups can be cost effective. The improvement in self-esteem, perceived quality of life, and perceived social support can be important in how individuals see their lives and can bring closure. There are positive outcomes for group facilitators, too; they improve their professional skills as agents of change and enhance their appreciation of history and of the individuals they are helping.

USING LIFE STORY CIRCLES TO PROMOTE CULTURE CHANGE IN LONG-TERM CARE

We are all living out our life stories. Our past experiences influence our present and future expectations, aspirations, struggles, and successes. Each person brings his or her life story to any culture or subculture that he or she is part of. This inevitably forms both positive and negative cultural patterns.

Valuing and encouraging the purposeful use of life story work with a focus on quality of life can be a powerful way to propel culture change. In fact, doing so can lead to the development of a culture that is unique and close to an ideal culture that is unique and reflective of the experience and needs of its members. This may help older adults achieve a point in life that Robert Butler (2005) calls "elementality."

Here are some ways a culture of "elementality" can be promoted in long term care settings:

- Jean is a direct care provider and has many clients who are farmers. To promote lifelong memories and reminiscences with these clients, Jean tells her own life story of growing up on a farm, milking cows, and planting crops. By reminiscing about her life experiences, she develops a reciprocal relationship with her clients that improves quality of life for her as well as for her clients.
- In a staff training exercise with other nursing assistants, social workers, nurses, and activity professionals, Gerry talks about a ball and glove his father gave him when he was a child, just before his father left the family and never returned. Gerry and the other group members are moved to tears. As they all share other significant stories, a special bond is formed between them that improves their quality of life in many ways.

- A long-term care facility establishes training in using reminiscence in groups with older adults with dementia. Staff members learn how to facilitate reminiscence work in formal and informal groups. Once the reminiscence groups have been established, family members watch videotapes of the sessions and are encouraged to spend more time reminiscing with their loved ones. As the process unfolds, supervisory staff notice increased use of naturalistic reminiscence being facilitated between residents and family members by staff of all levels. The administrator observes a dramatic improvement in communication and cooperation among the staff and increased family satisfaction with the facility.

Classic family and organizational systems theory posits that, if one person in the system feels positive or negative about being part of the group, it is likely that others feel the same way. As each person becomes part of the system, their history has a direct effect on the organizational culture. The examples above indicate how the use of life story work can improve that culture. Unfortunately, the use of life stories has often been perceived as unimportant or inconsequential by administrators and policymakers rather than as the core of forming intimate family-like settings. This may be an oversight or reflect a disconnect between the values of policymakers and administrators and established domains of quality of life for those they wish to provide for.

The development of life story circles as regular exercises and activities for board members, staff members, volunteers, and families with a distinct focus on development of quality of life for everyone within the system could help facilitate quality of life in long-term care facilities. Life story circles should encompass and incorporate participants' life history, values, and needs in a synergistic process that forms a culture most reflective of those involved and unique to the individual and group cultures within the system.

WAYS TO USE REMINISCENCE AND GROUPS

1. To explore and share with others end-of-life wishes to prompt thoughts and values.
2. To support families and individuals to cope with specific disease processes such as dementia, Parkinson's disease, and diabetes.
3. To work with families to resolve old hurts and leave a legacy.
4. To work with individuals who are depressed and living alone to reestablish friendships and search for meaning.

5. To support clinicians who work with frail elders to establish and identify value structures.

6. To support individuals who suffer major losses in their lives.

7. To identify periods of strength in one's life and help to use those strengths to face a current situation.

8. To confirm one's life and to more clearly see the positive contributions one has made by recalling periods in life or one's total life.

EXERCISES

Reminiscence Activity

Prepare a constructed reminiscence activity for your next family gathering or social engagement with close friends.

1. Select a photograph, videotape, music, food, or any other media that you believe will create a reminiscence match.

2. Present this to the group without telling them why you're doing so.

3. Notice how the group reacts and what effect the reminiscence activity has on the gathering.

Accessing Therapeutic Resource States

This activity can be done individually or in group settings. It is important that each person has a chance to share his or her experiences while knowing that they have every right not to answer any questions or share anything with others if they are not comfortable doing so.

1. Stretch your arms, roll your neck, take a deep breath, and let it out.

2. Close your eyes and let your mind begin the recall of a safe place from some time in your past—maybe yesterday, last month, a decade ago, or when you were a little child.

3. Form a picture of this place in your mind. See the colors, shapes, textures near you and at a distance.

4. Begin to hear the sounds—around you and in the distance—in this safe place.

5. Begin to feel what it feels like to physically connect with the sights and sounds of this place from your past, and let yourself feel the emotions associated with this experience.

6. Continue to see, hear, and feel the aspects of this safe place while you become aware of any smells or tastes that go with your

presence in this safe place. Alternate your awareness from one of the five senses to another as you reexperience this safe place, remembering that this is a resource that you developed and that these resources are available to you at any time.

7. Look around this safe place and select an object that is there and within your reach. Grasp this object and bring it back (in your imagination) to the present.

8. Talk or write about the object. Notice how you feel and how others respond to you.

9. How is this helpful to you and your relationships with these individuals?

REFERENCES

Barrett, K. G., & Soltys, F. G. (2002). Geriatric social work: Supporting the patient's search for meaning. *Geriatric Rehabilitation, 17*(4), 53–64.

Birren, J. E., & Deutchman, D. E. (1991). *Guiding autobiography groups for older adults.* Baltimore: Johns Hopkins University Press.

Burnside, I. (1993). Themes in reminiscence groups with older adult women. *International Journal of Aging and Human Development, 37*(3), 177–189.

Butler, R., Lewis, L., & Sutherland, T. (1998). *Aging and mental health*, 346–365. Allym and Bacon: Boston.

Butler, R. N. (2005). The nature of memory, life review and elementality. *International Reminiscence and Life Review Conference 2005 Selected Conference Papers and Proceedings.* Superior: University of Wisconsin-Superior. pp. 9–18.

Burnside, I., & Schmidt, M. G. (1994). *Working with older adults: Group process and techniques.* Boston: Jones and Bartlett.

Coppola, S., Rosemond, C., Greger-Holt, N., Soltys, F. G., Hanson, L., Snider, M. A., & Busby-Whitehead, J. (2002). Area assessment: Evolution of teamwork for frail older adults. *Geriatric Rehabilitation, 7*(3), 13–28.

Erikson, E. (1980). *Identity and the life cycle.* New York: Norton.

Feil, N. (1992). *V/F validation: The Feil method, how to help disoriented old-old.* Cleveland, OH: Edward Feil.

Frankl, V. (1959) *Man's search for meaning.* New York: Simon & Schuster.

Galinsky, M., & Schopler, J. (1989). Developmental patterns in open ended groups. *Social Work with Groups, 12*(2), 59–67.

Haight, B., & Gibson, F. (1995) Preminiscence Group work. *Burnside's working with older Adults, Group Process and Techniques.* Boston: Jones and Bartlett., pp 397–415.

Kunz, J. (1991). Reminiscence approaches utilized in counseling older adults. *Illness, Crisis and Loss, 1*(4), 48–54.

Kunz, J. A. (1995). Social Worker Perspective. *Burnside Working with older adults: Group process and techniques.* : Jones and Bartlett. pp. 397–415.

Lucero, M. (2001). Grief therapy: A mission Dimension in Middle Stage Dementia Care. *Designing Our Future Conference Program.* San Francisco American Society of Aging, 101.

McMahon, A. W., & Rhudick, P. J. (1964). Reminiscing adaptational significance in the aged. *Archives of General Psychiatry, 10,* 292–298.

Orange County Department on Aging. *In praise of age* and *A touch of gray* Hillsborough, NC (919–942–2005).

In Praise of Age (1994). Passmore, J., Producer. Chapel Hill: People's Channel. A television show wher the producer, hosts, and hostesses are all volunteers. A community effort with the people's Channel to inform and share with elder residents. Some hosts include Bob Seymour, Jerry Passmore, and Florence Soltys. Shultz, M.

A Touch of Gray (1992). Shultz, M.(ed) Chapel Hill Newspaper. Chapel Hill: McClathcy Newspapers. A weekly newspaper column by local professionals and elders in the community covering local, state, and national issues relating to aging.

Parker, M., Ouinn, J., Viehl, N., McKinley, A. H., Polich, C. L., Hartwell, S., Van Hook, R., & Detzner, D. F. (1992). Issues in rural care management. *Family Community Health, 14*(4), 40–60.

Perednia, D. A., & Allen, A. (1995). Telemedicine technology and clinical application. *Journal of the American Medical Association, 273*(6), 483–488.

Romanick, M., & Romanick, J. Q. (1981). An analysis of reminiscence function and triggers. *Experimental Aging Research, 7*(4), 477–489.

Rowe, J., & Kahn, R. (1998). *Successful aging.* New York: Dell.

Schopler, J., & Galinsky, M. (1990). *Groups in health care settings.* Binghamton, NY: Haworth Press.

Soltys, F. G. (1999). Telemedicine is people: Not just technology. Paper presented at the International Reminiscence and Life Review Conference, New York.

Soltys, F. G., & Coats, L. (1994). The SolCos model: Facilitating reminiscence therapy. *Journal of Gerontological Nursing, 20*(11), 11–16.

Soltys, F. G., Reda, S., & Letson, M. (2002). Use of groups' process for reminiscence. *Journal of Geropsychiatry, 35*(1), 51–61.

Tippett, M. K. (1991). *Kentucky babe.* Unpublished memoirs.

Toseland, R. W. (1995). *Group work with the elderly.* New York: Springer.

Williams, M. E., & Pedrecdnia, D. A. (1995). Telemedicine Technology and Clinical Application. *Journal of American Medical Journal, 273*(6), 485–488.

Williams, M. E., & Thompson, B. G. (1996). Geriatric healthcare in the 21st century. North Carolina Medical Journal., *57*(6), 368–371.

Yalmon, I. D. (1995). *The theory and practice of group psychotherapy.* New York: Basic Books.

CHAPTER SIX

Life Stories as Heirlooms: The Personal History Industry

Anita Hecht and Mary O'Brien Tyrrell

- In the United States within the next 25 years, the elderly population will double, representing nearly 20 percent of the total populace.
- Recording one's life story in late life is becoming a cultural trend.
- Many resources are available to the general public to assist in recording one's own story or the story of another.
- For those seeking assistance in recording a life story, a burgeoning personal history industry provides a multitude of formats and workers from a variety of backgrounds.
- Samples of case studies from the personal history industry illustrate some special needs and considerations.
- Within the personal history industry, there is a need for research to provide data as training and practice standards are developed.
- When the life story product is unveiled, holding a special event to celebrate an elder's life has been well received.

Authors' note:

In this chapter, the cases cited are real. To protect privacy, fictitious initials and names have been used and permission has been received from the families involved.

OPA

Several years ago, my (Hecht) mother found an old cassette tape of her father talking about his military service in Germany during World War I. At first, I didn't play the fragile, 30-year-old tape; I feared it might break, the contents then lost forever. I knew I had a treasure in my hands, though. I immediately digitized the tape, improved the audio quality, and made CD copies for my whole family.

Opa, as we had affectionately known him, died when I was a child after a long and difficult life as a Holocaust refugee. Now, many years later, the tape not only revived memories of an old man who loved us very much, but revealed things I had never known about his life experiences and his values. For instance, he had fought patriotically on behalf of Germany during World War I, only later to be racially persecuted by his own country. As my family kept listening, we were drawn together not only by our shared past, but by the larger sweep of history as it had played out in the life of our very real ancestor. This treasure continued to have its effect on the next generation. Opa's great-grandson began to ask questions about World War I, a distant event brought suddenly alive and made relevant by the voice of his great-grandfather speaking across time. This was a more precious gift than any I could remember.

It was unquestionably fortuitous that the recording had ever been made. The circumstance was a typical Sunday afternoon meal in the late 1960s. My brother had bought a new tape recorder and asked Opa to help him try it out. Although the tape recorder would be considered a dinosaur by today's technology, the impulse to record Opa's stories was prescient of a burgeoning interest in preserving the life stories of our elders.

This modern trend has led to the development of what is today called the personal history industry. A growing cadre of life story professionals and memoirists known as personal historians help others to not only tell the stories of their lives, but document, archive, and pass them on to present and future generations.

STORIES AS HEIRLOOMS

Along with the study and practice of reminiscence and life review in retirement communities and health care settings around the world, the private sector has begun to address the very human need to honor our elders and preserve their life stories. When a family member dies, we are often left with little else than their material possessions. Today, however, families and personal historians alike understand that a written memoir or a recorded life history is at least as precious as, if not more valuable than, a gold watch, Grandmother's china, or a disorganized shoebox of letters.

In 2030, the elderly population in the United States is projected to be twice as large as it was in 2000, growing from 35 million to 71.5 million, and representing nearly 20 percent of the U.S. population (Federal Interagency Forum on Aging-Related Statistics, 2004, p. 2). Yet, increased mobility has dispersed families and generations across large geographical distances. And, as our daily lives speed up, the oral traditions of storytelling around the home and hearth have been replaced by e-mail and answering machines. The mass-produced, impersonal products of film and television have further eclipsed personal and communal stories. While the recent growth of the personal history industry parallels our aging society, it also indicates a strong recognition of the importance and fragility of human bonds.

LITERATURE ON WRITING MEMOIRS AND FAMILY HISTORIES

Many books and articles have appeared in recent years around this growing trend. An article in the *New York Times Magazine* suggests that "the triumph of memoir" is a recent manifestation of the particular American longing to discover who we are (Atlas, 1996, p. 25). An article in the *World Almanac Book of Facts 2002* claims that "Family history is one of Americans' favorite pastimes" (Hantula, 2002, p. 719). In *Living a Life That Matters: Resolving the Conflict Between Conscience and Success,* Rabbi Harold S. Kushner (2001) proposes a universal reason for our growing interest in personal histories:

> We don't have to find the cure for cancer to make a difference to the world, and we don't have to write great novels to be noticed by God. We only have to share our lives with other people, and choose generativity over stagnation. (p. 145)

Or, as Daniel Taylor (2001) puts it in *Tell Me a Story, The Life-Shaping Power of Our Stories,* "Sometimes what we need most is simply to laugh and celebrate ourselves" (p. 118). Indeed, there have been a number of books written to aid people interested in writing memoirs or family narratives. One popular book, *To Our Children's Children* (Greene & Fulford, 1993), provides a helpful list of themes and questions to explore different facets of personal and family stories. In print for more than 30 years, Frank P. Thomas's *How To Write the Story of Your Life* (1984) reflects his belief that "Writing should be a positive experience devoid of nit-picking and [that] rules can only be guidelines" (p. 3). Thomas guides readers through an extensive process—from making a simple outline to crafting a narrative to finding a bookbinder.

In a more therapeutic venue, the Hospice Foundation of America (1994) has produced a comprehensive workbook called *A Guide for Recalling and Telling Your Life Story*. It offers thematic worksheets developed around different life history themes and encourages family members and caregivers to guide narrators through the storytelling process. In another comprehensive resource, *Writing Family Histories and Memoirs*, Kirk Polking (1995) argues,

> As a writer, you have a unique opportunity to change history from sterile dates and facts into a living chronicle of what you or your family left as a legacy for future generations. You are the only one who knows the communities you lived in, the history you were part of. Who but you know the personal struggles you faced, the successes you achieved? (p. 2)

Other resources for recording life stories include *Keeping Family Stories Alive,* by Vera Rosenbluth (1997), which describes the skills needed in the delicate task of interviewing: "The interviewer's aim is not to challenge the teller's memory or point of view, but to provide the opportunity for full exploration of the person's life" (p. 75).

Indeed, current research shows that a full exploration of one's successes and challenges holds significant therapeutic value for the narrator. Although personal histories are not to be confused with psychotherapy, reminiscence and life review can be effective in decreasing late life depression. In a meta-analysis of 20 studies, Bohlmeijer, Smit, and Cuijpers (2003) conclude that,

> Reminiscence and life review are potentially effective treatments for depressive symptoms in the elderly and may thus offer a valuable alternative to psychotherapy or pharmacotherapy. Especially in non-institutionalised elderly people—who often have untreated depression—it may prove to be an effective, safe and acceptable form of treatment. (p. 1088)

The definitions, practice, and effectiveness of personal history work, life review, and reminiscence are ripe for further academic, clinical, and evidence-based research. Some books offer a course curriculum for life writing groups. In *Telling the Stories of Life Through Guided Autobiography Groups,* James E. Birren and Kathryn N. Cochran (2001) offer a series of workshops organized around topics that are "common threads in the fabric of just about anyone's life" (p. viii). The themes include topics such as family, the role of money, career, and health.

All the literature on recording life stories encourages the sharing of day-to-day details in the narrator's world. Descriptions of a childhood home, the modes of transportation used, the types of discipline employed, and the current events of the day all enrich a life story with tone, setting, and history, bringing to life the living conditions of the past for future generations.

An overview of the personal history movement is found in the 2002 video documentary, *The Joys and Surprises of Telling Your Life Story*, developed under a grant from the Metropolitan Life Foundation and produced by John Kunz of the University of Wisconsin–Superior. Noted academicians, personal historians, narrators, and families discuss various aspects of personal history work, reminiscence, and life review (Kunz, 2002).

In addition to the literature and resources referenced, various community agencies and places of worship offer workshops and writing classes for people wishing to preserve their life histories. Local history centers often provide archiving and preservation tips on how to ensure that family documents, photographs, and other memorabilia are properly archived and accessible to future generations.

THE PERSONAL HISTORY INDUSTRY

Elder storytellers are often eager to respond to the entreaties of younger family members to write or record their life stories, but they are sometimes discouraged by what seems a daunting and time-consuming endeavor. For those who lack the skill, time, or energy to produce life histories on their own, the personal history industry has arisen to meet their needs. A competent personal historian can guide elders and their families through the process of producing a life history in a manner that is fruitful, comprehensive, respectful, and enjoyable.

A 2002 article in *Time* magazine featured several families who hired personal historians to write or record personal histories for themselves or a loved one (Stich, 2002). All the families placed great value on the collected stories. One family in particular stressed the significance the personal history gained after the death of the narrator. "Our dad died about a year after we did his history, but in this book he lives on" (p. A2).

Personal historians include journalists, psychotherapists, social workers, nurses, videographers, gerontologists, and people from other helping or writing professions, who have developed a passion for recording life stories. Their increasing numbers led to the founding of the Association of Personal Historians in 1995, a trade association dedicated to the development, education, and marketing of the personal history craft and business. Today the association boasts almost 600 members and holds annual conferences to educate members about the skills, challenges, and new research in personal history work. The association also has a Web site (www.personalhistorians.org) that lists the services of member professionals who are available to assist families and organizations in recording their histories.

Personal historians offer a wide variety of services, from full-scale video and print productions to partial services and hourly consultations on project planning and design. Full-scale projects assume all the production work required to produce an heirloom document. The narrator's only job is to answer the questions posed by the personal historian. Partial services may include recommendations and operation of professional recording equipment; transcription services for recorded interviews; and editing, digitizing, or publishing existing documents and recordings. Personal historians often teach classes, offer training, and provide assistance to individuals, families, and community groups. In many cases, the need for professional services exists.

When choosing a professional service, there is no replacement for the often intangible but essential trust necessary to any successful working relationship. A preliminary meeting between the personal historian and narrator will often reveal whether there is a good fit in terms of personality, communication styles, comfort level, and shared vision.

Given the wide variety of services, skills, and formats available, the following questions can be helpful when choosing a personal historian:

1. What training, background, interviewing experience, and professional affiliations does the personal historian possess?
2. Can the personal historian provide samples of his or her work and references from previous clients?
3. How will the information for the life history be collected?
4. How long will the process take, from start to finish?
5. In what format will the final product appear?
6. How long can the final product be expected to last?
7. What happens if either the client or the professional is unable to complete the project?
8. How much will the service cost?
9. How much input and responsibility will the client and/or narrator have in the creation of the final product?
10. Does the personal historian have experience in working with any physical and/or mental challenges that might factor into a particular case?

PRODUCING THE LIFE HISTORY

A recent cover story for the *Wall Street Journal Quarterly Report* (Zaslow, 2006) reports that, "Memoir writing is being celebrated as a cathartic, enlightening, late in life exercise that leaves a precious legacy" (p. R1). How exactly is this precious legacy produced? Outlined below are the various steps and considerations taken by most personal historians to help ensure a successful and satisfying outcome to a personal history project.

Project Goals

Most personal history projects begin with a collaborative assessment of goals by the client, narrator, and personal historian. The personal historian leads the family and narrator in a preinterview meeting to discuss the scope, format, length, and cost of the final product. The assessment is especially important if the client (i.e., the one paying for the service) is someone other than the narrator. At this juncture, family dynamics often come to the fore. In some families, there may be differing memories and opinions of events, people, and shared experiences. Thus, the paying client may be interested in preserving his or her version of history, rather than allowing the narrator to tell his or her own story. However, since it is the narrator's story that is to be documented, professional ethics dictate that it is the *narrator's* story—that is, his or her "truth"—that must be accurately presented and respected. Discussing and defining the project goals in advance is essential to clarifying what and *whose* stories will be told, and to remedy any unrealistic expectations.

Mr. S's daughter hired a personal historian to write her father's memoir. Mr. S was initially reluctant to tell his story since a cousin of his had recently completed a detailed family genealogy. Mr. S did not want his life story to appear as competition or one-upmanship. Thus, the personal historian helped Mr. S identify his personal goals. The production was collaboratively designed to focus on stories about Mr. S's recently deceased wife and the times they shared in over 50 years of marriage. It would not include a family genealogy. When the memoir was completed and distributed at an annual family reunion, Mr. S had the marvelous sense of honoring his beloved wife, and his descendants gained a new understanding of his dedication to marriage and family.

In addition to clarifying goals, personal historians also use the preinterview meeting to gather preliminary family and personal history information. Simple brainstorming and history-gathering exercises help define project themes and structure. Some of the common topics explored during a preinterview meeting include maternal and paternal family history, childhood memories, significant relationships, education, work history, and stories of children and parenting.

A personal historian can also help a narrator decide whether to include information about a myriad of delicate topics. Topics such as illness, divorce, suicide, or family secrets may conjure up shame for the narrator or for other family members. If handled judiciously, discussion and inclusion of these topics in a life history can be of great value to the narrator in the telling, and to his or her descendants in the listening. At the same time, if handled inappropriately, such issues could cause great conflict among family members. For these reasons, working with a neutral, nonjudgmental, and sensitive personal historian can provide valuable safety and objectivity to the life history project.

Finally, the personal historian can use the preinterview meeting to determine whether psychological obstacles are present that could impede a successful project. It might become apparent, for example, that the narrator is dealing with unresolved trauma or has a conflicted relationship with a living family member. It takes a trained professional to navigate these waters skillfully, in order to prevent personal vendettas or traumatizing events for the narrator or his or her family. Such cases are the exception rather than the rule, yet it is the opinion of these authors that professional standards and training are needed in this burgeoning industry. It is important for personal historians and families alike to understand that, while life story work may be therapeutic, it is not psychotherapy and is not intended as such. A personal historian should help safeguard psychological safety, personal expression, and a person's right to privacy.

In summary, a basic preinterview assessment with the personal historian should include the following questions:

- Will the scope of a project cover an entire family history—including genealogical information—or will the project cover only certain aspects of the narrator's life, such as his or her professional life, military experiences, or major life events?
- Will the final document include existing materials and memorabilia, such as photos, old video recordings, or the writings of ancestors?
- Will the document be shared only within the family or with other more public community institutions and historical societies?
- Are there any mental, psychological, or physical health considerations that the personal historian should be aware of, which could affect the production or outcome of the project?

Audience

Consideration of audience helps in designing a successful life history project. Most often, personal histories are created for a private audience of family and friends. Thus, more intimate experiences and values are explored in the interview—stories about birth, death, relationships, and spiritual beliefs. If the audience includes the narrator's grandchildren, a personal historian will also ask questions about childhood, favorite games played, sibling relationships, and school experiences. Such topics help to bridge the generations with stories of shared interest.

If, however, the personal history is to be part of a public archive such as a church, synagogue, or community organization, the interview questions may focus less on the narrator's personal life and center more on his or her affiliation with the institution, specific historical events, or values related to the larger community.

Sometimes moments of insight and surprise occur as a personal history project unfolds. In her life story, Mrs. B talked about losing her younger brother during World War II. He had been lost at sea when his ship was torpedoed. After distributing her memoir to family and friends, the book found its way to a surviving sailor who had been aboard the same ship. Through this unexpected contact, Mrs. B learned the details of the attack on her brother's ship. This information was more than the family had been able to learn in over 60 years.

Documentation

It is beyond the scope of this chapter to discuss the various types of equipment and the many interviewing, recording, writing, and editing skills involved in producing high-quality printed or recorded personal histories. The general options are outlined below. With today's technology, the archiving, transfer, editing, research, and educational capabilities are enormous with digitally stored information, regardless of the chosen format. We have reached a time when the production of historical documents does not belong only to the powerful, wealthy elite. It is accessible to all.

Although most personal history projects are not produced for broadcast television or commercial publication, personal historians generally recommend using the highest quality recording and print materials available. Not only do high-quality materials ensure a long-lasting, archival document, they emphasize the value placed on one's stories and, more importantly, on the loved ones who receive them.

Personal histories are typically produced in one of three formats—or a combination thereof: print, audio, or video documents. Time, cost, archival quality, and equipment are important elements in the selection of formats. Some families are delighted with loose-leaf notebooks filled with favorite recipes and newspaper clippings. Others choose well-crafted narratives preserved in archival, hardbound books with high-end photo reproductions. Mr. P, an accomplished jazz musician and successful businessman, chose to produce a personal history memoir, as well as a CD sample of his musical performances from the 1940s. The CD fit safely into an archival sleeve in the back cover of the hardbound book.

Undoubtedly, the interview itself is the heart and soul of the personal history project. Whatever the chosen format, a highly trained and experienced interviewer is essential to building a successful relationship with the narrator and eliciting illustrative and meaningful stories.

Print

With centuries of proven longevity and accessibility—the only necessary equipment being the human body and an adequate level of literacy—the written word may be the most permanent format for preserving life histories. Many personal historians and their clients choose to produce printed memoirs based on oral history interviews.

Written documents can be crafted on, preserved on, and printed from computer hard drives. Computer formats are increasingly powerful, because they allow for book publishing as well as easy distribution via e-mail and family Web sites. Furthermore, with current graphic design software, written documents can be artfully presented to give lasting beauty and a personal touch to the stories shared. Personal historians offer a huge variety of print services, each with their unique strength and style.

Audio

Although historically print has been the most commonly used format, some personal historians offer oral history interviews on CDs and other audio formats. In audio formats, not only are the stories captured, but so are the narrator's unique voice and manner of speaking. Many clients comment that these "live" recordings draw them into a sense of presence with the narrator in a way that surpasses the written word.

Most personal historians recommend digital over analog recording formats. Modern digital technology offers exquisite sound quality, as well as numerous transfer capabilities across formats, and thus more durability and permanency. Unlike analog cassette tapes that degrade with increased wear of the magnetic tape, digital signals can be played and transferred regularly without loss of sound quality. Unlike copies made from analog tapes, a fourth- or fifth-generation digital copy will be as clear as the original recording.

Digital audio signals may be stored in a variety of ways—on computer hard drives, audio CDs, and MP3 players—as well as preserved in any number of file formats, such as AIFF and WAV files. Digitally mastered CDs and mini-discs can be delivered with written subject logs and printed interview transcripts for clients who want backup print materials. Lastly, interviews may be preserved in multiple forms, such as raw, unedited interviews or edited programs that include tracks, time codes, and navigation menus.

Video

Many clients and personal historians choose to produce videotaped personal history documents, which offer the advantage of preserving the stories, sounds, and unique facial expressions and visual characteristics of the narrator and his or her surroundings. Across the globe, younger generations come of age with film, television, and digital photography. We all know the power of visual media to capture our attention and imagination.

The production of meaningful videotaped personal histories requires both a sophisticated level of technical knowledge and the ability to make a story and storyteller come alive on screen. Along with a skilled interviewer and videographer, the basic pieces of equipment needed for a video production are a digital video camera, a lighting kit, external microphones for high-quality sound, a video monitor, possibly an audio mixer, and all needed supplies. For subsequent edited programs, one must have access to and knowledge of current video editing software and hardware. Many personal historians offer postproduction editing services along with their interviewing and videotaping services.

Sometimes clients and narrators express a legitimate concern that recorded formats will be inaccessible over time, recalling their old reel-to-reel recordings, 16mm home movies, and 8-track cassette players. Certainly, the risk of outdated media storage exists. Yet, digital video and sound files are unlikely to be lost if there is a family member or personal historian who is dedicated to the upkeep and transfer of the interviews to the latest digital technology.

Special Needs and Considerations

Because personal history narrators are often elderly, a trained personal historian should consider the physical, cognitive, psychological, and cultural experiences that may impact and inform the narrator's storytelling. Physical impediments such as hearing loss, stroke, or chronic pain may necessitate shorter interview sessions and quiet working environments to reduce distractions, extraneous noise, bright lights, and interruptions.

Second, personal historians should be sensitive to the fact that talking about life stories may result in frustration or embarrassment for the narrator, especially if he or she struggles with cognitive dementia or cannot perform certain tasks. While the narrator may be able to remember events in the distant past, he or she may not be able to remember the reason for the project. Conversely, narrators in the early stages of cognitive illness can experience a significant increase in self-esteem if their stories are recorded while early memories are still intact.

A third area of special consideration involves psychological issues, in which the personal history of the person may signal the need for caution. Severe mental illness, childhood loss of a parent, or a past traumatic event may require competent assessment and handling. Over the past few decades, mental health professionals have gained a deeper understanding of posttraumatic stress disorder. Remembering traumatic events may arouse unwanted symptoms decades after an event occurs. Individuals who have survived war, severe accidents, rape, or other such horrors may be subject to severe stress, flashbacks, or psychosis. Such cases may require consultation with a psychotherapist and an assessment of the narrator's ability to safely participate in the life review process.

Mr. S, a Holocaust survivor, told the story of returning to his family home after hiding in the woods, only to find his parents and his four siblings killed and hanging from a lamppost in front of his house. Sixty years later, after recounting this story for the first time, Mr. S began experiencing increased sleeplessness, anxiety, and paranoia. Upon the recommendation and referral of his personal historian, Mr. S sought and received treatment from a psychotherapist skilled at working with Holocaust survivors. His symptoms subsided and his life story was successfully completed and distributed among grateful family members.

Certainly, recounting significant and difficult life events can result in positive and healing outcomes. As mentioned earlier, however, recording a life story may be therapeutic, but it is not a substitute for therapy. Personal historians and clients alike should be aware of this distinction. In the introduction to her book *The Past in the Present*, Faith Gibson (2004) states,

> There will be some people who, because of disabilities or special circumstances, may need assistance in telling their story and being heard. It is important that skilled help is available to those who need it so that they can tell their own story, in their own way, and in doing so feel enriched rather than diminished. (p. xvi)

Again, more research and professional training are needed in this growing industry. Additionally, as the general area of late-life reminiscence develops, personal historians have the opportunity to work with geriatric psychotherapists in cooperative development of a nomenclature for life review, reminiscence, and oral history, which will undoubtedly elucidate professional boundaries.

A fourth area of consideration is for people who are facing a terminal illness and may or may not be willing to tell their life story. Although one might anticipate that a terminally ill person would eagerly tell a life story, such is not always the case. The American cultural taboo of death is ubiquitous. End-of-life caregivers often insist that hope is never taken from the client. Telling a life story may seem tantamount to admitting that death is around the corner. Moving through the multiple stages of loss is complex. Narrators and their families may be moving at different rates through a process that is not well understood. Below the surface may lurk resistance and fear that when a life history is finished, the person's life may be over too.

A personal historian must assess the narrator's readiness to record a life story in the context of the dying process and treat his or her pace and wishes with respect and dignity. After Mr. and Mrs. T learned that she was terminally ill with a projection of only several months to live, Mr. T wanted his wife to write a life story with the help of a personal historian. Mrs. T initially agreed but became reluctant when the personal historian arrived for the interviews. Gently leaving behind a business card with several means of contact, the personal historian promised to return when Mrs. T was ready. After a delay of several weeks, the interview was initiated at Mrs. T's request. Upon completion, she was delighted to have her legacy passed down to her family. They now find it a priceless treasure.

A fifth area of consideration is the ethnic and cultural background of the narrator. Personal historians can be helpful in eliciting culturally significant stories, if they are aware of the history and issues of that particular culture. Cultural and ethnic backgrounds affect a multitude of personal choices regarding food, holidays, attitudes toward health and illness, success, family, and spirituality. These topics can be rich with story and will be of special importance to future generations who may grow up in the "melting pot."

Some stories are not as positive. A Polish narrator, World War II prisoner of war, and postwar refugee, Mrs. C experienced racial prejudice when trying to enter the United States to meet her American fiancé. Historically, many immigrant groups have experienced painful discrimination and racist attitudes. In this case, the personal historian was careful to record the painful details of the immigration so readers would be fully informed of the difficult experience and the context in which it occurred.

FINAL STEPS—EDITING, DUPLICATIONS, CELEBRATIONS

In the editing stages of a project, personal historians can assist narrators in deciding what information to include in or delete from the final document. Each life is filled with a myriad of events, but having too much data can sometimes discourage a recipient from viewing or reading the content. It is wise to recall that a poet is often revered for one special poem. It is the essence of a person's life story and not every single detail that will be treasured as a priceless heirloom for generations to come.

Some narrators choose to have the entire interview content preserved in the finished product. Others desire light to heavy editing of their life story. Separating the wheat from the chaff is another significant and essential skill of the personal historian. Many personal historians are well-trained writers, editors, publishers, and producers. If handled well, the editing process can transform a limitless project into a stunning, well-crafted life story.

After the editing process is complete and the narrator approves the final document, duplication and distribution are addressed. Often personal historians will assist in the design, printing, and binding of the written materials. In the case of recorded interviews, the personal historian supervises the packaging, assembly, and distribution of the finished programs.

Personal historians may recommend that the final product contain a formal dedication to people in the narrator's family or friendship circle. Sometimes storytellers dedicate their projects to long-deceased parents, while others dedicate their work to future great-grandchildren. Other times the finished product is dedicated to an agency or organization that has been meaningful in the narrator's life. Whatever the case may be, formal dedications help ensure the document's safekeeping and may also begin a formal tradition of passing on the heirloom documents.

In most cases, the family network is abuzz while a project is underway and the outcome is greatly anticipated. Celebrations are a wonderful way to honor the completion of a life history project, even in a situation in which the project is completed posthumously. Personal historians often help arrange book signing parties and video screenings, where the finished product is unveiled. Such events offer families and communities an opportunity to gather and honor the life of the narrator.

CONCLUSION

There are many aspects to recording personal histories in the private sector that have only briefly been touched upon here: interviewing skills, publishing considerations, technical pitfalls, legal agreements, and so on. This new field begs for more study, research, and practice. The rewards of creating personal histories are worth the effort. Based on comments from authors, narrators, families, and community groups, the creation and preservation of life stories is one of the greatest experiences we can have, as well as one of the most meaningful gifts we can pass on to current and future loved ones. In response to his own book signing party with 75 family members present, 91-year-old narrator George put it this way, "This is the best day of my life!"

REFERENCES

Atlas, J. (1996, May 12). The age of the literary memoir is now. *New York Times Magazine*, p. 25.

Birren, J. E., & Cochran, K. N. (2001). *Telling the stories of life through guided autobiography groups*. Baltimore, MD: Johns Hopkins University Press.

Bohlmeijer, E., Smit, F., & Cuijpers, P. (2003). Effects of reminiscence and life review on late-life depression: A meta-analysis. *International Journal of Geriatric Psychiatry, 18*, 1088–1094.

Federal Interagency Forum on Aging-Related Statistics. (2004). *Older Americans 2004: Key indicators of well-being*. Washington, DC: U.S. Government Printing Office.

Gibson, F. (2004). *The past in the present*. Baltimore, MD: Health Professions Press.

Greene, B., & Fulford, D. G. (1993). *To our children's children: Preserving family histories for generations to come*. New York: Doubleday.

Hantula, R. (2002). Tracing your roots. *World almanac and book of facts 2002*. New York: World Almanac Books.

Hospice Foundation of America. (1994). *A guide for recalling and telling your life stories*. Miami Beach, FL: Author.

Kunz, J. (Producer). (2002). *The joys and surprises of telling your life story* [Video]. Superior, WI: International Institute of Reminiscence and Life Review.

Kushner, H. S. (2001). *Living a life that matters: Resolving the conflict between conscience and success*. New York: Knopf.

Polking, K. (1995). *Writing family histories and memoirs*. Cincinnati, OH: Betterway Books.

Rosenbluth, V. (1997). *Keeping family stories alive: Discovering and recording the stories and reflections of a lifetime*. Vancouver, Canada: Hartley and Marks.

Stich, S. S. (2002, November 11) Stories to keep. *Time, 160* (20), pp. A1–A3.

Taylor, D. (2001). *Tell me a story. The Life-Shaping Powers of our Stories*. St. Paul, MN: Bog Walk Press.

Thomas, F. P. (1984). *How to write the story of your life* (6th ed.). Cincinnati, OH: Writer's Digest Books.

Zaslow, J. (2006, June 26). Memoir vs. memoir. *Wall Street Journal Quarterly Report*, p. R1.

CHAPTER SEVEN

When Words Are Not Enough: Art-Based Methods of Reminiscence

Renya T. H. Larson and Susan Perlstein

Art-based reminiscence models:

- Offer a nonverbal way to access and explore memory.
- Trigger powerful sense memories. Sensory stimuli (colors, photos, fabrics, perfumes, music, foods, etc.) carry powerful associations for most people.
- Offer a "safe space" for reminiscence because the arts are both "real" and "not real." This allows older people to remember while at the same time containing their memories in an aesthetic form. Some older people may be better able or more willing to reminisce under these circumstances.
- Provide older adults with social engagement. Research indicates that social engagement is essential for healthy aging.
- Provide older adults with lifelong learning. Participants acquire and hone aesthetic skills.
- Bolster the individual identities of older adults.
- Can reintegrate older adults into their communities. Art-based reminiscence creates a tangible legacy for future generations.

Humans experience the world through taste, touch, sight, smell, and sound. Memories of sensory experience are often visceral, vivid, and nonverbal. Recall, for example, the precise smell of a person that you love or the taste of your favorite food as a child. These sensory memories may quickly trigger a flood of other details about the past and rekindle its emotional associations.

Art-based models of reminiscence are well-suited to tap such memories because art, by definition, heightens the senses. Painting, for example, heightens perception and expression of sight; music does the same for the sense of sound. In art-based reminiscence, we heighten the senses and trigger sensory associations. This process can evoke frivolous or whimsical memories—it can also evoke memories so potent or complex that words alone cannot express them. In an art-based reminiscence group run by Elders Share the Arts, for example, the facilitator played holiday music and asked the participants what memories it evoked for them. "In my mind," answered one, "I can see my family in a big circle in a big house with a big backyard." She was silent for a moment, overcome by the power of her memory: "it gives me such a feeling."[1]

In another art-based reminiscence session, facilitator Marsha Gildin used a daffodil to stimulate visual sense memories. Participants transformed their memories into poems such as this one:

I'm thinking of a dress I once had.
It was my favorite
I had it when I was a teenager.
Yellow organdy! Sheer and crispy!
It looked good on me!
And when I wore it and walked into the Savoy
A gasp filled the room.
And then I danced the night away.[2]

Clearly, the senses are a strong conduit of memory. But the goal of art-based reminiscence is not only to evoke memories, but also to examine their meaning. Like many other models of reminiscence, some art-based models derive directly from the theories of psychologist Erik Erikson and gerontologist Robert Butler. Readers of this chapter are almost certainly aware of Erikson's (1997) concept of ego integrity, which theorized that reflecting on past experiences provides people in the last stage of life with "a meaningful interplay between beginning and end as well as some finite sense of summary and, possibly, a more active anticipation of dying" (p. 63). Readers will also recognize the groundbreaking contributions of Butler (1963), who linked Erikson's concept of integrity to the presumed propensity that seniors have for reminiscence—a propensity heretofore dismissed by psychiatrists and psychologists as obsessive or even pathological. Butler hypothesized that reminiscence should be not only tolerated in older adults, but encouraged; this hypothesis sparked a shift in professional attitudes toward reminiscence and paved the way for its infusion in the field of gerontology. Many models of reminiscence, some art-based models among them, have attempted and achieved the positive clinical outcomes defined by Erikson and Butler. Other reminiscence models, again including some that are art-based, do not measure outcomes by clinical standards, but rather attempt to promote a more general intellectual, emotional, or social engagement. What distinguishes art-based reminiscence models from nonart models is, therefore, not theory but methods: art-based reminiscence evokes and examines memories in the aesthetic form.

Art-based reminiscence emphasizes creative expression as a vital component of healthy aging. Research has begun to recognize that healthy aging requires more than physical fitness and disease prevention. A study by Glass, deLeon, Marottoli, and Berkman (1999), for example, found that social activities as significantly impact "all cause mortality" as physical fitness activities. In *Successful Aging*— the most extensive and comprehensive study on aging conducted in the United States—Rowe and Kahn (1998), named continued engagement in relationships and productive activities as one of the three key components of successful aging. (The other two components of successful aging are minimization of disease and disability and maintenance of physical and cognitive function.) Gene Cohen (2000) expanded on this research with publication of *The Creative Age: Awakening Human Potential in the Second Half of Life*. Cohen's book documents discoveries in neuroscience that radically challenge conventional assumptions about the aging brain. For example, studies have shown that it is not the number of neurons that dictates brain function, but the number and strength of the *connections between* neurons. While the human brain does, in fact, lose neurons throughout life, it does not lose its capacity for forming and deepening connections between the neurons that remain. In fact, studies have found that, between one's early 50s and late 70s, there is an increase in both the number and length of branches from individual neurons in different parts of the brain that are involved with higher intellectual functioning. However, neuroscientists believe that, in order for the brain to maintain connections between its neurons, and especially to forge new connections, it needs challenge. In other words, it is not old age per se that reduces the brain's functioning. It is stagnation that threatens the brain, such as the stagnation that occurs when older adults are cut off from meaningful opportunities for stimulation and growth.

Cohen (2005) expanded his defense of the potential of the aging brain with the publication of *The Mature Mind: The Positive Power of the Aging Brain*. In this book, Cohen introduced the concept of developmental intelligence, a "maturing synergy of cognition, emotional intelligence, judgment, social skills, life experience, and consciousness" (p. 35). According to Cohen, developmental intelligence is comprised of three types of thinking that improve with age:

- *Relativistic thinking* (the capacity for synthesizing disparate views). With increasing developmental intelligence, older people abandon absolute truth in favor of more realistic relative truths.
- *Dialectic thinking* (the capacity to hold opposites in mind without judgment). Older people who have developed this component of developmental intelligence are able to uncover contradictions in opposing views while accepting both as valid.
- *Systematic thinking* (the capacity for "seeing the forest as well as the trees"). This component of developmental intelligence prevents those who have developed it from undue focus on personal and petty issues.

The Mature Mind also offers a prescription for cognitive health in later life. To prevent age-related cognitive decline and enhance developmental intelligence, Cohen recommends:

- Mental exercise
- Physical exercise
- Challenging leisure activities
- The pursuit of "mastery" (of a skill, etc.)
- Strong social networks

How can creative engagement specifically contribute to healthy aging? Cohen (2005) completed a 3-year longitudinal study—the first of its kind—to answer this question. The study is named "Creativity and Aging: The Impact of Professionally Conducted Cultural Programs on Older Adults," and it used well-established psychological and medical indices to measure the impact of professionally implemented arts programming on seniors. The study was initiated in the fall of 2001. One hundred and fifty older people participated in the intervention group (arts programs run by professional artists) in three locations: Elders Share the Arts in Brooklyn, New York; the Center for Elders and Youth in the Arts in San Francisco, California; and the Levine School of Music in Washington, DC. A second group of 150 older people who did not participate in these arts programs comprised the control group. The median age of participants at the start of the study was 80 years. The preliminary results indicate that the intervention group, in comparison to the control group, experienced:

- Better overall health
- Fewer falls and less hip damage
- Fewer doctor's visits
- Diminished use of medications
- Diminished vision problems
- Better scores on a geriatric depression scale and a loneliness scale
- Increased involvement in activities

These initial trend data are all the more impressive given the advanced age of the participants. Cohen notes that gerontologists would expect general declines in functioning (given that participants' average age was 80) due to normal aging processes (increased risk of disease, etc.). A cultural intervention that is able, therefore, to not only slow the rate of decline, but, in some areas, reverse it, is highly significant.

The initial data reflect findings from the Washington, DC, site. Because this study had a staggered start, the data from the sites in Brooklyn and San Francisco (sites with later start dates) are still being analyzed. However, early analysis suggests that these two sites will yield data reflecting related outcomes. We believe the final results, once published, will encourage further research and increased interest in art-based work with older people.

Already, there is increased interest in the theory and practice of creative work with older people. When Susan Perlstein conducted her first Living History Theater workshops in senior centers in 1979, she had few colleagues or contemporary precedents. Many of the professionals she encountered would observe her artistic work with older people and ask, "Why bother?" At that time, gerontology conceived of the last years of life as years of inevitable decline, marred by disease and senility. Scant attention was given to quality of life or lifelong learning concepts that are so popular today. Only in the past few years, with groundbreaking research and the baby boomers nearing retirement, have these concepts gained currency. American ideology, quite possibly, is on the verge of a transformation.

Unfortunately, at present most senior centers and nursing homes offer little more than rudimentary arts and crafts programming. Although many host arts activities such as sing-alongs and dances, they don't generally offer participants rigorous or sustained outlets for creative expression. These activities are entertaining, but they don't offer the full benefits of creative expression.

What, then, are the full benefits of creative expression? In addition to the physical and psychological benefits suggested by the aforementioned research, arts programs have the potential to benefit older adults in several key ways. First, arts programs can be a tool for lifelong learning. Rather than merely engaging participants in artistic busy work, they help older adults hone new aesthetic skills and strive for new levels of sophistication in the art forms they have already mastered. In other words, these model arts programs defy the cultural misperception that stagnation is inevitable in old age. Second, arts programs can bolster participants' identities by giving them the opportunity to explore their unique identity, and to celebrate that identity in works of art. This is critical given that many of the benchmarks of aging generally weaken the older adult's links to his or her former self: retirement, diminished social roles, decreased self-sufficiency, institutionalization, the death of friends or a spouse. Finally, the arts can provide older people with a tangible legacy to leave to future generations. Our society provides few outlets for older people to contribute; creating artwork is one way that older people can overcome this deficiency to ensure that their unique talents and insights will be remembered.

MODEL PROGRAMS

This section begins with an overview of several outstanding arts programs for older people and then focuses specifically on programs that have developed art-based models for reminiscence.

ArtWorks, an artist-in-residence program sponsored by the Goldman Institute on Aging in San Francisco, provides workshop and performance opportunities for over 600 older adults in the Bay Area each year through a variety of residences, all taught by professional artists. At the On Lok Nursing Home facility, for example, the extraordinary work of Asian American resident artists from ArtWorks led participants to produce exquisite Chinese brush-paintings. Each painting demonstrated technical skill and an individual artistic vision. ArtWorks required that On Lok designate permanent wall space to exhibit the participants' work. ArtWorks professionally framed and displayed the paintings with the name of the artist, a photo, and a statement of artistic vision. Such professional touches are a hallmark of ArtWorks. The displays impress upon viewers in the institution—and upon the participating older adults—that old age is no barrier to artistic mastery.

Across the country, several senior centers have taken it upon themselves to develop high-quality arts programming: two are Center in the Park in Philadelphia, Pennsylvania, and Senior Arts in Albuquerque, New Mexico. At both centers, the extensive visual arts curriculum has led to the creation of works of art that reflect the cultural heritage of the participants (Center in the Park largely serves African Americans, and Senior Arts serves Native Americans). These artworks are displayed throughout the centers. As at On Lok, these displays help affirm the individual and cultural identities of the participants.

Few quality arts programs exist for older adults; fewer still ground their theory and/or practice in reminiscence. Across the country, the majority of reminiscence-based arts programs for older people are story-telling troupes who generally perform for youth audiences. Stagebridge Senior Theatre Company, for example, trains older people in the San Francisco area to perform in local schools in a program called Story-bridge. This nationally recognized program is funded by local foundations, the state arts council, and the U.S. Department of Education. While the older storytellers do tell traditional and well-known stories, they also share living-history stories from their own lives. The goal of the program is two-fold: it bridges a generation gap that has too often left young and old with few opportunities to interact, and it enlivens the curriculum with first-person perspective and nuance.

Stagebridge advertises for older adults to volunteer as storytellers in a dozen partner elementary schools in the Oakland area. The volunteers receive weekly training in the skills of storytelling, including how to tell their stories in schools and ways of shaping the stories from their own lives. The stories vary in theme; examples include a time they got in trouble for cutting school or how they grew up on a farm with a cow for a pet. Through these stories, children learn how much life has changed over the decades, but also how older people are really a lot like them. Stereotypes are broken down on both sides. Students are encouraged to interview their own grandparents and enter the Stagebridge Grandparent Tales Writing Contest. Discovering their grandparents' stories strengthens and creates new bonds between the generations. Formal evaluations show that the program helps increase students' language arts and reading skills.

Stagebridge also develops original senior theater productions. Some of these productions are based, either in whole or in part, on the actors' reminiscences. Similarly, Roots&Branches is an intergenerational theater company that devises original productions from the reminiscences of company members. The company is in residence at F·E·G·S Health & Human Services System in New York City and brings together a troupe of elder actors and acting students from the Tisch School of the Arts of New York University. Founder Arthur Strimling created Roots&Branches to build understanding and connection between generations. Each academic year, the two generations meet regularly to share stories from their lives and to engage in theater improvisations. The tape-recorded sessions are transcribed and shaped into a script by a professional playwright. Each spring, the original production is fully mounted.

The Roots&Branches model demonstrates how arts-based models of reminiscence can easily weave true-life stories with fantasy and imagination. For example, in 2002 Roots&Branches produced *Playing Lear,* an original production that used Shakespeare's tragedy (*King Lear*) as a springboard for exploring the theme of conflict and reconciliation between generations. The company read and studied scenes from the play to create scenes and monologues based on their life experiences. In the final script, the actors' reminiscences were woven together with material generated from improvisation and from Shakespeare's text. Clearly, unlike other models of reminiscence, art-based models allow participants to depart from the "facts" of a memory to explore its associations, implications, and thematic resonances. Such a model allows participants to reap the benefits of reminiscence *and* fantasy, play, and imagination.

Model programs in the arts disciplines of storytelling and theater most obviously lend themselves to reminiscence-based work, but model programs do exist in other disciplines. Perhaps the best known is the Liz Lerman Dance Exchange, an intergenerational dance company that often uses personal stories of company members and community participants as a key element. In 1975, Dance Exchange founder Liz Lerman created "Woman of the Clear Vision," a dance about her mother's death featuring professional dancers and adults from a Washington, DC, senior center. In this dance, Lerman discovered two passions that distinguished her from the mainstream of modern dance. The first passion was to incorporate narrative and the spoken word into her choreography, often drawing on the life experiences of cast members. The second passion was to include dancers of all ages in her pieces. Lerman finds human movement fascinating across the life span; while older people are largely excluded from mainstream modern dance, Lerman began to develop dances that showcased the distinctive expressive qualities of people at every stage of life, effectively opening up the dance stage to senior adults. In 1976, Lerman established the Dance Exchange. By the mid-1980s, the company was touring extensively, sometimes with the *Dancers of the Third Age,* an adjunct troupe of older dancers that also performed on its own for many years.

The Dance Exchange develops a wide range of professional and community-based dance projects in its home city of Washington, DC, nationally, and internationally. Not all of the company's work is relevant to the scope of this chapter; for our purposes, what is significant is that the Dance Exchange pioneered a wide range of techniques for incorporating personal story and memories with elements of movement in ways that celebrate and value people of all ages and that the Dance Exchange has continuously evolved these practices through myriad projects over the course of 30 years.

For example, one of the Dance Exchange's recent projects is *Near/Far/In/Out*, a performance work driven and inspired by dialogue among four generations of the gay, lesbian, bisexual, and transgender (GLBT) communities. Personal stories of one era intersected with those of another to reflect moments of history and individual change, generating a theatrical event that incorporated text, movement, metaphor, and music. A team of Dance Exchange artists, led by co-artistic director Peter DiMuro, were joined by members of the local GLBT communities at sites across the country to create and perform this innovative work.

Near/Far/In/Out invited its participants to explore memories on a theme that is often taboo (sexuality). Arts-based models of reminiscence are uniquely suited for exploring such memories, because, when facilitated with skill and sensitivity, the arts provide a safe space for this exploration.

Psychologist Donald Winnicott (1971) makes note of this benefit in his seminal work *Playing and Reality*. Specifically, Winnicott noted that play (like creativity) is a transitional space somewhere between reality and fantasy where we are free to explore our thoughts, feelings, and memories without fear of real-world consequences. We are also able to express our thoughts, feelings, and memories in nonlinear ways. For example, a memory of the first stirrings of a taboo crush could be expressed in movement: a bouncing gait, a flutter of eyelids, a hand placed over the heart.

One final example of an organization with a long-standing dedication to arts-based reminiscence is Age Exchange, based at the Reminiscence Centre in South East London. One highlight of the Centre is the hands-on museum of everyday life in the 1930s and 1940s. The Centre also hosts a gallery where three-dimensional interactive exhibitions are created around the memories of older Londoners from many cultures. Age Exchange is the focus for a wide range of cultural activities for older people, undertaking projects with day care centers, residential homes, schools, and youth groups, and running training courses for community and health workers. Under the direction of founder Pam Schweitzer, Age Exchange develops original dramas with The Good Companions, a group of older volunteers. Exhibitions, workshops, and publications often accompany the plays. Age Exchange has produced publications from the memories of older people such as the following titles: *Across the Irish Sea, Good Morning Children, Living Through the Blitz,* and *What Did You Do in the War, Mum?*

This section has described the range of art-based reminiscence models that exist as well as the individuals and organizations that developed them. We now turn to an in-depth exploration of one organization and its art-based reminiscence programs. That organization is Elders Share the Arts.

ELDERS SHARE THE ARTS

Elders Share the Arts (ESTA) is a nonprofit organization dedicated to affirming the time-honored role of elders as bearers of history and culture by using the power of the arts to transmit their life stories and life experiences in diverse communities throughout New York City. In ESTA's signature living history arts programs, participants transform their memories into artworks of all kinds: quilts, paintings, collages, murals, songs, dances, poems, and plays.

In 25 years of experience, ESTA's programs have provided participants with the benefits proposed by Erikson and Butler. In addition to promoting ego integrity, ESTA discovered that art-based reminiscence models are powerful conduits for building community. Quite early on, ESTA decided that building community would be a central component of all its arts-based reminiscence programs, because ESTA strongly believes that contemporary America offers too few venues for genuine and sustained interaction between the generations. Older adults do not often have opportunities to share their accumulated life wisdom. This fact denies them a natural and meaningful role in the wider society and reinforces their generalized isolation. When older adults transform their memories into works of art, however, they create a tangible legacy for future generations. The benefits extend far beyond the individual older participants to the community at large. We advocate for arts-based reminiscence not only to serve elders, but also to serve ourselves.

Transforming the Culture of Our Institutions: Arts-Based Reminiscence in Nursing Homes

Too often, the residents of nursing homes are isolated or depressed, sitting alone in the halls or remaining in their rooms. Over 15 years, ESTA has conducted art-based reminiscence groups at the Isabella Geriatric Center in Washington Heights, Manhattan. This nursing home strives to create a culture of community; over the years, the ESTA programs became one of the strongest forces for nurturing community at Isabella. ESTA conducted art-based reminiscence programs on all floors at Isabella and also trained youth volunteers to engage the residents.

One reminiscence group at Isabella called itself "The Love Group." The group consisted of 12 to 14 residents who gathered each week in the eighth-floor day room. The diverse group consisted of African American, Latino, Caribbean, Jewish-Irish, and Italian seniors. Each week, the facilitator led the participants through a greeting, a warm-up, the creation of a group poem, an artistic exercise, and a closure.

For example, in one session, the group explored the theme "music in our lives." The session began with a movement warm-up accompanied by Glen Miller's *In the Mood*. Wheelchair-bound residents stretched each part of their body: arms, hands, legs and toes, head, chest, trunk, and bottom. After the movement warm-up, the facilitator led the group in creating a poem together. Each participant contributed one line to this group poem about their reaction to the music:

Music in Our Lives

Listening to music from the big band days reminds me of dancing the
Lindy hop
With five or six different gals. They were all good partners.
It makes me think of when I was young—Glen Miller was a favorite
of mine.
I think of the Savoy ballroom up in Harlem—
Thursday night was ladies' night—that was MY night!
I saw many performers there:
Count Basie, Louis Jordan, and sometimes the Duke.
Yes, those were the big band days.
Dancing! The rumba, the Charleston, tap dancing,
I see myself dancing in Lucy, Jamaica—a special place I love so well.
I love dancing to Spanish music—
And then we would run to American music.
Oh! Dancing. My god what I liked.
I don't dance—I never did. But I watch others.
Going from church to church suited me fine.
I love waltzing around the floor—
I'm waltzing now.
I'm in a chair now, but I still enjoy a good spin.
Music in our lives.[3]

The Love Group was a powerful outlet for many residents at Isabella. One group participant named Joan, for example, rarely left her room before she joined the group. After she joined, she developed friends with whom she could engage in various social activities. As Lucille and other participating residents became less isolated, the culture of the nursing home as a whole began to shift. The staff and non-participating residents appreciated the music and laughter that spilled out of the day room during Love Group sessions, and staff and residents came to sing and talk together over lunch. A Love Group bulletin board displayed photos from the sessions and quotes from the poems and stories.

Bringing Community to Homebound Seniors:
Legacy Works

Homebound seniors face enormous challenges. Many have few or no support networks and therefore face extreme isolation. ESTA has developed an arts-based reminiscence model to meet the specific needs of this population: Legacy Works. ESTA artists first train family members or professional or volunteer caregivers (e.g., home health aides, friendly visitors, teen volunteers) to interview homebound elders about their life experiences. The trainees then learn the art of collage and work with the elders to transform their life experiences into this visual art medium.

One of the agencies that has partnered with Legacy Works is Union Settlement House, a multiservice agency that offers a range of programs for its primarily Latino and African American clientele. Under the auspices of the New York City Department for the Aging, Union Settlement House runs a senior services program that includes senior centers and services to homebound elderly. Homebound elders receive Meals-on-Wheels, friendly visitors, and shopping assistance. Through foundation support, ESTA has brought Legacy Works to the homebound elders served though Union Settlement. In one program, pairs of teens were assigned to visit an elder 4 days a week for 30 weeks. Each meeting lasted 1 to 2 hours. The project culminated in an art opening and exhibit at the Union Settlement gallery.

This particular model often succeeds in forging deep relationships between young people and homebound elders. In the Union Settlement House partnership, a touching friendship emerged between Rosa, an adolescent girl, and a frail 87-year-old woman named Marie who had been debilitated by arthritis. In her first visits with Marie, Rosa discovered that both of them were part Puerto Rican and part African American. She also discovered that they both had a persistent yearning in common: to leave New York City and find a life where the sun and the sea could comfort them. This initial bond deepened as Rosa recorded Marie's memories. The young woman's intense interest in Marie's past reduced Marie's isolation and bolstered her identity.

The ESTA staff had trained the teens to create family tree collages with their assigned elder. Because of her arthritis, Marie couldn't easily draw the details of her tree, and she asked Rosa and Rosa's partner, Eduardo, to help her. Together they drew thick, deep umber roots, branches covered with forest green leaves, and scarlet birds flying away into the blue sky. All three developed newfound artistic skills. Working on the collage also gave Rosa and Marie the opportunity to speak with each other and deepen their bond. The ESTA staff noticed that, over time,

Marie became Rosa's surrogate grandmother. Rosa confided in Marie, and Marie offered the young woman her insights and her advice. This example of the Legacy Works model clearly exemplifies that it can foster strong, mutually beneficial relationships. For homebound elders, this one-on-one relationship may be their only link to the wider community.

Building Bridges in Fractured Communities:
The Intergenerational Model

ESTA has also developed an intergenerational model of arts-based reminiscence called Generating Community that links generations and cultures through the creation of memory-based art. One of ESTA's longest community partnerships has been in Flushing, Queens. This 15-year partnership first began at the Rosenthal Senior Center, a center founded to serve aging immigrants. These older immigrants are predominately of European descent; some are Holocaust survivors. Over the years however, the demographics of the surrounding neighborhood have changed dramatically. Only one block away from Rosenthal, for example, at Intermediate School 237, students come from over 60 countries and speak over 50 different languages. Before ESTA began its partnership, these two factions of the Flushing community had few opportunities to engage with each other. In fact, cultural, racial, and generational factors all contributed to a mutual distrust.

ESTA has helped to ease this distrust through ongoing cultural exchange between the seniors at Rosenthal and the youth at the nearby school. Each year, the seniors and the youth spend the first weeks of the project apart, each group exploring its assumptions and prejudices about the other. When the two groups eventually meet, they learn oral history interviewing skills and gather each other's life stories. In the first year of the project, the seniors and students shared stories of leaving their native countries as well as their first experiences as immigrants in the United States. In the second year, the group explored "everyday heroes." Every year since then, the seniors and youth have explored a theme that reflects their collective interests and that arises from the life stories that they share with each other.

The seniors who participate in the Flushing project report that they feel needed, useful, and creative. The project provides them with a meaningful social role to play in their community, thus reducing their isolation. As they collaborate with young people to transform their stories into art, seniors are restored something of their traditional role as conveyers of cultural heritage. As role models and mentors to the young people, they have the opportunity to care for others at a time when they are often faced with increasing dependency themselves. Without such opportunities for reciprocal caring, seniors may feel that they burden their communities and have nothing to offer in return. Older adults in the Generating Community program have something valuable to offer, indeed: their stories. For immigrant youth, these stories can inform and inspire their transition in a foreign land. Further, the program reduces the young peoples' fears of aging. For some, the program offers their first real friendship with an older person.

CONCLUSION

As stated at the beginning of this chapter, the arts are uniquely suited to engage older people's senses and to thereby evoke sense memories. This process is often vivid and visceral. An arts-based approach may encourage older people to not only recall but to nearly reexperience their reminiscences. This is a benefit—and also a danger—of an arts-based approach. These approaches engage older people vividly and viscerally, so they must be facilitated with skill and care.

At the same time, arts-based approaches can offer older people a uniquely safe way to reminisce. This is because the arts contain reminiscence in an aesthetic form that is separate from "reality." The arts also offer a way to reflect and communicate nonverbally; therefore, older people can reminisce about things they cannot—or will not—put into words.

We are delighted that the authors of this volume chose to include a chapter on arts-based approaches to reminiscence. Although these approaches offer the specific and unique benefits we have outlined, they, unfortunately, are not always valued in our society. As readers know, our society also undervalues its older people. We hope that this chapter will contribute to a revaluation of both. We are encouraged by recent research that highlights the potential for healthy aging and also by research that demonstrates the role that the arts might play in this process. Most of all, we are encouraged by the extraordinary work of the organizations cited in this chapter. We have included contact information for these organizations below; we encourage readers to stay abreast of their innovative and important work.

EXERCISES

Activity: Hands Poem

This activity draws sensory awareness to the hands—through sight and touch—and triggers memories associated with them.

1. Begin by asking the participants to look at their own hands. Draw attention to the shapes, colors, and textures. Give them time to notice as many details as possible: wrinkles, lines, pores, veins, scars, calluses, rings. Make sure participants look at their fingers, their fingernails, their palms, and the backs of their hands.
2. After participants have had time to carefully examine their hands, ask them to close their eyes and touch their hands. Are their hands cold or warm? Are they moist or dry? What about the texture—is it rough or smooth? Is the texture of the back of the hand different from the palm? From the fingertips?
3. Ask participants to keep their eyes closed and think of activities that they have done with their hands. What did their hands do in childhood? What about when they were a young adult?
4. Ask participants to open their eyes.
5. Invite (but don't force) participants to share a memory of what their hands have done. Each contribution becomes a line in a group poem.

The following is an example of a hands poem:

These Hands

These hands!
These hands have changed many diapers.
These hands!
These hands have made many delicious salads every day of my life.
These hands!
These hands have added and subtracted plenty of figures—30 years with the labor council.
These hands!
These hands have painted beautiful canvases of color—they hung on the walls of my home.
These hands!
These hands have knitted sweaters, and when I got older—hats.
These hands!
These hands have drawn pictures, written poetry, and sang.
These hands!
These hands have lovingly cleaned many tushies.
These hands!
These hands have learned to work on a computer.
These hands!
These hands have gotten into everything.
These hands![4]

138   TRANSFORMATIONAL REMINISCENCE

NOTES

1. Isabella Nursing Home Love Group, December 18, 2000. Elders Share the Arts, Marsha Gildin, facilitator.
2. Isabella Nursing Home NF3 Group, April 5, 2002. Elders Share the Arts, Marsha Gildin, facilitator.
3. Isabella Nursing Home Love Group, October 16, 2000. Elders Share the Arts, Marsha Gildin, facilitator.
4. Living History Drama Group, November 26, 2001, Penn South Senior Center, Marsha Gildin, facilitator.

REFERENCES

Butler, R. (1963). The life review: An interpretation of reminiscence in the aged. *Psychiatry,* 26(1), 65–76.
Cohen, G. (2000). *The creative age: Awakening human potential in the second half of life.* New York: Avon Books.
Cohen, G. (2005). *The mature mind: The positive power of the aging brain.* New York: Basic Books.
Erickson, E. H. (1997). *The life cycle completed.* New York: Norton.
Glass, T. A., deLeon, C. M., Marottoli, R. A., & Berkman, L. F. (1999). Population based study of social and productive activities as predictors of survival among elderly Americans. *British Medical Journal, 319,* 478–483.
Rowe, J. W., & Kahn, R. L. (1998). *Successful aging.* New York: Dell Publishing.
Winnicott, D. (1971). *Playing and reality.* London: Routledge.

TRAINING MANUALS OF THE NATIONAL CENTER FOR CREATIVE AGING/ELDERS SHARE THE ARTS

Golden, Stephanie, with Susan Perlstein. *Legacy Works Training Manual.* National Center for Creative Aging, 2002.
Larson, Renya. *A Stage for Memory: A Guide to the Living History Theater Program of Elders Share the Arts.* National Center for Creative Aging, 2004.
Perlstein, Susan, and Jeff Bliss. *Generating Community: Intergenerational Partnerships Through the Expressive Arts.* Elders Share the Arts, 1994.

Contact Information for Model Programs Referenced in This Chapter

Age Exchange
The Reminiscence Centre
11 Blackheath Village
London SE3 9LA
United Kingdom
020-8318-9105 (telephone)

administrator@age-exchange.org.uk
www.age-exchange.org.uk

Elders Share the Arts
138 South Oxford Street
Brooklyn, NY 11217
718-398-3870 (telephone)
www.elderssharethearts.org

Liz Lerman Dance Exchange
7117 Maple Avenue
Takoma Park, MD 20912
301-270-6700 (telephone)
301-270-2626 (fax)
mail@danceexchange.org
www.danceexchange.org

Roots&Branches Theatre
Arthur Strimling, Artistic Director
315 Hudson Street
New York, NY 10013
212-366-8032 (telephone)
212-366-8033 (fax)
Roots&Branches@fegs.org
www.fegs.org/news_events/news/rootbranches/index.html

Stagebridge Senior Theatre Company
2501 Harrison Street
Oakland, CA 94612
510-444-4755 (telephone)
info@stagebridge.org
www.stagebridge.org

SECTION THREE

Content Versus Process

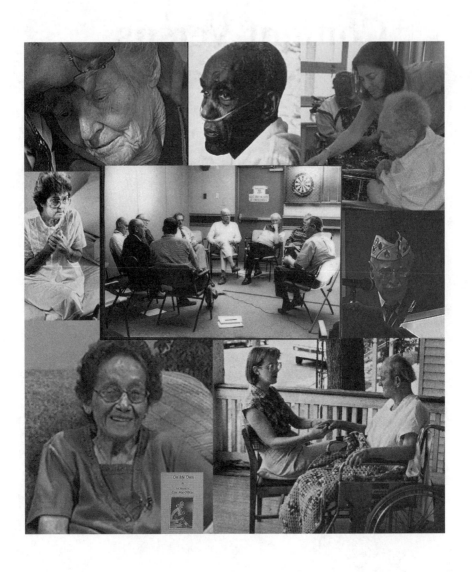

CHAPTER EIGHT

Cultural Aspects of Reminiscence and Life Review

Daniel W. L. Lai

- While the population ages, it also becomes more culturally diverse.
- Older adults are different in many ways, including in their past life experiences.
- Culture plays an important part in the life development of older adults.
- Older adults from different cultural backgrounds conceptualize aging differently, according to their current cultural context, as well as the cultural context that they have lived in in the past.
- For ethnic minority older adults with different cultural values and beliefs, particularly those who emigrated from another country, culture is an integral component of their aging process.
- Theories on ethnicity and aging have identified both the benefits and challenges experienced by ethnic minority older adults.
- Understanding the benefits and challenges experienced by culturally diverse older adults is essential to practitioners working in a multicultural setting.
- Through understanding the specific cultural contexts of the reminiscence, practitioners can immerse in the worldviews of ethnic minority older adults.
- The application of life review should take into consideration the cultural characteristics and meanings of past experiences expressed by older adults.

- To solicit or facilitate reminiscence, materials and tools that are consistent with the cultural preferences of older adults should be chosen.
- Understanding the worldviews of culturally diverse older adults can be achieved through practitioners achieving a better understanding of the cultural milieu of their clients.

The aging population is becoming more and more culturally diverse. The implication of this trend is that professionals working with older adults must take into consideration that older adults are not homogeneous. Older adults bring with them their various life experiences, which are also very culturally diverse. It is important for service providers to offer services or interventions that meet the unique cultural characteristics of the older adults they serve. The usual practice approach of one size fits all is no longer suitable. Intervention approaches that have their origin or foundation based on Western knowledge and theories must be critically revisited for their cultural appropriateness in applying to ethnic minority older adults.

Service providers are not just working with individuals or groups who are ethnically different. Older adults from different cultural backgrounds often have different values, beliefs, and worldviews. It is imperative for practitioners to understand not only cultural traits and characteristics of their clients, but also the impacts of these traits on the responses, outcomes, and meanings of their interventions.

An increasing number of older adults, even within the same age cohort, have diverse cultural backgrounds, so it is vital for practitioners to understand the interplay of culture on the application of life review and reminiscence. This chapter examines the importance of understanding cultural contexts when working with older adults from different cultural backgrounds. The relationship between cultural diversity and application of life review and reminiscence with older adults from ethnic minority backgrounds is also examined.

CULTURE AND AGING

Aging is a normal and inevitable process. However, aging is not simply an isolated process. It can be affected by numerous factors and different circumstances, such as losses of friends, family, roles, employment, the ability to drive, and the independence of maintaining a house. From a holistic perspective (see Figure 8.1), these factors and variables continue to influence whether healthy aging can be achieved.

FIGURE 8.1   A holistic perspective of healthy aging.

Research has consistently indicated that both physical and mental health affect the quality of life of older adults (Newsom & Schulz, 1996; Stein & Barrett-Connor, 2002). Older adults with a better health status tend to age more successfully than those with poorer health (Rowe & Kahn, 1995). In addition, research consistently shows that women report a poorer health status than men (Cummings, 2002). Financial status is an important factor in the well-being of older adults. Older adults with a better financial status often report higher levels of well-being (Nelson, 1994; Winkleby, Jatulis, Frank, & Fortmann, 1992). Education, often considered the key to financial success, is also associated with health and well-being among older adults (Winkleby et al., 1992).

Social support refers to both the size of social networks and the quality of care that older adults receive from their families, relatives, friends, and significant others. Social support is not only a tool for buffering stress and mitigating negative events or circumstances (Cobb, 1976; Dean & Lin, 1977), it offers both tangible and intangible resources that are beneficial to the well-being of older adults (Krause, 1990). As well, older adults with a religious affiliation tend to report higher levels of well-being (Fry, 2000).

In addition to individual factors, a number of social factors affect the aging process: attitudes held by society toward aging and older adults; attitudes held by society toward ethnic minorities; and physical, political, economic, social, and cultural environs. These factors most often interact to affect the aging process of individuals.

Among all these factors and variables, culture has often been overlooked or neglected by practitioners serving the older adult population. One of the most common reasons for people to overlook the importance of culture is that culture is considered a *personal* domain of individuals. Particularly in North America, there is a persistent myth that, if someone would like to immigrate here, one must be willing to become acculturated and to adopt the same set of cultural values and beliefs as the mainstream population. As a result, too little attention is paid to understanding individual variations and cultural diversity in the population.

Older adults from different ethnocultural communities are unique in their values, beliefs, and norms. For example, Native American elders have traditionally played an important leadership role in their communities and are respected for their wisdom, experience, and knowledge of tribal history and customs. They are well known and appreciated for using stories to share values and familial continuity. Asian American older adults frequently are strongly supported socially and economically by younger generations. Filial piety is an expected cultural norm within many Asian cultures such as Chinese, Japanese, and Korean. Advice and wisdom from older adults are valued as important familial and cultural assets. Therefore, older adults are usually seen as a treasure to the family and community (Chow, 2001; Ikels, 1990). In African American culture, older women represent the strength of the community through their involvement in their extended families. The elders in the community are renowned for their resiliency in supporting their families. Additionally, in Hispanic communities, spirituality in the form of traditional religion and morality is strongly supported. Oral history is a common method for sharing experiences and identities.

In 2000, the percentage of ethnic minorities among all elderly people aged 65 years or older was 8.1% for African Americans, 2.3% for Asians, and 5.0% for Hispanics. Projections to 2010 for ethnic minority populations predict growth of 13.0% in the African American population, 33.3% in the Asian population, and 34.1% in the Hispanic population. It is expected that the elderly population of these ethnic minorities will multiply at the same rates (United States Census Bureau, 2000).

Culture is a political issue. Although ethnic minority groups have gained some political and human rights, their voices are not necessarily respected by majority political machines. Requests for basic rights are often viewed as "preferential treatment," "special interests," or even threats to the well-being and stability of the mainstream majority. Particularly for ethnic minority older adults, their power and status are often ignored in a society that places much emphasis on individualism, utilitarianism, and a speedy pace of life.

Helping professions often fail to address the importance and issues of culture and ethnicity in their education and training curriculum, resulting in students' impression of issues regarding cultural diversity being at the fringe of their professional practice.

IMPLICATIONS OF CULTURE ON LIFE EXPERIENCE

Culture can be defined as sets of values and beliefs that guide the behaviors of groups and individuals. These values and beliefs often form the context in which meanings of events and social interactions are defined. While culture can be represented through customs and norms, it is imperative to understand that culture is more than just external traits and characteristics. Behaviors and ways of thinking are often based on the cultural meanings to which they have been assigned.

Culture itself serves a major function in linking to a cultural heritage that defines how things are done and how social relationships should be arranged (Gelfand & Barresi, 1987). Therefore, culture is the sustainable root for many older adults who may have lost some of their other social roles in the aging process, particularly for those who immigrate to a country that shares a different set of cultural values and beliefs. Older adults from culturally diverse groups often retain the values, languages, and practices of their cultural heritage. At the same time, through being mentors and role models, these older adults play an important social role in passing their history and cultural assets to younger family members and their community. The role of the grandparent is also important, because, in addition to providing surrogate parental care to their grandchildren, grandparents provide a link for the future generation to their family history.

On the other hand, culture-specific expectations of older adults may shock and frustrate some younger people. For example, as noted by Gelfand and Barresi (1987), the cultural expectation of living with children may not be met when adult children in ethnic minority communities no longer share those values or do not have the financial resources to live with their older parents in a nuclear-centered society. From this perspective, culture held by ethnic minority groups may create problems for older adults.

Due to the insensitivity of various societal systems, discrimination, and racism, ethnic minority older adults often encounter additional pressure and distress in the aging process. Some researchers have described the experience of ethnic minority older adults as a kind of double-jeopardy in which they must simultaneously endure the negative implications of being an old person and being a member of an ethnic minority group (Havens & Chappell, 1983).

Due to the fact that research on successful aging focuses mainly on older adults in the mainstream population and pays little attention to the situation of ethnic minority groups (Roos & Havens, 1991; Rowe & Kahn, 1995), a comprehensive approach of understanding successful aging in minority groups is underdeveloped. Yet, on the other hand, practice innovations and initiatives examining the applicability of intervention approaches with different ethnic minority older adults are growing and will enrich the knowledge base of practitioners who work with culturally diverse older adults.

CULTURE AND LIFE REVIEW

Little empirical research has been done on life review in ethnic minority groups. However, some practitioners have cited successful examples of using life review as an intervention approach for working with older adults from ethnic minority backgrounds (Haight, Nomura, & Nomura, 2000; Zuniga, 1989).

The process of reminiscence is a normal developmental task of later adulthood (Butler, 1963). Through the mental process of returning to the consciousness of past successes, achievements, and unresolved conflicts, these experiences are surveyed and reintegrated (Butler, 1963).

The theme of life review focuses on allowing older adults to build, consolidate, or rebuild their self-esteem and self-worth through reviewing past life experiences and incidents. Remembering and sharing both happy and painful experiences carry therapeutic benefits of helping clients to celebrate achievements and to heal emotional scars. For older adults in many ethnic minority cultures, the functions and concepts of life review and reminiscence are often consistent with their cultural values and practices.

Cultural values and experiences are integral to the lives of ethnic minority older adults. However, for ethnic minority older adults, particularly immigrants, their cultural roots are often either left behind or are far and distant. The cultural shock and pressure to assimilate or acculturate can create undue threats to their interests of maintaining their cultural heritage. Many older immigrants do not expect to have to abandon their past and cultural heritage. For some, the experience of being an immigrant is not entirely appealing. In addition to struggling for their economic survival, many of them have to strive to maintain the social and cultural existence of their ethnicity within their communities.

Because reminiscence and life review link the past and present for older adults, the process is useful for helping ethnic minority older adults establish cultural linkages between their heritage and their current life in a country where the dominant culture is different from their own. Reminiscing serves the function of transmitting cultural heritage, building self-esteem, resolving conflicts, establishing a sense of life achievement, and facilitating interaction and understanding across generations.

The lives of ethnic minority older adults, including those who were born in the United States, can be challenging. Discrimination and unfair treatment is common in many of their life experiences. Reminiscence and life review allow them opportunities to deal with the pain and suffering that they have lived through. From a healing perspective, reminiscence and life review are beneficial in allowing minority older adults to relieve the distress, burdens, and unresolved grievances that they faced during the earlier stages of their lives.

Many cultures rely on oral history as a means of educating the next generation and continuing their cultural heritage of stories, life experiences, and knowledge. In Western society, knowledge is often transmitted in written forms, and interests of the dominant majority in studying and recording stories and experiences of minority groups are not guaranteed. Ethnocultural minorities often face the danger of losing their cultural assets if their stories and experiences are left untold. Through life review and reminiscence, older adults from minority cultures can pass on their experiences and cultural knowledge to the next generations and build a stronger ethnic identity for their ethnic group.

In North America, achievements and contributions to society are typically measured using the mainstream standards. Ethnic minority older adults who followed life paths different from the older adults in the dominant culture are sometimes not recognized for their contributions to the society. Reminiscence and life review enable ethnic minority elders to recognize their life achievements and contributions within their own cultural context. Such processes serve an important function in helping minority elders to reestablish their self-respect and to revalidate their values in the contemporary society.

Mei Fung

Mei Fung, an 82-year-old woman of Chinese heritage, immigrated to the United States with her adult children 20 years ago from Hong Kong. Mei Fung was born and grew up in a small village in Mainland China.

At the age of 19, she left home to attend university in a big city. After finishing university, she worked as a teacher, got married, and gave birth to two boys and a girl. To escape World War II, her family moved to Hong Kong.

Life in Hong Kong was tough for Mei Fung, particularly after the death of her husband in 1950, when she was left with three children. Two years after her husband's death, her eldest son died of meningitis.

Single-handedly, Mei Fung raised her other two children through university. Twenty years ago, Mei Fung's son received a job offer from a major international corporation in San Francisco. She then migrated to the United States with her son's family, while her daughter decided to stay in Hong Kong.

Life in the United States was not smooth for Mei Fung. Despite the fact that she was highly educated, her English language skills were very limited. She spent a number of years adjusting to a different culture. Living with her son's family was another challenge, probably due to the incompatibility between the cultural values of Mei Fung and her two American-born teen-age grandchildren.

On the other hand, by visiting a Chinese senior center, Mei Fung became quite involved in her own ethnic community. In addition to making friends, she volunteered to help newly arrived elderly immigrants from China and Hong Kong.

Due to a stroke one year ago, Mei Fung lost her physical mobility. She became highly dependent in terms of her daily living and personal care needs and had to move to a long-term care facility. To work with culturally and ethnically diverse older adults like Mei Fung, there are care guidelines and suggestions that the practitioners may use.

GUIDELINES FOR PRACTITIONERS IN USING LIFE REVIEW WITH ETHNIC MINORITY OLDER ADULTS

1.   Place the client's experiences and stories in context.

Culture is an important component of one's sense of self. Although the goal of life review and reminiscence is to help older adults rediscover their sense of self by walking through their life histories, the meanings of these histories must be understood within the cultural context of the past events. Based on the case example of Mei Fung, practitioners using life review should put Mei Fung's experiences in the context of her life not only in the United States, but also in China and Hong Kong, where she lived most of her life.

2. Pay balanced attention to both achievements and unresolved regrets.

Mei Fung was relatively isolated and helpless in the long-term care facility, and her life seemed desperate. She was unable to do things that she used to do. Her sense of self-worth was affected due to her dependency on others. Yet, in the context of her past experiences, Mei Fung manifested a great deal of endurance and resiliency. Her ability to support her family and raise two children through university was a major success for her. However, through the process, she probably suffered from some pain, helplessness, and regrets—many of which may never be resolved. Mei Fung's educated background was an exceptional success for a woman in a traditional Chinese society. But her credential was also a burden, because most people at that time, particularly women, were mostly illiterate. Practitioners should maintain a balanced approach in addressing these experiences by not only focusing on the positives but providing opportunities for Mei Fung to resolve the negative issues that she experienced.

3. Be sensitive to the underlying cultural implications of experiences.

Practitioners' sensitivity to the cultural implications of their clients' life experiences is crucial to their ability to truly understand the feelings of ethnic minority older adults. For example, in the case of Mei Fung, losing her husband was a devastating experience. Losing her eldest son brought additional guilt and shame to Mei Fung. As a Chinese widow, Mei Fung was expected to protect her children, particularly her eldest son, who was supposed to extend the family's lineage. In addition to her grief over the death of her son, Mei Fung probably also endured the condemnations of relatives and family friends. The meaning and experiences of being a widow in traditional Chinese society carried many negative implications in Mei Fung's life.

4. Educate significant others.

Despite the benefits of life review and reminiscence, practitioners must understand that not many young people, including adult children, understand such benefits. Some may think that reminiscence indicates that their elders are not able to accept their current reality and that they are stuck in the past. Some may think that reminiscing is a pathological symptom, without realizing the elders' need to express themselves by going back to their past. Therefore, education for family members is needed to ensure that older adults are given the opportunity to express themselves in the context of their past.

In conducting life review with ethnic minority seniors, it is helpful to keep the following points in mind:

- The focus of life review and reminiscence should go beyond the surface of the incidents and into experiences.
- Histories, experiences, and memories are meaningful only when they are understood in the cultural context of the older adult who has brought up the reminiscence.
- *Meaning* is the most important component of life review. Older adults from different cultures will probably assign different meanings to a similar experience.
- Consider the cultural background and exposure of the older adults when selecting tools or materials for triggering memories and reminiscence. For instance, the music of Elvis Presley may not be effective with elderly immigrants from another culture.
- If life review is done in a group setting where most members are older adults from the dominant mainstream culture, do not single out an ethnic minority older adult. This experience could be intimidating and embarrassing.
- Use the tools and materials for facilitating life review and reminiscence appropriately, taking into consideration the compatibility of the tools with the cultural environments in which the older adults lived.
- Be aware of the fact that older adults from a similar cultural background might not share the same experience. It is important to respect each client's individuality and uniqueness.
- Focus not only on successful stories, but also pay attention to clients' hidden regrets, concerns, and unresolved negative issues.

EXERCISES

As previously noted, working with culturally diverse seniors requires practitioners to be sensitive to their cultural upbringing and background. The development of such sensitivity cannot be achieved overnight. It relies heavily on the openness of the practitioners to accept differences. In addition, it is important for practitioners to reach out to culturally diverse seniors to learn about their cultural contexts. The following are some suggested activities that practitioners could do in order to familiarize themselves with the culture of older adults in ethnic minority communities:

Identify an Ethnic or Cultural Group of Interest

It does not really matter which cultural group you choose to understand. This is merely a first step. Once you are familiar and comfortable with the process of this exercise, you can follow the same steps to understand older adults from other ethnic minority backgrounds.

Make the First Contact in the Community

Immerse yourself in a selected ethnic minority community by walking in the neighborhood, dining in a restaurant, and going to a grocery store. This immersion will let you form an initial impression of the experience. Identify and write down the feelings underlying any observations and experiences that you have in the immersion process.

Conduct Library Research

Starting in the children's section of the library, find books on general customs and characteristics of different ethnic minority groups in different countries. Keep in mind that culture is more than custom, diet, costume, and festivals. Practitioners should be sensitive to the underlying assumptions, values, and beliefs of cultural norms and activities. Practitioners should also be aware of the diversity within each of the culturally diverse groups.

Talk to the Experts

Identify some experts in the ethnic minority community who have the cultural resources to provide you with some general knowledge about the ethnic group. They might be community leaders, community workers, or service providers. Pay them a visit, chat with them, ask them questions about things that you do not understand. These cultural resource persons are crucial to practitioners for building a working alliance with ethnic minority communities.

Make the Second Contact—Interact with the Older Adults

Visiting a senior center in an ethnic minority community is one of many way to interact with the seniors. Contact the senior center to seek permission to attend some of the social and recreational functions. You can also volunteer so that you gain the direct experience of serving and interacting with the older adults.

REFERENCES

Butler, R. N. (1963). The life review: An interpretation of reminiscence in the aged. *Psychiatry, 26*(1), 65–76.

Chow, N. W. S. (2001). The practice of filial piety among the Chinese in Hong Kong. In I. Chi, N. L. Chappell, & J. Lubben (Eds.), *Elderly Chinese in Pacific Rim countries.* Hong Kong: Hong Kong University 125–136.

Cobb, S. (1976). Social support as a moderator of life stress. *Psychosomatic Medicine, 38,* 300–314.

Cummings, S. M. (2002). Predictors of psychological well-being among assisted-living residents. *Health and Social Work, 27*(4), 293–302.

Dean, A., & Lin, N. (1977). The stress-buffering role of social support: Problems and prospects for systematic investigation. *Journal of Nervous and Mental Disease, 165,* 403–417.

Fry, P. S. (2000). Religious involvement, spirituality and personal meaning for life: Existential predictors of psychological wellbeing in community-residing and institutional care elders. *Aging & Mental Health, 4*(4), 375–387.

Gelfand, D. E., & Barresi, C. M.. (1987). *Ethnic dimensions of aging.* New York: Springer.

Haight, B. K., Nomura, T., & Nomura, A. (2000). Life review as an Alzheimer's intervention: Results of an American-Japanese project. *Dimensions, 7*(4), 4–5, 8.

Havens, B., & Chappell, N. L. (1983). Triple jeopardy: Age, sex and ethnicity. *Canadian Ethnic Studies 15,* 119–132.

Ikels, C. (1990). Family caregivers and the elderly in China. In D. E. Biegel & A. Blum (Eds.), *Aging and caregiving: Theory, research, and policy* (pp. 270–284). Newbury Park, CA: Sage.

Krause, N. (1990). Perceived health problems, formal/informal support, and life satisfaction among older adults. *Journal of Gerontology, 45*(5), 193–205.

Nelson, M. A. (1994). Economic impoverishment as a health risk: Methodologic and conceptual issues. *Advances in Nursing Science, 16*(3), 1–12.

Newsom, J. T., & Schulz, R. (1996). Social support as a mediator in the relation between functional status and quality of life in older adults. *Psychology & Aging, 11*(1), 34–44.

Roos, N. P., & Havens, B. (1991). Predictors of successful aging: A twelve-year study of Manitoba elderly. *American Journal of Public Health, 81,* 63–68.

Rowe, J. W., & Kahn, R. L. (1995). Successful aging. *The Gerontologist, 37*(4), 433–440.

Stein, M. B., & Barrett-Connor, E. (2002). Quality of life in older adults receiving medications for anxiety, depression, or insomnia: Findings from a community-based study. *American Journal of Geriatric Psychiatry, 10*(5), 568–574.

United States Census Bureau. (2000). Population projections. Retrieved August 30, 2006, from www.census.gov/ipc/www/usinterimproj.

Winkleby, M. A., Jatulis, D. E., Frank, E., & Fortmann, S. P. (1992). Socioeconomic status and health: How education, income, and occupation contribute to risk factors for cardiovascular disease. *American Journal of Public Health, 82*(6), 816–820.

Zuniga, M. E. (1989). Mexican-American elderly and reminiscence: Interventions. *Journal of Gerontological Social Work, 14*(3/4), 61–73.

CHAPTER NINE

Mental Health Applications of Reminiscence and Life Review

John A. Kunz

- An estimated 20 percent of older adults living in the community suffer from depression. (APA, 2006).
- Up to 50 percent of older adults living in long-term care facilities may be depressed. (APA, 2006).
- The majority of older adults who are depressed remain undiagnosed and suffer in silence.
- Symptoms of depression may include lack of energy, neglect of responsibilities, loss of appetite, sleeping difficulties, concentration problems, irritability, agitation, feelings of hopelessness, lack of pleasure in life, exaggerated self-blame or guilt, delusions or hallucinations, headaches, backaches, digestive upsets, and other physical complaints.
- Suicidal thoughts are also a symptom of depression, and suicide is more prevalent among older adults than any other age group.
- Sometimes what appears to be depression may be delirium caused by inappropriate medications or the interaction of medications and/or alcohol.
- *Dementia* means the loss of brain function and can be caused by a variety of reasons, including Alzheimer's disease. Sometimes depression can cause someone to appear as if they have dementia. Many people with a type of dementia also may be

depressed. Evaluation and treatment of dementia and depression must occur conjointly.

- Caregivers of those with a dementing illness such as Alzheimer's disease are at risk for becoming depressed. They need to be aware of the symptoms of depression and reach out for help and support when needed.
- Society may unjustifiably expect older adults to be depressed and may believe the symptoms of depression cannot be treated successfully. Mental health professionals can closely evaluate mental health needs, offer recommendations, and make referrals.
- Utilizing reminiscence approaches during the assessment process can bolster older adults' confidence and self-esteem and help ease what can be a humiliating process.
- Reminiscence and life review approaches can be integrated into a number of treatment approaches, including cognitive behavioral therapy.
- These approaches are effective in individual, group, marital/family, and milieu therapy modalities.
- Clinicians can make conscious use of reminiscence material that results in the development of therapeutic resource states that facilitate change.
- In looking toward one's future, it is possible to conduct a life review with a keen eye for what types of reminiscence topics and life experiences could provide comfort and assist the maintenance of self-esteem and mental health during the aging process, especially if one develops dementia.
- Reminiscence approaches can help obtain and maintain attention and rapport for those who want to educate older adults about mental health issues.

I grew up having Sunday dinners with grandparents, aunts, uncles, cousins, and the rest of our family, where we heard stories from the past, ate memory-laden foods, and listened to my grandparents, my mother, and others harmonizing to songs from the 1920s, 1930s, and 1940s. As a teenager with a then-novel small cassette tape recorder, I got it all on tape.

Following the passing of my grandfather, who had been married to my grandmother for almost 68 years, I worried about how Grandmother would get along. She did well, and at Sunday dinners loved to hear the tapes of when she was singing with my grandfather. She would cry and laugh and sigh and get on with her life. Then, after my grandmother's funeral, our family ate her Norwegian version of "Chinese hot dish" and white "monkey hair cake" while listening to tapes of both of my grandparents singing their old songs. We cried and laughed and went on with our lives. That's when I first learned the potential healing power of reminiscence and life review, which I incorporated into my practice as a psychotherapist, teacher, and author for over 20 years. I later learned the ways in which these joys may also turn to sorrow or lead to other startling outcomes.

LORETTA

Suddenly widowed in her late 50s, Loretta went on to build the country home she and her husband had dreamed about. Once completed, the home seemed empty, and her fantasy that the new home would bring her late husband back in some way was unfulfilled. She would play their old songs, cry, drink, take tranquilizers, and cry even more. As Loretta sank into a psychotic depression, her delusions grew more vivid and she accused her neighbors of repeated travesties. Further isolation drove her deeper into a depression that could only be treated with electroshock therapy.

Loretta's obsessive reminiscence was a symptom of unresolved grief and her eventual depression. Family members and professionals working with her did not realize that this type of reminiscence was symptomatic of what eventually became serious and life-threatening mental illness. Later, while Loretta was being treated for depression, she participated in group therapy, which used reminiscence and music. At many sessions, she played a record of the song "Are You Lonesome Tonight." Instead of being alone and isolated, she was sharing her feelings with a group of other people her own age. Slowly she became able to work through her grief, cherish the fond memories, and move on with her life.

AL

In the same group, Loretta met Al. He had been an alcoholic all of his adult life. At age 67, he started treatment that included the reminiscence group. The group did a timeline exercise, which, starting with participants' earliest memories, identified significant milestones or markers in their lives. When faced with this exercise, Al was overwhelmed and sobbed uncontrollably. Without alcohol to mask his emotions, he was now confronted with decades of sorrow that he acknowledged was largely brought on by his regrets. As his children grew up, he had not been there for them, his wife divorced him, and the rest of his family gave up on him. Without the support of the treatment program and the incorporation of these issues and feelings into his 12-step and other work, Al likely would have begun drinking again or quite possibly committed suicide. Most people have seen the intoxicated person at a bar, alone, crying about the life they have led. Al, however, with the help of the treatment team, was able to emotionally process these issues—and begin to move on.

SHIRLEY

Shirley came to a program that involved telling one's life story. She said she was from Germany, where she survived the Holocaust, and stated that "some things are best not remembered." However, her family wanted her to write her life story and she didn't know how. She hired a life story professional who had a strong background as a mental health nurse. Shirley was able to work through her confusion about the past, put her story in order, and eventually be at peace.

This process of facing the content and detail of horrific experiences was very difficult for Shirley. As she wrote her story, she endured sleepless nights, anger, and intense feelings of fear, anxiety, and depression. The personal historian kept in close touch and assured Shirley that her feelings and reactions were natural. Had these symptoms of posttraumatic stress disorder continued or worsened, the professional would have referred her for further mental health assessment and treatment.

IDA

Shirley's younger sister, Ida, who also survived the Holocaust, had a more difficult time handling her traumatic memories. She had Alzheimer's disease and was very confused. With little or no short-term memory remaining, she reverted to her long-term memories and reexperienced the trauma of her past. Those caring for her identified activities and physical environments that triggered her traumatic memories and avoided them. For example, they never exposed her to the kind of stainless steel shower room that would evoke images of the cold, frightening facilities of her past. Instead, they attempted to trigger happy and secure memories by singing children's songs that her sister Shirley remembered from their childhood. They also used lots of towels and lotions, making bath time a happy and soothing experience for Ida.

These examples illustrate both the natural and delicate aspects of the processes of reminiscence and life review. For practitioners in aging, it is important to keep in mind the context of their relationship with the person who is reminiscing. For example, a family friend or fellow club member will reminisce with someone much differently than that person's psychotherapist would.

AGING AND MENTAL HEALTH

"Those gremlins! Those little green gremlins are jumping all over the room! Don't let them do that!" The neatly dressed woman pleads with her home health nurse to make the gremlins stop.

As she does this, family members who are witnessing the episode wonder what it means. They ask the nurse whether the outburst is a sign of Alzheimer's disease, if their mother has become psychotic, whether this is a ploy for attention, and if the problem could be caused by the combination of medications she takes.

The nurse consults with the woman's physician, who is well aware of her history. The physician concludes that she most likely developed another urinary tract infection and as a result has become delirious. After receiving the results of laboratory tests, the physician prescribes antibiotics that should clear up the infection and make the gremlins disappear in a day or two.

The Three *Ds*

This real-life anecdote illustrates the complexities of establishing a differential diagnosis for patients who are experiencing mental health symptoms. All health care professionals who work with older adults must understand the three *Ds* of geropsychiatry—delirium, depression, and dementia. These conditions can be difficult to diagnose, because they often manifest the same symptoms. In addition, a patient may suffer from all three disorders plus other conditions that can further complicate diagnosis and treatment.

Delirium

Delirium is described as acute or temporary confusion and has many causes, including the shock associated with a change in a person's living situation, infection, fever, toxic medication levels, and the interaction of prescription drugs with over-the-counter medications or alcohol.

The symptoms of delirium may be similar to those of dementia and depression. However, the onset and resulting behavior change is usually sudden. Giving the patient time and placing him or her in a consistent, familiar environment is often the best approach to treating delirium. A small amount of medicine or a reduction in medication also may help.

Recently, a family friend, George, who was about to celebrate his 80th birthday, began to complain about seeing "green geckos"—as portrayed in an insurance ad on television—lurking around his lake home in northern Minnesota. He thought his son or grandson had brought them from Florida and was bothered but not fully upset by them being around. He is diabetic and has trouble keeping his blood sugar under control. He was also about to have angioplasty due to clogged arteries in his heart and resulting poor circulation. This combination of physical problems most likely caused him to be delirious and thus see the geckos. Family members were relieved to understand the reason for these symptoms and to be reassured that this was most likely not the result of Alzheimer's disease or another type of dementia. It is also interesting to note that the family was divided over whether George was, in fact, hallucinating or whether a family member had actually brought geckos into his house.

Just over 1 percent of community-dwelling individuals age 55 or over are thought to be experiencing delirium. About 25 percent of older adults are believed to be delirious upon hospital admission, and 10 to 30 percent of postoperative patients experience delirium following major surgery (American Psychological Association, 2006).

It is extremely important to rule out delirium before considering any other psychiatric diagnosis, because many of these symptoms may appear the same and older adults are more susceptible to this condition than younger adults.

Depression

Depression is a medical disorder that is often misunderstood by the general public and underdiagnosed by health care professionals. Whether an individual becomes depressed because of stressors in his or her life or because of endogenous reasons, the resulting state is characterized by a change in brain chemistry. This results in abnormal thought patterns, mood disturbances, and changes in basic functioning.

Symptoms of depression may include disturbed sleep, changes in appetite and weight, decreased interest levels, irritability, outbursts of anger, uncontrolled crying, anxiety problems, obsessive thinking, difficulty concentrating, memory problems, delusions, hallucinations, and suicidal or homicidal thoughts.

Certain types of depression or mood disorders, including pseudo dementia, have symptoms that are very similar to those of dementia. Therefore, it is important to rule out depression, which is often treatable, before diagnosing dementia. A combination of antidepressant medication and psychotherapy is effective in most cases.

Albert had a history of recurrent agitated depression. His wife and family knew that, when he started to obsess about the crack in their basement foundation that had been fixed 30 years ago, he would soon need another series of electroconvulsive therapy. The more he obsessed about whether he had made the correct decision about the basement so long ago, the less he slept, the less he ate, and the less he was interested in reading or spending time with family and friends. This change in his life-style caused him to become even more obsessed with the basement, and this viscous cycle of depression became worse. At this point, Albert doesn't think there is anything wrong with him because all he can think about is the basement. Fortunately, his wife and family have seen this before, and they get him help as soon as possible. Once the treatments he receives get his brain chemistry "unstuck," he is able to let go of his obsessive thoughts and get on with his life. Follow-up talk therapy helps him and his family heal but would have done little good until his brain chemistry had been changed through some sort of medical treatment.

Although there is only a 1 percent prevalence of major depression, such as the type Albert had, in community-dwelling older adults and a 2 percent prevalence of dysthymia (low-grade depression), as many as 30 percent of older adults have mild or minor depression. It has been estimated that up to 50 percent of individuals in long-term care settings are depressed (American Psychological Association, 2006).

Older adults have the highest rate of suicide of any age group in the United States. Their suicide attempts are usually lethal, but they also make many more passive attempts such as by discontinuing medication, having "accidents" that were in fact suicide attempts, starving themselves, or simply giving up. Suicide occurs more often in men and is often seen in combination with alcohol or other drug abuse. Interestingly, 75 percent of older adults who complete suicide had, in fact, seen their physician within 1 month prior to the event (American Psychological Association, 2006).

The good news is that 90 percent of individuals respond well to treatment if and when the diagnosis is made. The best form of treatment is a combination of psychotherapy and medication (American Psychological Association, 2006).

Dementia

Dementia is the loss of brain function. It may be the result of a number of reversible and irreversible illnesses. Symptoms of dementia include confusion and disorientation to person, place, or time; memory disturbances (usually short-term rather than long-term); and difficulty functioning.

Alzheimer's disease and vascular dementia are the two most common forms of dementia, comprising 90 percent of dementia diagnoses. The remaining 10 percent are comprised of over 100 types and include vitamin deficiency, multiple infarcts, Pick's disease, encephalitis, and Parkinson's disease. Some types of dementia are treatable and reversible, but most are progressive in nature. Individuals with dementia often have depression as a secondary diagnosis (American Psychological Association, 2006).

When a girl forgets her jacket at school, we say she is forgetful. When an older man forgets his coat at the club, his family may worry he has Alzheimer's disease. For most people, the word dementia is very frightening, and, unfortunately, many people believe that developing dementia is inevitable. This is a myth. The majority of older adults will not develop dementia, but its prevalence does increase with age. Six to 8 percent of those over age 65 have some type of dementia. This doubles every 5 years after age 65 to the point that, at age 85, about 30 percent of Americans have some type of dementia. Many of these people are still living in their own homes or in lightly supervised settings (American Psychological Association, 2006).

Dementia needs to be managed over time. With appropriate expectations and a supportive environment, many older adults with dementia can flourish. Intervention and, at times, medication may be necessary to manage problematic behaviors.

Differential Diagnosis

Depression, dementia, and delirium often occur simultaneously. This makes an accurate diagnosis and appropriate treatment challenging. Furthermore, older adults have unique developmental needs requiring specialized approaches. A thorough, multidisciplinary diagnosis is critical in determining appropriate expectations and treatment approaches and care plans.

Other Disorders and Special Needs

Some older adults may have a history of bipolar disorder, schizophrenia, recurrent depression, or other disorders. Therefore, it is crucial to obtain each patient's history as well as a thorough history of physical and mental disorders within his or her family before making an assessment. It is believed that a larger-than-expected percentage of older adults have problems with substance abuse or dependence. Counselors often divide these individuals into two groups. One group is the lifelong alcohol or other substance abuser who may or may not have received treatment in the past. The other group is made up of older adults who have just started abusing chemicals, often in response to a major change in life-style or the loss a partner or other significant person in their lives. The first category usually would be referred for traditional treatment, and the latter category would focus more on resolving their immediate grief issues.

Personality Patterns

Lifelong personality patterns or problems may complicate both assessment and treatment. For example, a lack of interest in social activities may be a symptom of depression for an individual who normally enjoys being with others. Such behavior would not indicate depression in an individual who has always engaged in solitary activities and spends time alone.

Some personality patterns are so strong and set that they are diagnosed as personality disorders. In most instances, these have been lifelong disorders and have had strong effects on the individual's mental health and social relationships.

Behavioral Problems

Behavior problems of older adults, especially those living in long-term care settings, are increasingly becoming the focus of attention. Long-term care providers can no longer medicate or restrain the problem away, nor can facilities simply "dump" the problem resident on another facility. Family members of older adults with behavioral problems are often embarrassed and frustrated and feel even more humiliated if their family member is sent to a mental health unit for evaluation. The most appropriate place to assess and treat mental health problems of older adults, particularly with dementia, is where they are living. In many circumstances, the mental health or behavioral problems may have been prevented with an awareness of developmental psychological issues and use of reminiscence approaches. This is particularly the case with older adults with dementing illnesses.

As more individuals live longer, society must find ways to deal with older adults who have mental health and behavioral problems. Increased awareness of mental health issues and more stringent regulations have resulted in a greater need for long-term care facilities and social service organizations to find effective ways to assess and treat these conditions.

Unfortunately, ageism still affects the way many people, including health care professionals, perceive the mental health needs of older adults. For example, symptoms of depression are often attributed to what many mistakenly believe is part of the normal aging process.

USING REMINISCENCE AND LIFE REVIEW
TO PREVENT, ASSESS, AND INTERVENE WITH
MENTAL HEALTH PROBLEMS

Prevention and Assessment

Reminiscence and life review approaches can be directed toward preventing, assessing, and intervening with mental health problems of older adults. Efforts to engage older adults in the many forms of reminiscence and life review described in the earlier chapters of this book may often prevent older adults, especially those facing changes in their lives, from developing mental health symptoms. However, when such disorders are suspected, it is important for that person to be assessed by a qualified health care professional.

Most older adults have never seen a mental health professional before, and the experience may feel awkward or embarrassing or may even make them angry. The use of memorabilia, questions, and some self-disclosed reminiscence content from the professional can help establish rapport. If the health care professional takes a genuine interest in who these people really had been throughout their lives rather than just at this moment in time, it will lead the way to learning a great deal about who they are, what they value, what motivates them, and how they are feeling about their lives now. This information is essential for making an accurate assessment.

One way to proceed is to use the Reminiscence Engagement Process described in detail in chapter 3 of this book.

How many times have you been asked to count backward from 100 by sevens? It doesn't happen very often unless you are being given a mental status exam, and, in that case, let's hope you are good with math.

A 93-year-old woman with moderate dementia who goes by the name of Beana, was required to have a mental status examination. Having been the valedictorian of her high school class, Beana became immediately guarded and tense when told she was going to be given a test. Perhaps it was like going to class and having to take a "pop" quiz. As she struggled with answering questions about the current date and year, where she lived, and who was the president of the United States, tears rolled down her cheeks. Her inability to remember and process information became apparent to her as her weaknesses were revealed during this humiliating process.

Fortunately, she was accompanied by her nephew's wife, Nancy. Beana lives with her nephew, and he and Nancy are her care providers. During the interview, Nancy provided a great deal of emotional support for Beana and, after the interview, worked hard to bolster Beana's self-esteem by commenting on how goofy the questions were, etc. This helped bolster Beana's natural defense mechanisms and repair the assault to her self-esteem by focusing on her strengths rather than weaknesses, her abilities versus her disabilities. Hours later, however, Beana was still talking about the interview and how upset she was that she couldn't answer such simple questions that she could have answered when she was 15 years old.

When Florence Gray-Soltys does such an interview, she asks questions that are relevant to the client's life-style. For example, when she works with an older African American woman with little or no formal education, Florence may ask her to explain the directions for making homemade biscuits rather than asking her to count. It is important to keep the individual's educational, cultural, and historical background in mind during the assessment process. It is extremely important to focus on success rather than failure and, except when absolutely necessary, avoid putting a client in a humiliating situation.

As you get to know the individual through reminiscence, it is important to note his or her style of reminiscence to further the assessment process, develop a treatment plan, and evaluate the outcome of treatment. Being aware of these styles can help assess whether the client's disorder has moved him or her into a more negative style and hopefully determine whether the chosen treatment approach has moved the client to a more positive style. Again, lifelong personality patterns still come into play.

Reminiscence Styles

It is important to realize, however, that not all older adults want to reminiscence, and their interest in reminiscing and patterns of reminiscing may be an indication of either positive coping skills or dysfunction. Longitudinal research by Peter Coleman (1986) resulted in the establishment of four categories of reminiscence styles.

First were those who liked to reminisce. He found that they enjoyed this activity over the 10-year period of the study while they led healthy, relatively happy lives. These older adults would be excellent candidates for the use of reminiscence during assessment and intervention approaches. Most likely, if the ability to engage in natural reminiscence activities remains available, they are less likely to become depressed. If they no longer have the opportunity to engage in natural reminiscence due to changes in their life circumstances, then efforts to engage them in reminiscence activities may prevent the development of some mental health or behavioral problems. For example, it would be crucial to include in a reminiscence group a widowed 98-year-old nursing home resident who is the oldest living member of her family of origin and has lost touch with all her lifelong friends.

The second category of reminiscence styles included individuals who did not like reminiscing. They had striking life stories to tell but chose to engage in other activities instead. They also led healthy, relatively happy lives, but never chose to reminiscence. It might be appropriate to focus on the current interests of these individuals and certainly not force anyone to reminisce or discuss material they don't want to discuss. However, these individuals may reminiscence at times of emotional crisis or as a part of a reunion or other activity that promotes natural reminiscence.

An active retired professor in his 80s attended and audiotaped a workshop on reminiscence and older adults. He objected to the notion that older adults needed to reminiscence as part of normal human development. He emphatically stated that he preferred to remain involved in current, present-day affairs. However, he also quickly acknowledged that even he enjoyed and needed to reminiscence on occasion. As an example, he noted that a few of his former colleagues had just visited for a weekend, and they talked at length about the issues they had faced when they had been employed at the university. If individuals who normally don't reminiscence begin to, it may be a sign that they are working through some difficult emotional issues, grieving, or are substituting reminiscence for their daily interests. Because this would represent a change in their normal life patterns, this should be taken into account during a mental health assessment.

The third category of reminiscence style was a group who also chose not to reminisce—not because they did not want to, but because when they did so, they became depressed due to the feelings of a loss they experienced. This group lived shorter, less happy lives. Although further diagnoses of depression were not made in the study, it appears likely that these individuals were, in fact, depressed or had unresolved grief and loss issues. When older adults are in a depressed state, issues from the past that were once resolved often resurface and again become the source of emotional distress. Emotionally healthy older adults may recall past events with great emotion, but usually feel a sense of satisfaction and resolution when the process is complete. Older adults with depression or dementia may not be able to finish this process.

Coleman described the fourth category as "compulsive reminiscers." These were individuals who repeatedly and obsessively reviewed negative past experiences that had caused them emotional pain. They lived shorter, less healthy lives. This type of reminiscence might be seen in individuals with a lifelong obsessive-compulsive personality pattern. However, if this style of reminiscence was not a usual pattern, this could be a clear symptom of depression or dementia. An obsessive thought about past issues previously resolved is one common symptom of depression. The change in manner of reminiscence should be considered in making a diagnosis. This change in reminiscence style also may indicate that an older adult is identifying and working toward the resolution of grief and loss issues. The repetition of past life themes is also common with individuals who have dementing illnesses, in which case efforts should be made to identify and avoid the stimulus for such responses. An older man with recurrent clinical depression began having sleeping difficulties and spent most of the night berating himself for the business decision that lost him his business and put three good employees out of work 35 years ago. When he's not clinically depressed, he rarely thinks of his experience and, when he does, he dismisses the thought after a few moments. When he is depressed, he can't get these thoughts out of his mind and thinks and talks about them constantly. His wife knows he needs to resume treatment for depression.

Treatment Approaches

Once the initial assessment is complete and an appropriate treatment has been determined, reminiscence and life review approaches can and should be incorporated in the treatment plan. These approaches may be utilized at multiple levels. They may include the use of approaches described above as preventative. Individuals, their family members, and other care providers and treatment program providers may be directed to include specific approaches. Each intervention must be planned in keeping with the capabilities and limitations of the individual and his or her family/support system.

For example, an older adult who is experiencing a sense of worthlessness may be encouraged to tell his or her life story in some form. Since he or she may be overwhelmed with depression, health care professionals from a variety of disciplines can assist family members and close friends to encourage the depressed older adult to reminisce. A teenager who has an interest in making videotapes may be asked to tape his or her grandfather as he is interviewed about his life. Later, the teenager can edit the tape and the family can have a premiere celebrating the grandfather's life. This can be a very powerful intervention.

Beyond the creation of a therapeutic milieu that utilizes reminiscence and life review approaches, these strategies should also be incorporated with individual and group work, including integrating these approaches with solution-focused, cognitive behavioral therapy. A framework for such a treatment includes the use of reminiscence matches, resulting therapeutic resources states, and, in some cases, advanced psychological directives. These terms are further defined and illustrated below (Kunz, 1997).

Reminiscence Matches

The use of reminiscence triggers, props, and themes in individual and group work is frequently cited in the literature (Burnside, 1995; Osborne, 1989). These may be used in community presentations and in individual and group situations (Kunz, 1990). Bandler and Grinder (1975) studied the therapeutic communication of Milton Erikson and other noted therapists and, in what they called neurolinguistic programming, emphasized how each person perceives and interprets the world through the five basic senses: visual, auditory, kinesthetic, olfactory, and gustatory. Most individuals also use one of the five senses in particular as their preferred or primary sense for experiencing and understanding reality. To develop rapport quickly and effectively, Bandler and Grinder recommended determining the client's lead sense and then matching that lead sense by using language that is similar. For example, a depressed individual whose lead sense is visual might describe the future as dark and dim. The therapist would use language that is also visual by asking questions about what dark colors the client sees and leading him or her to see some variation in the darkness that might lead to some brightness. In contrast, a depressed client with a kinesthetic lead sense might say "I feel liked I'm bogged down in mud and slipping deeper and deeper." The therapist would use language laden with feeling content and eventually might help the client find a "strong, solid root to grab onto." In both of these examples, the depressed individual was describing symptoms of depression and simultaneously experiencing a deep state of depression. These types of emotional states have been described by Bandler and Grinder as "stuck states." Clients are stuck in their depression or other emotions. By using their lead system to first establish rapport and create a mood of understanding, the therapist is able to mirror or match the individual. Once this occurs, the therapist can then lead the individual to a more positive emotional state.

Following this framework, Kunz (1991b) defines a reminiscence match as a stimulation of one or all five senses. Pictures, old toys, radio equipment, music, food, flowers, and bread baking in an oven are examples of stimuli that might produce these matches. They happen naturally all the time but can be developed and used clinically in a number of ways.

These reminiscence matches connect individuals to positive or negative resource states, similar to the stuck states described by Bandler and Grinder. The stimulation of one or more of the five senses forms a match of current experience with past experience. For example, when grinding coffee in an old-fashioned grinder, the scent of coffee beans and the taste of the fresh coffee can elicit memories from several senses. As participants discuss their reactions to these types of experiences, they commonly discover unknown connections, and the conversation frequently goes in several directions.

Another example is that of a reminiscence group using a wind-up phonograph and old records. The facilitator played the *Skater's Waltz*, expecting a discussion of dances and romance. However, three women in their late 80s recalled skating to the music as young women and winning competitive skating matches. This connected them to a sense of competence and success and bonded them together as former athletes.

Often reminiscence matches are positive experiences. However, the more cognitively impaired an individual is, the more likely it is that negative reminiscence matches may be unintentionally stimulated. In these situations, the only method the confused individual may have to communicate this negative result is through a behavioral outburst (Kunz, 1997).

Therapeutic Resource States

The successful use of a reminiscence match allows individuals to access a resource state from their past. These may include coping skills, identity, past experience, courage, security, or spiritual values or beliefs. One way to make sense of these resource states is to use Maslow's (1968) hierarchy of needs. Resource states may include knowing that one's basic needs will be met; reassurance that one will continue to be safe; having a sense of connection, love, and belonging; and having a sense of self-esteem and value and a sense of self-actualization. By the time an individual has reached older adulthood, the "calling in life" that Maslow refers to is usually quite evident. This core of an individual's identity that can be found through reminiscence and life review work is the key to his or her emotional well-being. Through the structured use of reminiscence matches, individuals are helped to use their uniquely developed coping skills, identity, experience, courage, security, spiritual values, sense of purpose, and inner values to cope with current issues and problems. This process is especially helpful as older adults and others face dramatic life changes. The resource states may be used in an obvious, overt, or conscious manner, or in more subtle ways, with the individual less aware of the manipulation of reminiscence matches and resource states (Kunz, 1991b).

Because of their longer life histories, most older adults have a wide variety of resource states to draw upon. In fact, these resource states can be looked at as results of the successful resolution of each of Erikson's (1963) stages of human development. Individuals develop trust in Erikson's first stage. To know that one is loved and will be taken care of is important for everyone. Most older adults are "adult orphans" and may be facing traumatic changes in their lives. Using reminiscence matches to help them reaffirm the trust and security they developed long ago can be very helpful as they face these changes.

Similarly, the sense of competence developed in most individuals from the ages of 6 to 12 is needed throughout our adult lives. If older adults are having some physical or cognitive problems that result in their feeling a sense or inferiority, reminiscence matches can be employed to reaffirm their sense of competence through related resource states.

Reminiscence and life review approaches can be developed to affirm or strengthen an individual's sense of self at each of Erikson's stages, promoting increased feelings of competence, independence, initiative, identity, intimacy, generativity, and integrity. These are all integral to good mental health.

Reminiscence matches can also cause an individual to access a negative resource state from the past. A simple St. Patrick's Day party may be enjoyable for many, but for an individual who experienced trauma in his or her family on that day, participation in such a party may be stressful. Unresolved or partially resolved issues may be reawakened. An oriented older adult would likely use avoidance to cope with this situation. Individuals with dementia may not be able to explain why they didn't want to attend the party, resulting in their being further traumatized, and they may have a catastrophic outburst because an unsuspecting staff member brought them to the party. Social history and the observation of physiological and emotional reactions are keys to avoiding these negative matches. Communicating such events to family members and other care providers is also important.

Advanced Psychological Directives

The preceding example of a negative reminiscence match illustrates what problems could be avoided by the use of an advance psychological directive. Advance psychological directives ensure that one's psychosocial history is best utilized in future care. Older adults without cognitive impairment are usually able to say what they want or don't want. In contrast, if they are depressed or are having some other emotional problem, they may be less likely to apply the positive use of reminiscence and life review approaches. If older adults develop a dementing illness, they will become less likely to apply these approaches as their disorder progresses.

The best way to start the process of identifying advanced psychological directives is to use a workshop or other educational tool to sensitize older adults and their families to the value and use of reminiscence and life review approaches. Then, as follow up, individuals and their families should plan for the future by writing their own social history and developing guidelines about what activities and approaches should be avoided (such as the St. Patrick's Day party) and what activities and approaches should be emphasized. Other media besides writing can be utilized.

For example, if an individual has fond memories of being fed macaroni soup as a child and records this as an advance psychological directive and that person later becomes confused and agitated, care providers could try serving the individual macaroni soup as an intervention. This may or may not help, but the goal would be to create a visual, kinesthetic, olfactory, and gustatory reminiscence match for the individual that would result in a therapeutic resource state of love and security—with the hopes that the intervention would decrease the level of agitated behavior and improve the individual's quality of life.

The use of advance psychological directives increases the chances of maintaining a higher quality of life in the event an individual can no longer effectively advocate on his or her own behalf and also provides guidelines for concerned family members and guardians. It provides the additional benefit for individuals facing the potential of a dementing illness to be and feel more in control of their destiny during the early stages of the disorder. These concepts also help family members and friends find more effective ways of communicating and maintaining a positive relationship with their loved ones (Kunz, 1997).

Brief Therapy

Psychotherapy is often defined as a change in one or more of the domains of affect, behavior, or thoughts. The use of reminiscence matches to produce therapeutic resource states often results in an immediate change in one or all of these domains. Solution-focused or brief therapy (Watzlawick, Weakland, & Fisch, 1994) utilizes the client's own language and interpretation of the world to conceptualize the problems and contract for what changes the client wants to make. Fully oriented older adults are able to be verbally explicit in defining these changes. The more cognitively impaired an individual is, the more the clinician needs to interpret the "poetry" of that individual and look for meaning in verbalizations and behaviors about what he or she needs (Kunz, 1991a). The perspective of the therapist is often broader than that of the client and may include the input of family members, care providers, and other multidisciplinary professionals—particularly if the client has some cognitive impairment (Kunz, 1997). Brief therapy can result in desired changes in a single session.

Cognitive Behavioral Therapy

Cognitive behavioral therapy (CBT; Beck, 1995) is considered by many to be the most researched, respected, and funded form of psychotherapy.

Studies have shown effective use of cognitive behavioral therapy for older adults with depression (Dai et al., 1999), anxiety (Koder, 1998), intergenerational programs for cognitively impaired older adults (Camp et al., 2000), obsessive compulsive disorder (Carmin, Pollard, & Ownby, 1999), pain management (Cook, 1998), and sexual dysfunction (Crowther & Zeiss, 1999).

CBT focuses on changing dysfunctional cognitions (thoughts), emotions, and behavior and includes the following three assumptions: (1) Dysfunctional behavior is the result of distorted or negative automatic thinking often based on faulty logic or errors in reasoning; (2) these underlying negative thoughts can be changed through examining the underlying core beliefs or schemas; and (3) self-affirmations and other techniques can build positive behavior and reduce problematic behavior by counteracting the negative automatic thinking with positive thinking.

Three modifications of cognitive behavioral therapy in working with older adults have been suggested (Gallagher-Thompson & Thompson, 1996): (1) The therapist should remain more active in therapy than with younger adults; (2) the process should be expected to go more slowly; and (3) efforts must be made to compensate for cognitive or sensory deficits. Interweaving life review techniques in counseling oriented to mildly confused nursing home residents is recommended by Spayd and Smyer (1996). An example is provided by the work of Young (1990) and Young, Beck, and Weinberger (1993), who describe the use of a timeline life review technique to assist older adults in developing more functional schemas based on a detailed evaluation of their life history.

Integrating Brief Cognitive Behavioral Therapy with Reminiscence and Life Review

Medicare and other third-party health insurers are increasingly concerned about when and if psychotherapy is medically necessary for older adults. Butler (1995) and others fear that reminiscence and life review approaches in therapy will cease to be funded at some point in the future. Solution-focused cognitive behavioral therapy is an accepted framework for individual and group therapy with older adults (Beck, 1995). Integrating reminiscence and life review processes within this framework should further substantiate and justify the use of reminiscence and life review techniques in clinical work with older adults.

The following case summaries illustrate the integration of the reminiscence and life review techniques of reminiscence matches and resource states with a brief cognitive behavioral therapy framework.

PROMOTING ORIENTATION TO REALITY

Recall the story about Beana and her nephew's wife Nancy discussed earlier in this chapter. During the times that Beana would become despondent and disoriented, Nancy found that by helping Beana focus on the 1940s floral carpet that remained on the living room and bedroom floors, Beana would become better oriented to her current life situation. Now that Beana's nephew and Nancy have decided to replace the outdated carpet, they plan to make a large rug out of the 1940s carpet to be placed in Beana's room to help her become oriented to reality when needed.

CRISIS SITUATION

During a reminiscence group, an 82-year-old woman fell off the sofa and broke her hip. She was an avid storyteller and had many tales to tell about the community in which she lived. At the hospital, the emergency staff kept asking her questions and actively listened to her tales. Special emphasis was placed on eliciting reminiscence matches using all sensory modes. This approach helped the woman maintain identification with community leaders and changes in the community over the years. The reminiscence matches led her to a confident, successful emotional resource state. This recaptured schema allowed her to stay connected with her rational intellectual abilities, helping her avoid her feelings of emotional and physical pain, and reduced the potential for panic or other behavior problems at this time of crisis. Appealing to cognitive resources through reminiscence approaches reduced the potential for the development of dysfunctional behavior and/or being overwhelmed by negative emotions.

SITUATIONAL DEPRESSION

A young woman who was providing care for her grandparents called for assistance with what she was told was her grandfather's situational depression. The woman's grandfather and grandmother were in their late 80s. The grandfather had immigrated to the United States from Norway when he was a young man. He married and he and his wife raised a family. He was very successful in his industry and became moderately wealthy. He was always a good provider of strength for the marriage and family. However, at this later point in life, he was overwhelmed by his wife's behavioral symptoms of moderate Alzheimer's disease.

When I first met Sven, he was sitting in his study, where he slept much of the time. There was a large print on the wall depicting a bear that had been slain, with townspeople looking on in delight. It turned out that this print had been in his family for generations. In fact, Sven's grandfather had killed this bear in Norway because it had become a menace to the community in which they lived. Sven's grandfather had become an instant hero. Oddly enough, following in his father's and grandfather's footsteps, Sven also killed a bear that was feared in the Minnesota town where he and his wife and children lived.

This family heirloom, the print of the bear hunter, became a metaphor for Sven's intergenerational strength and ability to be strong in the face of a menacing bear—or, for that matter, Alzheimer's disease. Helping Sven get in touch with this part of his identity combined with education about Alzheimer's disease and his own situational depression, helped Sven make the decision to begin taking antidepressant medication. The medication helped change his brain chemistry to get him out of his depressed state so he could make decisions regarding changes in their lives and develop realistic expectations for his wife's behavior. As he recovered, he returned to his strong "bear hunter" persona and did his best to continue to be strong in a difficult situation.

PSYCHOTIC DEPRESSION

When listening and eventually dancing to Glen Miller's *Sunrise Serenade,* a withdrawn, 74-year-old psychotically depressed acute mental health patient began communicating and discussed the details of a time in her life when she lived in a large city where she worked, dated, and danced before returning to the region where she grew up to care for her aging parents. She wasn't able to grieve the changes and losses in her life and connect with the therapist and group members. This auditory, musical reminiscence match accessed the resource states of confidence, self-esteem, social skills, and lifelong values. Beginning in the group session, and without explicitly discussing the use of brief cognitive behavioral therapy processes, she was able to examine her self-worth and validate a schema that supported her self-esteem and value as an individual. This new level of self-affirmation resulted in more social behavior in other aspects of her treatment and life. These behavioral changes further supported and enhanced her improved emotional state that was also tied to her rediscovered, more functional schema. The continued use of music in subsequent therapy sessions reinforced this affirmation of her earlier identity and the more functional schema she had lost in her grief and subsequent depression. The therapist maintained individual contact during a 4-year follow-up period to this group work. This 4-year period was the longest time the patient had remained out of the hospital for 11 years.

ACUTE CONFUSION

An angry, withdrawn, 66-year-old psychotically depressed acute mental health patient receiving electroconvulsive therapy for a recurrent depression would become agitated, withdrawn, and uncooperative during the treatment process. She had reminisced about her mother's holiday sausage while attending a group with her brother one day. The next day, she had no recollection of that reminiscence group and refused to eat, bathe, and get out of bed for the day. When the therapist approached the patient with a platter of sausage that he had made from the recipe roughly described by her and her brother the day before, her affect immediately brightened and her behavior changed dramatically. She bathed, dressed, and attended the group, where she enjoyed the sausage, ate other foods, and socialized.

This simple intervention using the visual, olfactory, gustatory, and kinesthetic reminiscence matches helped this acutely confused older adult access her resource states of attachment, love, and belonging that she developed years ago in her relationship with her mother. During this time of confusion, fear, and anger, she was in desperate need of this more secure schema. The reminiscence intervention helped her find the resource of this schema. She was able to feel a sense of security in knowing that she was loved and belonged. Her behavior improved immediately, and her affect improved dramatically. Significant change had occurred in one therapy session.

MODERATE TO SEVERE CONFUSION

A moderately to severely confused older adult was observed pounding on the nursing station counter of the nursing home where she resided. She was demanding a train ticket immediately. She became more insistent about the ticket as her requests were ignored. When approached about her needs, she immediately wanted to talk about where she wanted to go. She wanted to ride a train to another community where her cousin, a teacher, lived and where she helped her with her children. She gradually calmed during this 5-minute conversation as the therapist asked simple questions and validated the significant relationship and role she had with her cousin. She became secure and confident knowing she was important to someone and needed. Her verbal and creative reminiscence helped her find these resources with the assistance of the effective communication techniques used by the therapist. Her affect changed, and she was no longer frustrated, angry, and agitated. She was calm and secure thanks to the more functional schema from her past. Her behavior followed suit as she sat down next to the other residents.

ACTIVITY GROUP

A group of assisted living residents was assembled to create a quilt. The group met weekly and received technical assistance from the group leaders. A photo of each member was taken and printed on a fabric square. Members then embellished their square with drawings, buttons, stitching, and other representations of their past experiences and values. The group possessed a myriad of reminiscence matches and resulting resource states. Lifelong schemas became graphically apparent and shared. This process resulted in enhanced or improved affect and improved the patients' self-worth.

IMPLICATIONS

Reminiscence matches, resulting resource states, and advanced psychological directives may be used to maintain and improve quality of life for older adults who range from being fully oriented to extremely confused. Such techniques may be used to develop rapport and maintain group attention. Using photographs and advertisements from decades ago with phone numbers that no longer exist—such as "Melrose 203" or "two longs and a short"—stereo-optic viewers from the turn of the century, or other props enable a clinician to gain and maintain audience attention when doing outreach education to groups of older adults. Using such an approach demonstrates the speaker's and the organization's understanding of older adult development and provides instant rapport with the audience. This primes participants to take in new information as well.

With this informational framework, older adults, family members, and friends can creatively develop a variety of plans to ensure that their quality of life is maintained and enhanced as they age, regardless of whether they ever become cognitively impaired. Family, community, and facility events can be fine-tuned to better meet the developmental needs of older adults.

The use of life history books, scrapbooks, photo albums, music, foods, smells, and other ways of stimulating the senses can be included in activities. If trained properly, community, teen, and children's service groups can use these approaches to develop intergenerational programs that provide deep levels of meaning and understanding for both the older and younger participants. Incorporation of these principles is useful in architectural designs and in planning and marketing strategies for assisted living and other programs for older adults. Increased use of these activities should prevent mental health problems from developing.

Scientific studies about the ongoing effects of such activities are needed. It would be helpful to establish a training protocol that incorporates these ideas for individuals initially diagnosed with Alzheimer's disease and their family members and friends and then tracks the progression of the disease, levels of caregiver and patient stress, level of care needed, and number of behavioral or mental health problems. It is imperative to train those caring for older adults in all capacities about the significance of these principles and approaches.

Training programs that allow care providers to experience a reminiscence match, resulting resource states, and advanced psychological directives is an excellent way for them to personalize the value of such approaches and incorporate such approaches in their daily work. Professionals responsible for planning the care of older adults should include such approaches in a multidisciplinary treatment planning process. These approaches should be used both individually and in group settings. Drawings, photos, bracelets made of special beads, quilts, collages, and other items may incorporate this material. For example, a collage of items representing the home he built for his wife and family can connect an older man with a schema of strength, accomplishment, and pride.

An edited video life review done while an older adult is fully functioning may prove useful as he or she ages, especially if cognitive impairment develops. This video could help the older adult maintain a connection with lifelong functional schemas. It would also be a tool to assist caregivers in better understanding the psychosocial essence of the individual for whom they are caring. This would be an excellent area for future research, particularly to determine the effect of watching the edited video life review on individuals as they face various changes in their lives or progress through the stages of Alzheimer's disease.

The use of these principles is even more crucial if an older adult has unresolved grief issues or is experiencing the most common forms of mental health problems: delirium, depression, or dementia. In these situations, the multidisciplinary treatment team should determine when any negative reminiscence may be causing or exacerbating the symptoms. They should also determine which reminiscence matches appear to improve the symptoms. A consistent treatment plan should then be developed that integrates the positive reminiscence matches and resulting resource states with a brief cognitive behavioral therapy approach. This plan should be reevaluated often and new approaches added or deleted depending on the results. Such an approach should be utilized in individual, group, couple, and family therapy. Comparative research evaluating the effectiveness of increased integration of reminiscence and life review techniques with brief cognitive behavioral therapy should be relatively easy, since these therapies already have a well-established research base.

The expanded use of reminiscence and life review approaches in caring for or treating older adults requires a great amount of energy. Likewise, a great deal of effort must be made to personalize the approaches for each individual. Many professionals and care providers have gained enormous satisfaction in doing so. Sometimes, however, professionals and care providers succumb to the same symptoms of depression and frustration that their clients are experiencing and don't challenge themselves to work even harder to apply these principles and techniques.

EXERCISE

This exercise may be completed individually or in a group. When possible, have participants imagine and carry out the roles of the variety of health and social service professionals who may be involved in this case.

1. Read this news article.

NEW YORK (Associated Press, July 26, 2006)—She wears torn night-gowns and sleeps on a couch that smells of urine. Her bland diet includes pureed peas and oatmeal. Her dogs, once a source of comfort, are kept locked in a pantry.

A court filing alleges that this is the life of 104-year-old Brooke Astor, the multimillionaire Manhattan socialite who dedicated much of her vast fortune to promoting culture and alleviating human misery.

Astor married into a family that at one time was among America's wealthiest and most prominent. Her late husband's father, John Jacob Astor 4th, died in the sinking of the Titanic; his grandmother, Caroline Astor, led New York society for 25 years during the Gilded Age of the late 19th century; and his great-great-grandfather, John Jacob Astor, became America's wealthiest man by 1840.

The court papers—filed last week and reported on Wednesday by the *Daily News*—blame the alleged misery and squalor inside Astor's Park Avenue duplex on her only child, Anthony Marshall, who controls her $45 million portfolio.

The accuser: Astor's grandson Philip Marshall.

He alleges in a sworn statement that his 82-year-old father "has turned a blind eye to her, intentionally and repeatedly ignoring her health, safety, personal and household needs, while enriching himself with millions of dollars."

The court papers—which were sealed on Wednesday—seek to remove Anthony Marshall as legal guardian and replace him with Annette de la Renta, the wife of Oscar de la Renta, and J.P. Morgan Chase bank.

A call to Anthony Marshall was not immediately returned. The former diplomat and Broadway producer declined to discuss the case with the *Daily News*, saying, "It is a matter that is going to be coming up in a court of law and it should be left to the court." A hearing was scheduled for Aug. 8.

Philip Marshall's allegations regarding his grandmother have the backing in sworn statements of such famous names as Henry Kissinger and David Rockefeller, who both attended Astor's 100th birthday gala four years ago.

"This is a remarkable and extraordinary woman who has given so much to so many, and he wants to see that in her last days she's given what she needs," said Rockefeller spokesman Fraser Seitel. "She can afford it, and she deserves it."

Astor ran the Astor Foundation after the death of her third husband, Vincent Astor, in 1959.

Brooke Astor gave millions to the New York Public Library, the Metropolitan Museum of Art, Carnegie Hall and the Museum of Natural History. But she also funded smaller projects such as new windows for a nursing home and was noted for personally visiting the places she helped out.

"Money is like manure, it should be spread around," was her oft-quoted motto.

Astor has faded from sight in recent years amid declining health, including two broken hips. Once she was confined to her apartment, court papers allege, she was denied many of the staples of her high-society life.

Her son allegedly replaced her costly face creams with petroleum jelly. A French chef was fired, leaving her at the mercy of an "unmotivated cook" serving pureed peas, liver, carrots and oatmeal, court papers say.

Her dogs, Boysie and Girlsie, have been confined to a pantry for the last six months to keep them from damaging the apartment, the papers say. Philip Marshall also alleges that nurses had to use their own money to buy hair bonnets and no-skid socks for the elderly woman when requests for the items were denied.

"Her bedroom is so cold in the winter that my grandmother is forced to sleep in the TV room in torn nightgowns on a filthy couch that smells, probably from dog urine," Philip Marshall said in his affidavit.

2. How could reminiscence and life review approaches be utilized to establish rapport and assess Mrs. Astor and this situation?
3. How could reminiscence and life review approaches help Mrs. Astor and this situation in individual, group, family, and milieu therapy modes?
4. How would reminiscence and life review approaches vary on the professional or personal role one would have in this situation? Think about the grandson, caregivers, social service worker, nurses and physician, pastor, attorney, or judge.

REFERENCES

American Psychological Association. (2006). Associated Press. Retrieved September 9, 2006, from www.apa.org.
Bandler, R., & Grinder, J. (1975). *The structure of magic: A book about language and therapy I*. Palo Alto, CA: Science and Behavior Books.

180   TRANSFORMATIONAL REMINISCENCE

Beck, J. (1995). *Cognitive therapy: Basics and beyond*. New York: Guilford Press.
Burnside, I. (1995). Themes and props: Adjuncts for reminiscence therapy groups. In B. K. Haight & J. D. Webster (Eds.), *The art and science of reminiscing: Theory, research, methods, and applications*. Washington, DC: Taylor & Francis 153–163.
Butler, R. N. (1995). Foreword: The life review. In B. K. Haight & J. D. Webster (Eds.), *The art and science of reminiscing: Theory, research, methods, and applications*. Washington, DC: Taylor & Francis.
Camp, C. J., Judge, K. S., Bye, C. A., Fox, K. M., Bowden, J., Bell, M., Valencic, K., & Mattern, J. M. (2000). An intergenerational program for persons with dementia using Montessori methods. *American Journal of Psychiatry, 157*, 1915–1924.
Carmin, C. N., Pollard, C. A., & Ownby, R. L. (1999). Cognitive behavioral treatment of older adults with obsessive compulsive disorder. *Cognitive and Behavioral Practice, 6*, 110–119.
Coleman, P. G. (1986). *Ageing and reminiscence processes: Social and clinical implications*. Chichester, England: Wiley.
Cook, E. A. (1998). Effects of reminiscence on life satisfaction of elderly female nursing home residents. *Health Care for Women International, 19*, 109–118.
Crowther, M. R., & Zeiss, M. (1999). Cognitive-behavior therapy in older adults: A case involving sexual functioning. *Journal of Clinical Psychology, 55*(8), 961–975.
Dai, Y., Zhang, S., Yamamoto, J., Ao, M., Belin, T. R., Cheung, F., & Hifumi, S. S. (1999). Cognitive behavioral therapy of minor depressive symptoms in elderly Chinese Americans: A pilot study. *Community Mental Health Journal, 35*(6), 537–542.
Erikson, E. H. (1963). *Childhood and society* (2nd ed.). New York: Norton.
Gallagher-Thompson, D., & Thompson, L. W. (1996) Applying cognitive behavioral therapy to the psychological problems of later life. In S. H. Zarit & B. G. Knight (Eds.), *A guide to psychotherapy and aging* (pp. 61–82). Washington, DC: American Psychological Association.
Koder, D. (1998). Treatment of anxiety in the cognitively impaired elderly: Can cognitive-behavior therapy help? *International Psychogeriatrics, 10*(2), 173–182.
Kunz, J. (1990). Reflections and memories: A counseling program for older adults. *Caring, 9*, 44–46.
Kunz, J. (1991a). Case reports: Counseling approaches for disoriented older adults. *Illness Crisis and Loss, 1*(2), 91–96.
Kunz, J. (1991b). Reminiscence approaches utilized in counseling older adults. *Illness Crisis and Loss, 1*(4), 48–54.
Kunz, J. (1997). Enhancing quality of life for older adults. *Ed-Cetera, 2*(2), 6–7.
Maslow, A. H. (1968). *Toward a psychology of being*. New York: Van Nostrand.
Osborne, C. L. (1989). Reminiscence: When the past eases the present. *Journal of Gerontological Nursing, 10*, 6–12.
Spayd, C. S., & Smyer, M. S. (1996). Psychological interventions in nursing homes. In S. H. Zarit & B. G. Knight (Eds.), *A guide to psychotherapy and aging* (pp. 241–264). Washington, DC: American Psychological Association.
Watzlawick, P., Weakland, J. H., & Fisch, R. (1994). *Change: Principles of problem formation and problem resolution*. New York: Norton.
Young, J. E. (1990). *Cognitive therapy for personality disorders: A schema focused approach*. Sarasota, FL: Professional Resource Exchange.
Young, J. E., Beck, A. T., & Weinberger, A. (1993). Depression. In D. Barlow (Ed)., *Clinical handbook of psychological disorders* (pp. 240–277). New York: Guilford Press.

CHAPTER TEN

Traumatic Memories and Life Review

Marvin J. Westwood and Holly B. McLean

- Many older adults have had traumatizing experiences during their lives. The revealing of memories related to these experiences should be anticipated and prepared for by anyone who is facilitating a life review process.
- Traumatic memories that are revealed during life review need to be handled with competence in order to minimize risks of retraumatization.
- It is prudent for facilitators of individual or group-based life review processes to have some understanding of the trauma recovery process and how life review can be beneficial in that process.
- It is essential that facilitators also have knowledge and skills related to how to act in a preventative way to reduce the risk of retraumatization, effectively manage the disclosure of traumatic memories, and promote healing for older adults.

Reactions to and Recovery from
Traumatic Experiences[1]

- The central experience of psychological trauma is one of disempowerment and disconnection from others.
- The basic premise of models of recovery from trauma is the healing power of authentic relationships.
- Recovery from trauma cannot occur in isolation. People who have been traumatized need to regain the capacities damaged by their traumatic experiences, including the ability to trust,

feelings of competence, identity, and intimacy. This can only occur in connection with supportive others.

- Although the process of recovery from trauma is not a straight-forward, linear process, it can be conceptualized to occur in three basic stages:

  - Establishment of safety

    - Includes physical and emotional safety

  - Remembrance and mourning

    - Telling the story of the trauma
    - Reconstructing the experience to bring a new interpretation that affirms the dignity and value of the individual
    - Grieving disturbing experiences and integrating the traumatic memories into the life story

  - Reconnection

    - Outcomes include the ability to engage more fully in relationships with others and a capacity to take pleasure in life as lived.

Life Review

- The life review process is consistent with models for assisting in the recovery from traumatic events.
- It is a meaning-making process that encourages self-disclosure and the generation of new perceptions of events, self, and others.
- Life review allows clients to write privately, organize their thoughts, and, in a sense, rehearse what will be shared with others—a key to emotional safety.
- The process of writing the story of the trauma helps with remembrance and mourning.
- Sharing of life stories promotes the realization of individual as well as commonalities of experience.
- There are demonstrated therapeutic benefits of engaging in life review that relate to outcomes for recovery from traumatic experiences.

Specific Strategies

- There are specific preventative and remedial strategies that facilitators of life review can engage in that will help ensure a healing life review experience for older adults as well as reduce the risk of retraumatization during life review.

- These strategies include building a safe relationship or group context for life review—where anxiety is mitigated; emotional expression is validated, encouraged, and contained when necessary; and individuals are referred to other resources as needed.

INTRODUCTION

Life review offers a relatively safe and effective means for older adults to integrate traumatic memories into their larger life story. Life review can be a therapeutic and beneficial process, fascinating, exciting, and freeing all at the same time. However, opening up of the painful memories associated with traumatic events during life review needs to be managed appropriately in order for healing to occur. Particular care needs to be taken because inappropriate responses by others to traumatic disclosures during life review can retraumatize older adults, resulting in further shame and suffering. The purpose of this chapter is to give life review facilitators strategies to manage the life review process and the revealing of traumatic memories in both individual and group contexts so that healing occurs and the risk of adverse effects is minimized.

Because of the high prevalence of trauma in U.S. society, practitioners often find themselves working with older adults who have experienced violence or have been victimized. Current research shows, for example, that in North America, as many as one in five women will be raped in their lifetime, and one in four women as well as one in six men were sexually abused as children (Briere, 1996; Schauben & Frazier, 1995). Early experiences of physical abuse and emotional abuse are unfortunately not uncommon in our society. Critical events such as experiences of witnessing the loss of a loved one through injury or violent death are also part of the history of some older adults. Older adults who have experiences in the military will also have been subjected to many potentially traumatizing events and situations, including active combat, witnessing of atrocities and torture, seeing friends and comrades killed, being taken hostage, casualty handling of civilian adults and children, and the retrieval and disposal of human remains (MacDonald, Chamberlain, Long, Pereira-Laird, & Mirfin, 1998). Life review practitioners need to be prepared for the disclosure of memories associated with these and other distressing experiences when working with older adults in the life review process.

In the words of a life review group participant, a World War II veteran named Gordon, "it is an honour to listen to the stories of people's lives." To not listen to the whole story, to respond incompetently or unethically due to lack of knowledge or fear is to deny the chance for healing, and could easily cause an older adult who has experienced trauma even more pain. Therefore, we focus in this chapter on the structure and skills needed to promote a safe, healing relationship and group environment for traumatic memories to be disclosed. Although most readers will not, and should not, anticipate engaging in trauma therapy with older adults, a brief review of typical reactions to trauma and the model for trauma recovery delineated by Herman (1997) is useful background knowledge for any professional working with older adults and provides the conceptual framework for the strategies for managing traumatic disclosures that are discussed in this chapter.

RECOVERY FROM TRAUMA

An experience, and the social context in which it occurs, can profoundly affect how people make sense of themselves and their world. Traumatic stress reactions result from real experiences that are psychologically overwhelming. The experience may be life threatening or may threaten the person's integrity as a human being. Today we sometimes use the term *traumatic* loosely to describe upsetting experiences, but truly traumatic events are so horrible and terrifying that the person experiencing the event feels absolutely no control, completely powerless (Herman, 1997). Many people who are exposed to traumatic events are somehow able to go on with their lives without being haunted continually by the memories of what has happened to them; however, that does not mean that the dreadful experiences had no impact. According to van der Kolk and McFarlane (1996), after exposure to traumatic events, most people become preoccupied with their experience of it. Intrusive memories are considered a natural way of responding to and integrating awful events. The replaying of upsetting memories over and over serves the function of mitigating the emotions associated with the traumatic event and, in most cases, creates a tolerance for the content of the memories. However, with the passage of time, some people are unable to integrate their experience and start to develop the specific patterns of avoidance and hyperarousal that are associated with traumatic stress reactions. Traumatic stress reactions are thus conceptualized as the "result of a failure of time to heal all wounds" (Van der Kolk & McFarlane, 1996, p. 7). Symptoms of traumatic stress reactions include sleep difficulties, difficulties relaxing, night sweats, exaggerated startle responses, irritability, depression, anxiety, and a host of other somatic complaints.

Two of the basic premises of models of recovery from trauma are empowerment of the individual who experienced the trauma and the healing power of authentic relationships. Given that the central experience of psychological trauma is one of disempowerment and disconnection from others, it makes sense to base recovery and subsequent thriving on restoring control to the individual (not controlling him or her) and the encouragement of connection. According to Herman (1997), recovery can take place only in the context of relationships; it cannot occur in isolation. In connection with others, individuals with traumatic experiences can regain the capacities damaged by the trauma, including the ability to trust, feelings of competence, identity, and intimacy. Just as these capacities are originally learned in relationships with significant others, they are reformed in the context of positive, affirming relationships with others.

Herman (1997) delineates three basic stages for the process of recovery from trauma, each stage having a central therapeutic task associated with it and appropriate therapeutic interventions. The task associated with the first stage is the establishment of safety, the second is remembrance and mourning, and the third is reconnection with ordinary life. Herman points out that, "like any abstract concept, these stages of recovery are a convenient fiction, not to be taken too literally" (p. 153). Recovery from traumatic experiences is a process that is inherently turbulent and complex. However, Herman stresses that, without the establishment of safety, the revealing of traumatic memories should not be encouraged. Safety includes both physical integrity and the perception of minimal risk of psychological danger (Briere, 1996): it is apparent to the extent that individuals feel valued and unconditionally accepted and supported by the therapist and, in the case of a group, other group members.

Once some degree of safety is established, the second stage of recovery involves telling the story of the trauma. This involves the reconstruction of the experience to bring a new interpretation of the trauma that affirms the dignity and value of the individual who experienced it. The goal of this phase is not "exorcism" of the trauma story, but "integration" of the traumatic memories into the broader life story (Herman, 1997, p. 181). The telling of the trauma story will inevitably release profound grief. This kind of reaction is a normal and expected part of recovery. With reconstruction and mourning, the memories and story of the trauma becomes another part of the individual's life story and no longer a distraction or impediment to full engagement in the world. The final stage of recovery thus focuses on desire and initiative. Herman relates that full resolution may never occur; however, the best indices of positive outcomes are the individual's restored capacity to take pleasure in life and engage fully in relationships with others. The individual becomes more interested in the present and the future than the past and is "more apt to approach the world with praise and awe than fear" (Herman, 1997, p. 212).

LIFE REVIEW

Life review methods have traditionally been researched and used with older adults—particularly those in long-term care facilities, who may have a variety of life experiences (Rife, 1998); however, we have found life review to be particularly effective with older adults and other individuals who have experienced trauma (Westwood, Black, & McLean, 2002). It is clear from our brief review of Herman's model that life review has many aspects that fit with the therapeutic process of recovery from trauma. A key component of life review is not just writing about one's experiences but sharing life stories with others either individually or in a group context. Being able to disclose oneself to others, and to feel transparent and validated by another when disclosing, is essential for realizing authentic relationships. By facilitating this process, life review promotes intimate connection with others. Yet it is also a structured process that allows individuals to engage and self-disclose at their own pace. The self-reflection and private writing in life review permits individuals to organize their thoughts and, in a sense, rehearse what will be shared with others. This opportunity to monitor affectively charged material that individuals choose to reveal in life review promotes emotional safety.

In addition, when engaged in effectively, life review facilitates the integration of new understandings about oneself, others, and the world (Brown-Shaw, Westwood, & deVries, 1999). Specifically, the themes and accompanying sensitizing questions that are often used in life review enhance recall of salient experiences and emotions and encourage the viewing of various perspectives on one's life story (deVries, Birren, & Deutchman, 1995). The act of writing and sharing the life story facilitates remembrance, the recalling of events that might have otherwise been forgotten, along with the feelings about events that have been suppressed. The therapist and other group members (in the case of group-based life review), assist in offering new perspectives on experiences and affirming the self-worth and value of the individual, his or her strengths and courage. Particularly in group-based life review, individuals gain new insights from the realization of their individuality as well as commonalities of experience. This can offer special relief for people who have been traumatized, who often feel separate and unworthy. They feel accepted by the group—and therefore "acceptable"—after revealing their story.

The therapeutic potential of life review for older adults who have had traumatic experiences, then, is quite apparent; and there is a substantial body of research that shows the measurable positive outcomes of the life review method (Silver, 1995). Birren and Deutchman (1991), for example, provide a summary of the benefits from 22 studies that used mostly older adults as participants in life review experiences. Some of these positive outcomes included increased sense of personal power and importance; reconciliation with the past and resolution of past resentments and negative feelings; resurgence of interest in former activities or hobbies; development of friendships with other group members; and increased role clarity, self-esteem, self-understanding, and greater sense of purpose and meaning in life. Other studies have shown life review has positively affected participants' sense of social connectedness, willingness to interact with others, and willingness to disclose to others (deVries, Birren, & Deutchman, 1995). Brown-Shaw, Westwood, and deVries (1999) also found that life review helps with the integration of unresolved issues that have restricted older adults from living their lives more fully. One life review group participant, a fighter pilot during World War II, put it most succinctly when he commented that the life review "helped lay some ghosts to rest." As highlighted above, life review can be a very healing experience for older adults who have traumatic experiences in their past; however, the disclosure of memories related to those experiences needs to be managed appropriately. We now delineate how to facilitate the remembrance of distressing events in a way that will lead to integration into the larger life story and avoid risks of retraumatization.

SPECIFIC STRATEGIES

It is useful to think in terms of "preventative" and "remedial" approaches to working effectively with the disclosure of traumatic memories during the life review process. Preventative actions include the way you set up the life review interview or establish the necessary group environment for the disclosure of traumatic memories to be honored and affirmed and not result in shame for the individual. These are the strategies for building safety—so that anxiety related to the life review process is lessened; incremental self-disclosure occurs so that individuals do not become overwhelmed; and a relationship or group environment where the expression of feelings is encouraged and respected, and yet contained if needed. A remedial strategy would be referring individuals to other resources and managing extreme reactions to the disclosure of traumatic memories. Although these kinds of reactions are rare, it is necessary as a professional to be prepared and ready for what may occur in the context of life review.

PREVENTATIVE: MANAGING ANXIETY

Mediating an individual's or group member's anxiety is a necessary first step in building safety for the conducting of life review, and this is especially so for those who have had traumatic experiences. Older adults will engage in a life review experience in the midst of various stages of readiness for the experience; still, it is important to recognize that even those who seem ready and willing to review their life stories may not be fully prepared for what this may entail in terms of their emotional responses. Many older adults know very little about what life review involves emotionally and will have only a minimal appreciation for what they are getting into. They may be willing to participate in life review in the hopes of "feeling better"—meaning less depressed or less lonely. They may want to connect with other people more fully and intimately but may not be aware of how much discomfort is involved in this process; and, of course, knowing about life review is quite different from actually experiencing it. It is critical, then, regardless of the older adult's apparent readiness for life review, that the initial session is geared toward helping him or her (or group members in group-based life review) to continue with the process. To accomplish this, facilitators of life review need to manage their natural apprehension and anxiety.

How do you manage anxiety? Life review facilitators strive to remove ambiguity in terms of the expectations for the experience and give the person (or people) they are working with a sense of control and protection. Following this basic premise, it is important in the initial life review session for the facilitator to clarify his or her role, goals, expectations, and structure for the life review experience. Because we work mainly in life review groups, an example of the format we follow for an initial life review group session is outlined below:

1. Welcome and introductions
    a. Informal welcome and introduction of group leaders.
    b. Housekeeping issues (washroom locations, parking, etc.).
    c. Explanation of purpose of first meeting and review of session agenda, including when breaks will occur.
    d. Introductory dyad activity: break into pairs with goal of introducing one's partner to the group. Suggested information to include in the introduction is the person's name and something unique about the group member that they would like the other group members to know about him or her.

2. Guidelines for speaking and listening in the group
    a. Set goals for the group. Elicit group members' input toward the goals of the group. General group goals could include the following:
        i.   For group members to get to know each other.

     ii.   To begin to write about experiences and provide an opportunity to share life experiences with peers.

     iii. To provide a supportive environment to tell life stories.

     iv. To help people feel less alone in their experiences.

     v.   To develop future goals and possibilities.

   b. Introduce the group agreement (see Table 10.1 for an example) as a means of clarifying group norms and responsibilities. Ask for input from group members.

3.   Sharing activity to introduce the life review process

   a. Introduce the idea of branching points and the branching points life review theme.

   b. Give group members an opportunity to jot ideas on an index card related to a branching point and then briefly share in the group.

4.   Expectations for the next session

TABLE 10.1. Life Review Group

Group Leaders: *[Insert names of group leaders and contact information.]*
Session Dates: *[Insert session dates and times.]*
Group Agreement
Guidelines to make this experience rewarding for everyone:

This group experience will be stronger if everyone attends all the sessions and arrives on time. We will notify each other in advance if we are unable to attend the group or will be arriving late.

To help everyone be comfortable with speaking in the group, we will keep what is said during the group sessions confidential. You have a right to this confidentiality and to your personal privacy. The names of people in the group and the things we talk about will be kept within the group; however, you are free to talk about your own experience outside the group, always being wary of breaching another group member's privacy.

You have a right to privacy within the group, too. If you don't want to participate in any discussion, you can "pass." If someone is directing comments or questions to you that make you feel uncomfortable, you can say "stop" at any time.

We welcome different beliefs and values within this group. We can respect and affirm each other by honoring our different viewpoints and not judging each other. We will speak only from our own experience, using "I" statements.

We will also endeavor in this group to make sure that everyone has equal time to have their voice heard.

Many of us are used to thinking that the way to support another person is through helpful comments, suggestions, and advice. In this group, no advice will be given unless specifically requested.

In summary, the importance of the first session to set the tone for the experience cannot be overemphasized. A systematic approach and activities for self-disclosure in the group provides a degree of purpose, reducing the anxiety and uncertainties prevalent in a less clearly focused group process (Johns, 1996). According to Borgen, Pollard, Amundson, and Westwood (1989), structured group activities also offer psychological safety because of the boundaries provided by each structured situation. Each activity becomes a complete entity with the consequences of a group member's way of being ending with that particular activity. A structured group process thus provides the sense of safety that can make it easier for group members to engage and disclose at their own pace. This is particularly important when working with older adults who have had distressing experiences. An important task for life review facilitators is to ensure that the older adults feel comfortable to take some risks in disclosing but at the same time are held back from overdisclosing during life review sessions. By establishing a safe relationship and group environment, alleviating as much initial anxiety as possible, the facilitator takes the necessary steps to prevent premature disclosure of distressing experiences and helps older adults to continue with the life review process.

PREVENTATIVE: HONORING EMOTIONAL EXPRESSION

Birren and Deutchman (1991) remind us that older adults are not as emotionally frail as might be indicated by the many attitudes and stereotypes in Western culture. Life review facilitators should not discourage the expression of strong emotions that are a common and expected aspect of interpersonal sharing and, as mentioned above, a very normal part of the grieving process in recovery from trauma. However, a group leader will want these feelings to emerge as naturally as possible and for the people he or she is working with to feel safe sharing their feelings. Facilitators do not want older adults to feel overwhelmed or ashamed of intense feelings. A therapeutic life review is one in which there is incremental disclosure by the participant so that the intensity of feeling deepens naturally. In group-based life review, Birren and Deutchman (1991) speak of this in terms of "developmental exchange" or a mutual sharing among group members whereby the group members "move from tentatively and guardedly alluding to important features of their lives toward an increasingly open sharing" (p. 45). Life review facilitators need to be attuned to the level of personal sharing of the people they are working with, normalizing the expression of emotions and containing them if needed. The specifics of how facilitators do this are described below:

1. Normalizing the process
   a. Before the reading of life stories starts, the facilitator should tell the older adult that, as personal experiences in the past are told, there is often the accompaniment of a wide range of feelings. These may be surprising and may feel somewhat uncomfortable at times.
   b. This is *normal!* Remind the participant that expressing emotions is a natural way of communicating and being congruent. Strong feelings are expected and okay.
   c. Give an example, such as "Often people may begin to cry when recalling a loss."
   d. Name the feeling. When someone begins to read his or her story, the facilitator may acknowledge emotional expression by using an empathic statement that will help the reader identify feelings in the moment. A basic empathic statement acknowledges a person's feelings and the context; for example, "It sounds like you are feeling very sad right now." By naming the feeling, the facilitator models support for the expression of emotion, and the participant will tend to feel less uncomfortable with feelings that are being expressed.
   e. This is not therapy! Life review facilitators should not probe for feelings that do not emerge spontaneously or process with more than acknowledgment through a basic empathic statement. For example, facilitators should not try to suggest feelings other than the one(s) expressed: "It sounds like you are feeling very sad right now and I wonder if there's some anger there too." This kind of intervention is part of necessary exploratory work in therapy, but it is not appropriate when traumatic memories are revealed in the life review context. The facilitator should not open up something that the individual is not ready to cope with and that the facilitator may not be able to follow up on with appropriate processing.
   f. Do not attempt to shut down feelings. Life review facilitators want the person or people that they are working with to be able to trust that the facilitator can handle their emotions; this is essential for psychological safety. There should be a box of tissues within range so the individual can reach for them if needed, but the facilitator should not jump in with a tissue at the first sign of tears. Facilitators should maintain appropriate eye contact and wait until the individual is finished speaking before responding. Facilitators should lean forward, if they are not already doing so. In a group, they should prevent other group members from jumping in with tissues and statements such as "I'd like to make this better for you" or "you'll get over it" or

"you just need to go on." All of these types of behaviors interfere with the individual's experience and convey a message that it's not okay to express feelings.

g. Offer reassurance to the individual who is experiencing the effects of earlier trauma of the normalcy and congruence of their experience. Individuals are often frightened by some of the feelings that can emerge suddenly with traumatic memories. Statements of reassurance give the individual a sense of mastery of being able to tell his or her story and be emotional without being judged. For example, "To cry when you talk about this experience to me is very normal, and, in fact, I feel closer to you right now."

As highlighted, the expression of feelings should be encouraged and is a normal and expected part of remembrance of tragic events during life review. However, facilitators need to be vigilant to signs of very strong feelings that are potentially overwhelming an individual's capacity to cope. In the event that participants exhibit any of the following behaviors, the facilitator needs to actively intervene to help them contain their feelings: crying so hard that they are struggling a bit to catch their breath; say they are feeling "out of it," "not here," "fuzzy," or "a little faint"; or all of a sudden they go completely quiet, frozen, or blank.

2. Containment of feelings
   a. *Tell the reader to stop:* Use an empathic statement: "Sounds like you are feeling a little overwhelmed right now, let's stop reading for a while."
   b. *Offer reassurance* and normalize the experience: "I find this sometimes happens when people talk about very disturbing experiences like this."
   c. *Move to immediately ground the reader* by asking him or her to take some deep breaths and put their head down if needed. Tell the individual to take a few moments and help him or her get reoriented to the room. Ask the older adult to focus on squeezing his or her toes and fists. Direct him or her to notice and focus on objects in the room and silently repeat the object's name (e.g., "Notice the chair you are sitting in, the light fixture ..."). This will help bring the person back to the present moment.
   d. *Redirect the reader's attention:* This involves shifting the individual away from focus on the trauma to other aspects of the story. Remind him or her of another part of the story and just chat for a few minutes before seeing whether he or she wishes to continue or finish another time.

e. *Highlight the individual's strengths:* Give validating and affirming feedback to the individual regarding his or her courage in sharing this story.

In summary, the primary goal of a facilitator of a life review experience is to ensure the safety of the individual or individuals that one is working with. Traumatic memories can result in feelings that overwhelm individual's capacities to cope and facilitators need to be alert to signs that this may be the case and intervene as needed. There will also be times when it will be appropriate to refer individuals for further therapeutic work with a helping professional who specializes in working with traumatized clients. Working with trauma requires extensive training and supervised practice, and it is prudent to investigate possible sources for referral before initiating life review with older adults. The next section briefly describes remedial actions such as how to broach the topic of referral to another helping professional and what to do when extreme reactions to the emergence of traumatic memories occur.

Remedial: Broaching the Topic of Referral

Many older adults view seeking professional help negatively, and especially the seeking of help from psychological professionals. Life review facilitators can, therefore, anticipate some resistance when they broach the topic of referral to other resources. If the older adult has started to form a good relationship with the facilitator, he or she may feel like he or she is being passed on, dismissed, rejected, or abandoned. These feelings may result is expressions of anger or annoyance. There are also many misconceptions about therapy in our culture, and older adults might worry that the suggestion of psychological referral means they are "crazy" and that they may lose any freedom they have and be locked away—all of which can result in older adults downplaying their distress. Reminding themselves and being aware of the sensitivities surrounding this topic will help facilitators broach the subject of referral with compassion and empathy.

a. *Normalization:* Explain that there are common reactions to distressing experiences that have lasting effects. These reactions are a normal response to abnormal events and do not mean that a person is crazy or weak or somehow flawed. Explain that sometimes these reactions can intensify when the story of the event is told and that this is natural.

b. *Recommend specific resources:* Let the individual know that relief if possible. The facilitator should explain that he or she knows people who specialize in helping those who have these

kinds of experiences. Ask the older adult to consider speaking
with one of them.

c. *Offer reassurance* to the individual that speaking to someone
further about these issues is a sign of strength. Stress a desire for
the older adult to receive the best care possible and a commitment to continue to be involved in their care as needed.

d. *Watch nonverbal reactions* and offer empathic understanding
based on the individual's reaction. Also use immediacy to bring
issues to the surface (e.g., I notice you are frowning and looking
away; are you feeling angry with me right now?).

e. *Develop a contract:* Don't press for a decision right away, but
make sure the participant agrees to discuss the topic again next
time.

Ethical guidelines in most helping professions are meant to ensure
that individuals will not be harmed by an experience. It is, therefore,
ethically incumbent on the facilitator of life review to be aware if someone is at risk as a result of sharing a traumatic memory. Providing a safe
relationship and group context we feel is the best way to reduce risks for
life review participants; however, remedial action may be needed, and it
is critical to follow-up with referrals to other resources for individuals
who have revealed unresolved trauma and who are struggling. In the
most extreme situations in which an older adult becomes at risk for
hurting him- or herself, it is the facilitator's responsibility to ensure that
he or she receives immediate assistance such as providing accompaniment to hospital emergency. Facilitators will probably never need to do
this, but they need to be prepared should this unlikely event occur. A
detailed discussion of traumatic stress reactions is beyond the scope of
this chapter. Still, by having some basic knowledge of traumatic stress,
stages of recovery, and preventative and remedial strategies for managing the revealing of traumatic memories, we believe it is possible to
facilitate a truly rewarding and therapeutic experience for older adults
in life review.

Bob

At a meeting at the Royal Canadian Legion, a former life review group
member, a World War II veteran named Bob said the following:

> I wish now to speak to my six comrades who have taken part in the
> life review group. In what you have done, you have given something of
> profound value. Those of us present who are old enough to go back 70
> years and who are like me and grew up in a small town will remember
> that almost every mature male in town over 35 was a veteran of World

War I. Amongst them were several that people considered a bit "odd." For these men the comment offered was, "Oh, he was shell-shocked." This was not just a statement; it was verdict—and the door was then closed. Well, the door is now open. Now there is hope when for them there was none.

EXERCISE

Feelings Metaphor

The way to get a group started each session is to ask the members to share with the group a metaphor for how they are feeling at the moment. The prompt might sound like this:

> I want you imagine a metaphor for how you feel today. By that, I mean select a word, image, event, picture, tune, or whatever best captures how you feel at this moment. For example, you might feel like a balloon that is about to burst or a cat lying in front of a fire.

Let each group member have an opportunity to describe his or her metaphor to the rest of the group. Then encourage self-reflection with the following prompts:

> "Note how quickly these images communicate to others how we feel."
> "Notice how your own feelings change (or perhaps not) when you speak your metaphor to the group."

This activity is a good way to indirectly assess individuals' emotional states, and it enables creativity of expression and tends to deepen the feelings of inclusion and cohesion that are essential for building safety.

NOTE

1. Based on Briere (1996) and Herman (1997).

REFERENCES

Birren, J. E., & Deutchman, D. E. (1991). *Guiding autobiography groups for older adults: Exploring the fabric of life.* London: John Hopkins University Press.
Borgen, W. A., Pollard, D., Amundson, N., & Westwood, M. J. (1989). *Employment groups: The counselling connection.* Toronto, Canada: Lugus Press.

Briere, J. (1996). *Therapy for adults molested as children: Beyond survival.* New York: Springer.

Brown-Shaw, M., Westwood, M. J., & deVries, B. (1999). Integrating personal reflection and group-based enactments. *Journal of Aging Studies, 13,* 109–119.

deVries, B., Birren, J. E., & Deutchman, D. E. (1995). Method and uses of guided auto-biography. In B. K. Haight & J. D. Webster (Eds.), *The art and science of reminiscing: Theory, research methods and applications.* Washington, DC: Taylor & Francis.

Herman, J. (1997). *Trauma and recovery.* New York: Basic Books.

Johns, H. (1996). *Personal development in counselor training.* London: Cassell.

Macdonald, C., Chamberlain, K., Long, N., Pereira-Laird, J., & Mirfin, K. (1998). Mental health, physical health, and stressors reported by New Zealand defense force peace-keepers: A longitudinal study. *Military Medicine, 163*(7), 477–481.

Rife, J. (1998). Use of life review techniques to assist older workers coping with job loss and depression. *Clinical Gerontologist, 20,* 75–79.

Schauben, L. J., & Frazier, P. A. (1995). Vicarious trauma: The effects on female coun-selors of working with sexual violence survivors. *Psychology of Women Quarterly, 19,* 49–64.

Silver, M. H. (1995). Memories and meaning: Life review in old age. *Journal of Geriatric Psychiatry, 28,* 57–73.

Van der Kolk, B. A., & McFarlane, A. C. (1996). The black hole of trauma. In B. A. van der Kolk, A. C. McFarlane, & L. Weisaeth (Eds.), *Traumatic stress: The effects of overwhelming experience on mind, body, and society.* New York: Guilford Press.

Westwood, M. J., Black, T. G., & McLean, H. B. (2002). A re-entry program for peacekeep-ing soldiers: Promoting personal and career transition. *Canadian Journal of Counsel-ling, 36*(3), 221–232.

CHAPTER ELEVEN

Reminiscence, Grief, Loss, and End of Life

Florence Gray Soltys

- In early development, children learn from parents and others what is the acceptable response to losses.
- About 50 percent of all women are widowed by the age of 65, but only about 12 to 22 percent of males suffer widowhood.
- It is better to have loved and lost than never to have loved at all.
- The reaction to a terminal diagnosis or death of someone close is both an emotional and physical shock.
- Loss, grief, and mourning are three inevitabilities of human existence.
- It is estimated that 30 to 35 percent of all individuals seeking assistance from medical professionals are suffering from unresolved grief.
- The stresses of grief may be expressed in the form of somatic complaints.
- Grief is a healing process, not a disease, and is very individualistic; grieving is a dynamic evolving and fluctuating process.
- Reminiscing done either with an individual or in a group is a wonderful way to explore and clarify grieving.
- It is the little things that are the essence of life and in the end what become paramount.
- Hospice is a concept that includes the patient and family as the standard of care.
- The death rate is one per person.

- The fastest growing segment of the population is 100 years and above, and 4 out of 5 of these centenarians are women.
- Hope has been described as the chance greater than zero for a positive outcome.
- Depersonalization occurs when a person cared for is always on the receiving end. The caregivers need to share with the dying individual and allow them to reciprocate.

REMINISCENCE AND END OF LIFE

Reminiscing is a self-reflective process that involves the recollection of past events, experiences, and feelings. Everyone performs reminiscence, both silently and verbally. Those who face life-threatening illnesses sometimes feel a paramount need to bring closure and explore the meaning in their lives. When one realizes that there are fewer years left than already lived, the urge to quantify one's life and reestablish goals becomes important. Although simple reminiscing occurs in people of all ages, it is more common among older adults.

The life cycle is a basic biological resource from around which we create culture. Lives unfold over the course of decades into a series of roles and responsibilities. Our culture helps us get through discontinuities and transfers the experiences into an ensemble of discernable stages. Framed by rites and customs of passage, each stage brings specific development tasks that provide the basis for the creation of shared culture. Rites of passage are grounded in the life cycle and bring together family and community members bound by their sense of a common history, identity, and destiny. Culture is age-related in many ways. Age—like ethnicity, gender, geography, religion, and social class—is one of the variables that defines individuals within their culture in any given time and place.

Simple reminiscence is a recall of past events, remembering, or reflecting on the past—especially personally significant experiences. It may be recalling a long-forgotten experience and relating its significance to the current situation for assistance in problem solving, regaining strength to face a crisis, or for educational reasons such as solidifying intergenerational or oral histories. According to the seminal article by Butler (1963), reminiscence was first recognized as an important growth mechanism for the process of aging and the ending of one's life. Some definitions of reminiscence are vague and general, such as "the art or process of recalling the past" (Butler, 1974) or "a method of holding on to one's self while letting go of a personal situation" (Hammer, 1984). Others define the differences between reminiscence and simple remembering as "the process of memory with the added action property of reaching out to infuse others with these memories" (Butler & Lewis , 1973) or "developing on the past—retrospection both purposive and spontaneous." This may occur naturally, as Butler suggests, or may be what is referred to as social construction (Wallace, 1992).

Butler (1963) stated that, far from living in the past or exhibiting wandering of the mind as commonly thought, older people are engaged in the important psychological task of making sense of the life they have lived and memories, reminiscence, and nostalgia play a part in the process.

One reviews the past to understand the present. An awareness of mortality leads to a quest for finding meaning in one's life. Of course, not everyone struggles with the issues of meaning—various coping mechanisms, such as escapism or denial, may be used to avoid the issue. The awareness of mortality becomes the crucial defining moment in later life, and this awareness forces the individual to find or construct significance and meaning in life or to surrender to terror. On a practical level, older individuals are often intent on instructing their families about their estate, advance directives, and their particular wishes regarding death rituals. The individual wants to die in a way consistent with his or her values, wishes, and earlier life.

All of us want to leave the world feeling we have made a difference. We want to have the freedom to find meaning in our lives and share that meaning with our family, our friends, and the larger community. The process of self-reflection provides the opportunity to express our deepest feelings for those we care about. Reminiscence, whether done informally with loved ones or formally through cultural activities, helps us celebrate our living legacy at the end of our lives. As you age, your experiences and learning expand to an understanding that is sometimes referred to as wisdom.

Reminiscence helps people to say good-bye; express regrets and joys; appreciate all of the contributions they made to family, community, and society. As death nears, we become increasingly able to identify what is really important in our lives. Our families and friends become paramount. As Victor Frankl (1959) stated, "All of us need to leave knowing the things we've done, the things we've loved, the things we will leave behind with meaning, and the things we've believed in" (p. 115). "The person reviews the past, reappraises the present life structure, and explores options for change in view of new goals, hopes and circumstances" (p. 117).

Psychologist Erik Erikson (1968) suggests that, as we approach the end of our days, we need to bring together strands of our lives as a psychological preparation for facing death with a sense of life completed. Butler (2002) observed that individuals nearing the end of their lives seem to reminiscence more often. He further states that reminiscence is used to review the past events of one's life to address unresolved issues or to place events into an order that enhances self-esteem and a sense of personal identity through the recounting of personal achievements and experiences unique to the individual.

Reminiscence may be used to define one's value structure, addressing such questions as:

- What is most important to me?
- How can I be independent as long as possible?
- How can I live as long as possible?
- How can I be free of pain even if my life span is reduced?
- Can I make a contribution to medical science?
- How can I remain mentally competent and alert, staying true to my spirituality but letting nature take its course?
- How do I define what is important and leave good memories for family and friends? (Grudzen & Soltys, 2000)

Exploring values through reminiscence is especially important for the treating clinicians and the family, who may be involved in caregiving decisions. Reminiscence is also an effective way to explore these areas when assisting with the preparation of living wills and health care powers of attorney. It is helpful for health care providers to know the individual's values (through reminiscence, legal documents, or family knowledge) when making difficult decisions.

Advance directives, which vary by state, along with the health care power of attorney, give written instructions for choices but do not define in detail a person's complete personal values and beliefs. An adjunct to the advance directives, an ethical will, provides this opportunity. Baines (2002), who is a proponent of ethical wills, calls them a vehicle for clarifying and communicating the meaning in people's lives to families and communities. An ethical will can express one's moral underpinnings and record the thoughts of the heart, mind, and spirit. Baines suggests that personal narratives include such information as what is valued most, what is worth one's energy to defend, what lessons have been learned, what one is proud of, and mistakes with lessons learned. This process of introspection can put many areas into a new perspective and help one make sense of the experiences. The experience usually has a cathartic impact.

In terminal illness, two of life's crucial moments happen at the same time. The patient's body fails to function, and the patient and family face final separation—a life event that surpasses the importance of a birth, marriage, or rearing a child. Even if one hopes to face the end of life with courage, equanimity, competence, responsibility, achievement, humor, and the hope of giving support and comfort to one's survivors, most are caught unprepared when that time comes.

Pain is diagnosed in a broad framework encompassing the physical and psychological situation of the patient and family. The goal of pain management is to prescribe medications to control the pain while keeping the patient alert. The effects and interactions of drugs and their rates of absorption make it possible to prevent pain rather than just treat it.

Copp (1994) stated that care providers have a special obligation to assure palliation and compassion and that not doing so is not only inhumane but also negligent, raising many ethical questions. She defines five types of pain: life pain (death, separation, loss of income, loss of relationship, and loss of meaning in life); unexplained pain (pain that one imagines as far more threatening and life-threatening—that is, a headache means one has a brain tumor); disease-related pain (varies with the disease, how one perceives the illness, and one's personality); diagnostic pain (exists until one is driven to seek relief, and the pain of the workup may add to the already existing pain); and therapy-associated pain (may bring new problems such as added pain, diarrhea, loss of hair, invasions of the body, nausea, anorexia, and insomnia—sometimes the treatment seems worse than the disease).

People who experience pain sometimes express it to others who are ill-equipped to deal with it—the elderly, children, and already-exhausted caregivers. The pain is expressed in many forms: demands, irritation, rejection, recrimination, remorse, confession, and struggling for forgiveness and a fresh beginning. For the person in pain and the significant other, it is love tested and retested. The person in pain may not understand his or her own behavior, let alone be able to translate it and justify it to loved ones (Copp, 1994).

HOSPICE

As you ought not to attempt to cure the eyes without the head or the head without the body, so neither are you to attempt to cure the body without the soul. For the part can never be well unless the whole is well.

Plato (Mount, 1993)

You matter because you are you. You matter to the last moment of your life, and we will do all we can, not only to help you die in peace, but also to live until you die.

Dame Cicely Saunders (Corr & Corr, 1983)

Dame Cicely Saunders carefully and thoughtfully laid the foundation of palliative medicine and hospice care. In the mid-1960s, she started the first Center for the Care of the Dying to place equal priority on patient care, research, and teaching. She introduced the concept of total pain as a model for understanding chronic pain and, in doing so, went on to draw attention to the diverse variables that influence the pain threshold.

Patients who are restless, upset, anxious, fearful, angry, or depressed have a lower threshold for pain and thus feel more pain. Conversely, there is less pain when patients are rested, distracted, and other symptoms are well controlled. The use of analgesics along with support that allows patients to express their thoughts is imperative.

The use of reminiscence to clarify one's past experiences and value structure is crucial. Dame Saunders's model of hospice care advocated whole patient care in the tradition of geriatrician William Osler, who asserted that "It is better to know the person who has the disease than the disease the person has" (Balfour, 1993, p. 30).

Hospice is usually not a place, but rather a coordinated interdisciplinary program that addresses the physical, emotional, social, and spiritual needs of terminally ill individuals and their families (Soltys, Brookins, & Seney, 1998).

Pain management is possible in nearly all cases. The hospice concept is built on a patient/family standard of care, while the acute model focuses on the patient. The interdisciplinary team approach seeks to meet holistic physical, psychosocial, and spiritual needs.

The focus of care surrounding end-of-life care has changed dramatically as the model becomes more acceptable through the health care delivery system. Palliative care has become more common and acceptable as individuals, family members, and health care providers choose alternatives to continued treatment and suffering. The goals shift from care to comfort, and patients and their families are supported through this transition by a staff of trained professionals, including clergy, social workers, nurses, nursing aides, physicians, and volunteers.

Hospice offers patients and families an alternative to aggressive treatment, but they must agree to end curative treatment and move to the palliative mode. This includes radiation except for palliative reasons, chemotherapy, antibiotics, blood transfusion, dialysis, and any other treatment perceived as life prolonging.

Terminal illness can knock a lot of nonsense out of people; it induces humility and cuts us down to size. It frequently results in some inner discoveries about how often we rationalize our failures and weaknesses and dodge vital issues. For only when the way straightens and the gate narrows do some people discover their soul, their God, or their life work (Besch, 1956). The strong are able to take a crisis and use the experience to grow in strength and wisdom. Life can be a long lesson in humility.

While family and friends are losing just the person, the dying person is losing everything, which may generate depression. In older adult populations, depression may take many forms. Psychosomatic tendencies such as aches and pains or fears about physical well-being may dominate. Impairment in cognition may be present. Various losses and stressful life events can create a crisis. Loss of health, diagnosis of acute or chronic disease, the loss of a spouse and friends, and moving to a new living situation can shake create feelings of vulnerability and shake elders' sense of security to the core. Loss of control and independence, hope, and health, giving up on long-held goals, and making compromises to cope with all these losses contribute heavily to stress. Spirituality and religious beliefs may be challenged. Dealing with loss is never easy; however, with strong support, people can emerge stronger because of the crisis. The scars remain, but the individual may see new possibilities and act. It often depends on the loss, the person's personality, and the strength the person has left for regaining a feeling of wholeness.

Grief is:

- A healing process, not a disease.
- Very individualistic.
- Dynamic, evolving, and functioning.

Worden (2002) defines the mourning process as four tasks to be completed:

1. Accept the reality of the loss.
2. Work through the pain of grief.
3. Adjust to an environment in which the deceased is missing.
4. Emotionally relocate the deceased and move on with life.

Additional tips for working with dying individuals and their families are to:

1. Learn and respect the person's individual system, including religious, ethnic, family, and other cultural influences.
2. Become comfortable with your feelings about your own death.

3. Help the person find meaning in his or her life.
4. Know state laws on advance directives.
5. Get the information necessary to help the person negotiate the legal, health care, and insurance systems.
6. Encourage family meetings to talk about their lives and end-of-life issues. Be prepared to mediate or facilitate with individual family members and with the family as a whole.
7. Form teams or partnerships with health professionals to advocate for care that fits the person's values and beliefs.
8. Talk with others working with the dying and bereaved about a support group (Soltys & Danis, 1998).

Open communication is an important determinate in adjustment between health professionals, patient, and family. Education can provide the ill individual with knowledge to enhance, cope, and clarify expectations. We are usually less afraid when we know what to expect. This can allow experience, expression, and validation of feelings. A man in his 60s was in the final stages of lung cancer. He lived in two small rooms in a rented house. His two daughters (in their late 20s) assumed much of his care along with the hospice team. He spent many hours recalling his life with a reminiscence clinician. As his condition worsened, he was directly asked what he still needed to do. He replied, "I want to speak with my ex-wife to apologize for being irresponsible by not supporting the family, abusing her, and drinking heavily." Even though she had been remarried for many years, she agreed to come and speak with him. They spent a couple hours together. When she left, they both had been crying. She had forgiven him, and he died about 12 hours later. Reminiscing is an effective avenue to identify what needs to be done and to say we are sorry.

The need for meaning is a powerful motivator. Identifying a purpose to account for what is happening can greatly enhance one's coping skills (Frankl, 1959). An analogy might be the experience Frankl, a psychiatrist, had while living in concentration camps. He was able to muster the coping skills that allowed him to function and see himself coming to terms with the horrible conditions and his feelings and know that he had a future. This was possible for him even though he lost his entire family in the camps. But most individuals will have the gift of time by a family member, friend, or professional who will actively listen and confirm an individual's life, which can improve health. Through this process, people become empowered by their history, because their past is a vital source of strength, knowledge, wisdom, and maturity.

The interdisciplinary hospice team, which includes the family and the patient, works to understand everyone's physical, psychological, and emotional needs. In this way, the individual and family are able to face the crisis and begin to plan for the future. It is a time to share and express feelings that may have not been expressed before. Video-or audiotaping (if not previously done) can become important. As a grandfather told his grandson, "the time will come when these things we tell you will need to be heard again."

Most hospice and other clinics serving frail elders, outpatient clinics or home care providers present opportunities for flexibility and an enhanced sense of control for patients. The clinician sometimes becomes a guest in the patient's home. Without the rigidity of institutional rules, a very different picture of the person emerges in his or her own environment. Working in an alternative care setting can be a foreign experience to many professionals, and acceptance by them may require patience and understanding. The experience gives clinicians the unique opportunity to observe the support provided by the family—an important part of the clinical assessment.

> Only people who are capable of loving strongly can also suffer great sorrow, but this same necessity of loving serves to counteract their grief and heals them.
>
> Tolstoy (1886)

Mr. K

Mr. K was an 89-year-old man who lived with his 90-year-old wife of 62 years in a two-bedroom apartment. His wife had irreversible deafness that had begun in her 70s. Mr. K had a diagnosis of Parkinson's disease. Their one daughter lived about 500 miles away.

They retired to the southeastern United States when Mr. K turned 80, because living in the city had become too arduous for them. Mrs. K had been a children's librarian, and Mr. K had been a counselor of persons suffering from alcoholism.

As his disease progressed and her hearing deteriorated, they were increasingly unable to communicate with each other. Over the course of about one year, Mr. K spent many hours participating in reminiscence. Safety and communication devices were installed in the apartment, including a telecommunications device for the deaf so his wife could speak with their daughter. Mr. K felt a need to maintain control during the reminiscence and spent hours discussing his father, who had been an embarrassment to the family and provided poor support because of alcohol abuse.

After spending much time planning his funeral down to the most intimate detail, he revealed that he wanted to be cremated and his ashes divided. One half was to go in the local churchyard and a weeping cherry tree planted at the site, and the other half was to go to a small town in the Midwest and be placed on his father's grave as an expression of forgiveness and so Mr. K could be close to his father again. His wishes were carried out following his death two weeks later.

The use of reminiscence and Mr. K's ability to discuss and share his life made this resolution possible.

Mrs. C

Mrs. C, a 76-year-old widow, was brought to the interdisciplinary geriatric clinic by her family for evaluation. She had been diagnosed with a dementia of the Alzheimer's type. Over time, she had become more withdrawn and dependent on her family. At the beginning of her interview, she was withdrawn and gave slow, one-word responses to questions. She shared that her mother died when she was 9 years old and she dropped out of school in the fourth grade to care for her four younger siblings. At age 17, she married a tobacco farmer and they reared four children, all of whom were supportive and attentive to her. After more sharing, she quoted a poem about a cloud. She declared that she had 200 more poems at home, and this was the way she had managed stress over the years.

As she grew more comfortable, she shared that she "had visions from the Bible" and that she used red clay from her backyard to sculpt the visions.

She had been writing poetry and sculpting for 30 years, but, during the last 10 years, she had done neither. She had painted some of her sculptures with leftover house paint. She could not afford commercial clay. She wondered aloud, "are they worth anything?" She stated that the sculptures were in the tobacco house.

With her permission (and the family's), the curator for the local folk art museum went to Mrs. C's home, rescued the artwork, and found it to be wonderful. His assessment was that the sculptures could be sold on the commercial market or given to a museum. After conferring with her family, and despite limited resources, Mrs. C decided to give the art to two folk art museums so her great-great-grandchildren "will know who I am."

Needless to say, Mrs. C did not have dementia, but long-standing depression. With antidepressants, bags of clay, a return to sculpting, and much encouragement, she returned to her former self, becoming interactive again with family and friends. However, within 3 years, she again became depressed and was diagnosed with cancer following a fall (with hip fracture). She lived to the end with appreciation for her self and her accomplishments.

Mrs. C continued to reminisce and share her life as long as she was conscious. Mrs. C is an example for reminiscence clinicians of the challenges of discovery and the joys that reminiscence brings (Barrett & Soltys, 2002).

FACILITATING REMINISCENCE IN THE DYING

As death nears, people need to interact with others to reflect on and understand the meaning of their lives. Making meaning of the sum of our days is not a solitary vocation at the end of life. Unfortunately, our culture tends to isolate people at the end of their lives, and often we do not assist in making these meaningful connections. The results from reminiscence can provide reflection and meaning of one's life and family.

A documentary titled *An Unlikely Friendship* (Bloom & Soltys, 2001) contains interviews with a former president of the Ku Klux Klan (Mr. E) and the president of Welfare Mothers (Mrs. A). They recall their roles as co-chairs of desegregation plans for a small southern town in the 1970s. After a relationship with much anguish and hostility, they found they shared the value of quality education for their children, which made dramatic changes in their relationship, lives, and the community. Mr. E tore up his Klan card, and he and Mrs. A have remained friends for over 30 years. Their story has enriched the community through public television, in public classrooms, and in many community settings seeking greater understanding.

EDUCATION OF GRIEF PROCESS

With serious illness, people often reassess their lives and redefine where they may want to go and the legacy they want to leave. Recovery from death, a serious illness, or bereavement includes respecting and acknowledging an individual's soul and personal value structure. Exploring that system while respecting and adhering to an individual's desires can be a challenge for clinicians. Generally, people grow the most when confronted—whether emotionally, physically, or mentally. Even when an individual is very frail, the ability to face a major illness or death can be a powerful experience. It is the clinician's professional role to be there, respect the individual's values, recognize the person's contributions, and to let the individual know he or she is loved.

Clinicians need to be aware of and educate families about:

- Normalcy
- Dreams
- Need to tell story
- Uncontrolled emotions
- Inability to concentrate
- Hallucination

Good questions to ask yourself, the patient, and the family include the following:

- Who consoles you when you are upset?
- Who can you count on to help you in a crisis?
- Who can you count on to listen to you?
- With whom can you be totally yourself?
- Who appreciates you as a person?

Mrs. J was 78, widowed, and much loved by her family. She wanted to leave her thoughts for her family, and so 9 days before she died, she and I made a videotape. She shared many poignant moments, but some of the highlights of her life review were the influence of her mother, her husband and married life, her children both young and grown, the death of her husband, and her wishes for her family as she left them.

Mrs. J described her husband's illness and death at a young age (he was in his 50s) as well as their discussions and planning for her. After his death, she had frequent dreams of him and felt his presence. This was comforting for her. As her death became nearer, the dreams reappeared and brought much comfort. She strongly felt she would meet him and they would rejoin their happy relationship.

Her final message to her family was "to love each other and let them know you love them. I don't care about having lots of money but love is necessary." Mrs. J's message emphasized that "little things are the essence of life," and love conquers and lessens all fears. Mrs. J's story also demonstrates how dreams can be useful for resolving grief.

What follows are several poems that describe how reminiscence facilitates resolution at the end of life.

How do I know my youth is spent?
My get up and go has got up and went.
And yet—I can grin when I know where it's been!

Old Irish common saying

This I wish for all of us and the millions of elders,
Who are becoming greater in number each year!
Celebrating their lives with them is an honor and pleasure.
Man is like breath; his days are as a fleeting shadow.
In the morning he flourishes and grows up like grass.
In the evening he is cut down and withers.
So teach us to number our days that we may get a heart of wisdom.

Myerhoff (1980)

The following poem was found in the room of a nursing home patient in Scotland. The poem beautifully illustrates the need to respect the whole of one's life and the value of reminiscence.

What Do You See Nurse?

What do you see, nurses, what do you see?
What are you thinking when you're looking at me?
A crabby old woman, now very wise,
Uncertain of habit, with faraway eyes?
Who dribbles her food and makes no reply
When you say in a loud voice, "I do wish you'd try!"
Who seems not to notice the things that you do,
And forever is losing a stocking or shoe ...
Who, resisting or not, lets you do as you will
With bathing and feeding, the long day to fill ...
Is that what you're thinking? Is that what you see?
Then open your eyes, nurse; you're not looking at me.
I'll tell you I am as I sit here so still,
As I do at your bidding, as I eat at your will.
I'm a small child of ten ... with a father and mother,
Brother and sister, who love one another.
A young girl of sixteen, with wings on her feet,
Dreaming that soon now a lover she'll meet.
A bride soon at twenty—my heart gives a leap,
Remembering the vows that I promised to keep.
At twenty-five now, I have young of my own,
Who need me to guide and give a secure happy home.
A woman of thirty, my young now grown fast,
Bound to each other with ties that should last.
At forty, my young sons have grown and are now gone,
But my man's beside me to see I don't mourn.
At fifty once more, babies play round my knee,
Again we know children, my loved one and me.
Dark days are upon me, my husband is dead;
I look at the future, I shudder with dread.
For my young are all rearing young of their own,
And I think of the years and the love that I've known.
I'm now an old woman ... and nature is cruel
'Tis its jest to make old age look like a fool.
The body, it crumbles, grace and vigor depart
There is now a stone where I once had a heart.
But inside this old carcass a young girl still dwells,
And now and again my battered heart swells.
I remember the joys, I remember the pain,
And I'm loving and living life over again.
I think of the years ... all too few, gone too fast.

And accept the stark fact that nothing can last.
So open your eyes, nurse, open and see,
Not a crabby old woman; look closer ... see ME!!

My Reflection

I look in the mirror and what do I see?
Can that old woman really be me?
Whatever happened to that young smiling face?
Can this be the one that's taken its place?
How did the years go by so fast?
All that was the future is now in the past.
What will be left in this life for me?
Are all of life's pleasures just a memory?
Although the years have taken their toll,
and left me here so suddenly old.
In my mind there will always be that
young smiling face that used to be me.

Mezo (1998)

EXERCISES

Sentence Completion Exercise

This exercise encompasses several areas of the grief process, beginning with validating and normalizing one's symptoms; checking on his or her real or perceived support system; describing special days, life adjustments since the loss, lost dreams and broken plans, loved one's personality, first experience with death, family rules about expressing grief, coping skills, and personal goals.

I.   Recognizing Individual Feeling
    a. If I could talk with _____, I would say the following:
    b. My happiest time was _____.
    c. Holidays as they were and as they are now: _____.
    d. A dream I've lost is _____.
    e. I wish we could have _____.
    f. These memories make me feel _____.
    g. The times that I am reminded of you are _____.
    h. Since my loved one died, the ways I've changed are _____.

II. For Letter Writing, Discussion, and Audiotaping
    a. What I miss the most is _____.

b. What I do not miss is _____.
c. What I wish I had said; not said _____.
d. The happiest times of my life with you was _____;
the worst was _____.
e. When you died, I felt _____.
f. Times I always want to remember are _____.

III. Perceived Quality of Life

Discuss the five most important areas, persons, or things in your life. Rank in importance from one to five. Discuss your current satisfaction with each area. Discuss changes that you would like to make about your life.

IV. Photographs, Music, Art, Literature
   a. Use photographs to assemble a life story and review and discuss relationships.
   b. Use music to evoke thoughts, recall, and reminiscing.
   c. Use art and colors to express feelings.
   d. Literature is a nonthreatening way to enter the world of someone else. Use literature to apply the author's experience and situation to your own.

Grief and Loss Exercise

This exercise (developed by Kunz, 1997) may be done individually or in group settings. Most older adults don't need to do this type of exercise because they are living with grief and loss or have spent plenty of time anticipating such losses. It is, however, a tremendous tool to help sensitize younger people to grief and loss issues. Ask participants to write down their answers. Let participants know that they will have the option to pass or remain silent about their responses when group sharing is facilitated.

Step 1: Think about your life today. Become increasingly aware of all the people, activities, people, pets, hobbies, and interests you cherish. Think about your abilities, talents, and values you cherish. Think of the roles in life you play. Do what you need to acknowledge your spiritual beliefs about what life has given you.

Step 2: Now list the five most important things that came to mind when you completed the above tasks. Don't worry too much about how you categorize these things. Then prioritize them from the fifth to the most important thing in your life.

Step 3: Remembering that you still have all five of these important things in your life, now imagine that number five on the list no longer exists for you. Cross it entirely off the list. What happens inside? How do you feel? Are you laughing or using another defense mechanism to shelter your emotions? How many older adults do you know who have faced this loss or the real or perceived threat of this loss?

Step 4: Now imagine that number four on your list no longer exists for you. Cross it entirely off the list as well. Answer the same questions as in Step 3. How does losing both number five and four change your feelings?

Step 5: Going gradually and giving yourself enough time for reflection, continue imagining numbers three, two and one no longer existing for you, and cross them entirely off the list. With each new imagined loss, answer the questions from Steps 3 and 4. Notice the cumulative emotional impact that develops with each additional loss.

Step 6: Answer the following questions: What's left in your life now? How have your values changed? What is your purpose in being alive? Who are you now? These questions represent the many issues older adults face each day.

Step 7: Share your answers with at least one other person, even if you did this exercise by yourself. If you did it as a group, now is an excellent time for group sharing of the answers. Facilitators should use their judgment in deciding whether to break into small groups or process as an entire group. It is also sometimes helpful to process answers at each step.

Step 8: Give yourself a chance to again reflect on the reality of your current situation and again do what you need to do in terms of any spiritual acknowledgment of your feelings regarding your current situation.

Common Results and Discussion of This Exercise

When done in groups, there is usually a great deal of laughter during Steps 3 and 4. This is a good time to discuss laughter as a psychological defense mechanism, making sure to frame the discussion in a positive manner and then also talking about the fear, hurt, anger, and depression that is part of the grief process.

Job or school is usually the fifth most important thing identified in groups from ages 20 to preretirement age. Most older adults are no longer working full-time. Most older adults in long-term care facilities remember their work days as they relate to the various staff in the facility. Some older adults were forced to retire due to health changes or organizational policy. The friendships and relationships at work are not easily replaced. Furthermore, a significant part of the identity of many older Americans lies in their career or professional life. Acknowledging this and reminiscing about the individual's life work can be very helpful for caregivers; it is not only interesting for caregivers, but it also helps individuals access the more confident, secure resource state of their profession. Thus, they are responding as an adult and not in a less familiar, dependent patient role.

One's home is commonly listed as the fourth most important thing. Many younger adults are still collecting their items of interest, decorating, landscaping, or buying new homes. It's hard to imagine that in only a few decades they will be downsizing and getting rid of possessions and perhaps moving from their house to an apartment or other living arrangement. Many older adults have faced or anticipate the sale of the home in which they've resided for decades. Although this process provides a tremendous amount of reminiscence material and lends itself to life review processes, it is also a time for heavy grieving. The form of the grief will depend on the timing and how prepared the older adult was for this change. The more ready for the change and personal sense of control, the better.

The automobile and the independence it represents also frequently rates in the number four or five priority. Most older adults receiving in-home or long-term care have had to face giving up this part of their independent identity. Due to vision, hearing, and other changes, many older adults are forced to limit their driving or worry about the day they may have to stop driving altogether.

Pets also are often listed at the fourth or fifth priority level in this exercise. Research demonstrates that pets can have a significant impact on health, quality of life, and the longevity of older adults. One woman in her 80s who had lost her husband, had moved from her home to an apartment, had her only living sister diagnosed with Alzheimer's disease, and whose daughter received a promotion and moved 2,000 miles away said, "I don't know what I'd do without my little kitty." Throughout these cumulative losses, she'd increasingly relied on the bond with her cat.

REFERENCES

Baines, B. K. (2002). *Ethical wills.* New York: Persews.

Barrett, K.G., & Soltys, F. G. (2002). Geriatric social work: Supporting the patient's search for meaning. *Geriatric Rehabilitation, 17*(4), 53–64.

Besch, L. E. (1956). Spiritual insight. In C. F. Lytle (Ed.), *Leaves of gold* (p. 81). Williamsport, PA: Coslett.

Bloom, D., & Soltys, F. G. (2001). *An unlikely friendship* [Video documentary]. Chapel Hill, NC: Filmmakers Library.

Butler, R. N. (1963). The life review: An interpretation of reminiscence in the aging. *Psychiatry, 26,* 65–70.

Butler, R. N. & Lewis, M. (1973). *Aging and mental health*. Boston: CU Mosley Co.

Copp, L. A. (1994). Past endurance: A construct of pain and suffering. In I. Corless, B. Germino, & M. Pittman (Eds.), *Death, dying, and bereavement* (pp.228–238). Boston: Jones and Bartlett.

Corr, C., & Corr, D. (Eds.). (1983). *Hospice care principles and practices*. New York: Springer Press.

Erikson, E. H. (1968). *Childhood and society*. New York: Norton.

Frankl, V. (1959). *Man's search for meaning*. Boston: Beacon Press.

Grudzen, M., & Soltys, F. G. (2002). Reminiscence at end of life: Celebrating a living legacy, *Dimensions, 7*(3), 1–8.

Hammer, M. L. (1984). Insight, reminiscence, denial, projection: Coping mechanisms of the aged. *Journal of Gerontological Nursing, 10*(2), 66–68.

Kunz, J. A. (1997). *Grief, loss and older adults* [Videotape and workbook]. Mental Health Outreach Network.

Paul, R. and Elder, E. (2002). *Critical Thinking: Tools for taking charge of your professional and personal life*. Upper Saddle River: Financial Times Prentice Hall.

Mezo, H. (1998). My reflection. Gift to author Soltys.

Mount, B. (1993). Whole person care: Beyond psychosocial and physical needs. *The American Journal of Hospice and Palliative Care,* (Jan/Feb), 28–37.

Myerhoff, B. (1995). *Remembered lives*. Ann Arbor: University of Michigan Press.

Saunders, C. (1983). The last stages of life. In C. Corr & D. Corr (Eds.), *Hospice care principles and practices* (pp. 5–11). New York: Springer Press.

Soltys, F. G., Brookins, M., & Seney, J. (1998). Why hospice? The case for ESRD patients and their families. *ANNA Journal, 25*(6), 619–624.

Soltys, F. G., & Danis, M. (1998). *Helping families face the end of lives*. Adult Services Practice Notes. Jordan Institute. Chapel Hill: University of North Carolina Chapel Hill.

Tolstoy, L. (1886). *The death of Ivan Illych*. New York: New American Library of World Literature.

Wallace, J. B. (1992). Reconsidering the life review: Social construct of talk about the past. *The Gerontologist, 32*(1), 120–125.

Worden, W. J. (2002). *Grief counseling and grief therapy*. New York: Springer Press.

Index

Arts programs (continued)
  in senior centers, 127, 128
  U. S. Department of Education
    funding, 129
ArtWorks, 128
Association of Personal Historians,
  Web site, 2
Autobiography, 43, 69–70, 71
  in psychoanalysis, 72
Autonomy, 24, 25

Bahr, R. T., 71
Baines, B. K., 200
Bandler, R., 168
Barresi, C. M., 147
Beck, A. T., 172
Berkman, L. F., 125
Birren Center for Autobiography and
  Life Review, Web site, 3
Birren, James E., 71, 91, 110, 186, 190
Bitterness, 44
Blogging, 3
  intergenerational, 8
Bohlmeijer, E., 110
Boredom, 43
Borgen, W. A., 190
Boylin, W., 70
Brain
  development, 20, 30, 31, 32, 42
  functioning of, 42, 45, 125
Brief therapy, 171
  reminiscence/life review and,
    172–176
Brown-Shaw, M., 187
Butler, Robert N., 1, 2, 29, 31, 32,
  42, 43, 45, 67, 69, 71, 102, 124,
  125, 172, 198, 199

California State University, 3
Career, 26, 111
Caregiver
  depression and, 156
  ethnic minority, guidelines/
    exercises, 150–153
  life story/review and, 6, 9
  of older adult with dementia, 94
  support groups, 93

training, 94, 96, 97, 176–177
CBT. See Cognitive behavioral
  therapy
Center for Elders and Youth in the
  Arts, San Francisco, 126, 127
Change, 24, 46
  adapting to, 20
Childhood, 77
Children, reminiscence/life review
  and, 72
Cochran, Kathryn N., 110
Cognitive behavioral therapy (CBT),
  171–172
  reminiscence/life review and,
    172–176
Cognitive development, 11, 13, 20,
  22, 30, 31, 33, 44, 98
Cohen, Gene, 30–32, 32, 45,
  125, 126
Cohen's Four Phases of the Second
  Half of Life, 30–31
Coleman, P.G., 70, 71, 165
Commitment, 27
Communication, 34, 54, 204
  facilitator's skill of, 97
  intergenerational, 8, 53
Community, 87, 199
  building through arts programs,
    132, 135–136
Conscience, 25
Content, life review process v., 4,
  9–11, 72
Coping skills, 169
Copp, L. A., 201
"The Crabbit Old Woman," 74
The Creative Age: Awakening
  Human Potential in the Second
  Half of Life (Cohen), 125
Creativity, 126
Creativity and Aging: The Impact
  of Professionally Conducted
  Cultural Programs on Older
  Adults (Cohen), 126
Crisis, used for growth, 203
Cuijpers, P., 110
Cultural background. See also Ethnic
  minority

Critical Advances in Reminiscence Work

From Theory to Application

Jeffrey Dean Webster, MEd
Barbara K. Haight, RN, DrPH, FAAN

"This book is a mind opener to many important issues of human behavior."

—from the Foreword by **James E. Birren**

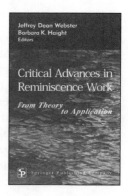

In this volume, Webster and Haight, along with multi-disciplinary contributors, point out ways of improving the quality of life through the processes of reminiscence. They present examples of cutting-edge treatments in reminiscence work.

Organized into sections, the book sets the stage with a valuable review of the literature and then focuses on conceptual issues, developmental/sociocultural contexts, special populations, and clinical applications.

Partial Contents:

Section One: Overview • A Continuing Review of Reminiscence, *S.A. Hendrix* and *B.K. Haight*

Section Two: Conceptual Issues • Reminiscence and Oral History: Comparisons Across Parallel Universes, *J. Bornat*

Section Three: Developmental and Sociocultural Issues • Reminiscing and Relating the Development of Parent-Child Talk About the Past, *R. Fivush* and *E. Reese*

Section Four: Special Populations • Themes of Continuity and Change in the Spiritual Reminiscence of Elder Catholic Women Religious, *S. Perschbacher Melia*

Section Five: Clinical Applications • Transformation in Life Stories: The Canadian War Veterans Life Review Project, *M.E. Shaw* and *M.J. Westwood*

2002 · 392pp · 978-0-8261-6992-1 · hardcover

11 West 42nd Street, New York, NY 10036-8002 • Fax: 212-941-7842
Order Toll-Free: 877-687-7476 • Order Online: www.springerpub.com

Geropsychological Interventions in Long-Term Care

Lee Hyer, EdD, ABPP
Robert C. Intrieri, PhD, Editors

Older people are entering nursing homes later and sicker than ever before, thus presenting as more physically fragile and complex residents and requiring more advanced care and treatment. To this end, Hyer and Intrieri have gathered together a group of health care professionals who are genuinely dedicated to the care and research of long-term care (LTC) environments. This group seeks to push the envelope for improved use of professional time, effort, and input and in this remarkable book, share their ideas with you.

By applying the Selective Optimization with Compensation (SOC) model to various care settings, the editors are able to examine current LTC practices and existing psychosocial issues confronting older LTC patients; either support or challenge them; and offer suggestions and strategies, such as Cognitive Behavior Therapy, for improving the LTC system and residents' physical, psychological, emotional, and social health.

Partial Contents:

Perspectives on Long-Term Care • Evolving Trends in Long-Term Care • Psychiatric Intervention in Long-Term Care • Treating Depression in Nursing Homes • "There is Still a Person in There" • Utilization of Self-identity Roles in Individualized Activities Designed to Enhance Well-being in Persons with Dementia • The Influence of Changing Emotional Goals on the Psychological Well-Being of Nursing Home Residents • Application of SOC Model to Care for Residents with Advanced Dementia • A Paradigm for Qualitative Research in Long-Term Care • Meeting the Needs of Nursing Home Residents and Staff • Cognitive-Behavioral Therapy for Long-Term Care Patients with Dementia • Consultations with Primary Care Physicians

2006 · 360pp · 978-0-8261-3845-3 · hardcover

11 West 42nd Street, New York, NY 10036-8002 • Fax: 212-941-7842
Order Toll-Free: 877-687-7476 • Order Online: www.springerpub.com

SPRINGER PUBLISHING COMPANY

End-of-Life Stories
Crossing Disciplinary Boundaries

Donald E. Gelfand, PhD, **Richard Raspa,** PhD
Sherylyn H. Briller, PhD
Stephanie Myers Schim, PhD, RN, APRN, CNAA, BC, Editors

This book provides a variety of narratives about end-of-life experiences contributed by members of the Wayne State University End-of-Life Interdisciplinary Project. Each of the narratives is then analyzed from three different disciplinary perspectives. These analyses broaden how specific end-of-life narratives can be viewed from different dimensions and help students, researchers, and practitioners see the important and varied meanings that end-of-life experiences have at the level of the individual, the family, and the community. In addition, the narratives include end-of-life experiences of individuals from a variety of ethnic and racial backgrounds.

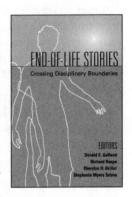

Partial Contents:

2005 · 218pp · 978-0-8261-2675-7 · hardcover

11 West 42nd Street, New York, NY 10036-8002 • Fax: 212-941-7842
Order Toll-Free: 877-687-7476 • Order On-line: www.springerpub.com

SPRINGER PUBLISHING COMPANY

Aging and the Meaning of Time

A Multidisciplinary Exploration

Susan H. McFadden, PhD and Robert C. Atchley, PhD, Editors

"What has life meant and how long is it worth living for? These and other questions are answered in the multidisciplinary survey Aging and the Meaning of Time, *a college-level text perfect for courses on philosophy and health alike. Chapters juxtapose the personal experience of aging with insights on philosophy, health, and metaphysics to provide an excellent survey. A top pick."* —**California Bookwatch,** August 2006

As we confront our own mortality, we might ask, "What has my long life meant and how have the years shaped me?" or "How long must I suffer?" Such questions reflect time-consciousness, the focus of this classic volume.

The authors, from diverse disciplines in gerontology, act as guides in the exploration of the realms of time in later life and their meanings. As they examine how the study of time can give new meanings to aging, they also consider the religious and spiritual questions raised when human beings consider the temporal boundaries of life.

Partial Contents:

Part I: Understanding Time and Aging • The Flow of Spiritual Time Amid the Tides of Life • Aging, Time Estimation, and Emotion • Meaning and the Tenses of Time: A Whiteheadian Perspective

Part II: Experiencing Time and Aging • Learning, Aging, and Other Predicaments • "It's 1924 and Somewhere in Texas, Two Nuns Are Driving a Backwards Volkswagen": Storytelling With People With Dementia

Part III: Effects of Religious Beliefs and Spiritual Practices on Meanings of Time and Aging • Discovering the Spirit in the Rhythm of Time • The Contemplative Context of Time • The Job Hypothesis: Gerotranscendence and Life Satisfaction Among Elderly Turkish Muslims • Chronos to Kairos: Christian Perspectives on Time and Aging

2006 · 280pp · 978-0-8261-0265-2 · softcover

11 West 42nd Street, New York, NY 10036-8002 • Fax: 212-941-7842
Order Toll-Free: 877-687-7476 • Order Online: www.springerpub.com